Foundations of Ajax

Ryan Asleson
Nathaniel T. Schutta

Foundations of Ajax

Copyright © 2006 by Ryan Asleson and Nathaniel T. Schutta

ISBN-13 (pbk): 978-1-59059-582-4
ISBN-10 (pbk): 1-59059-582-3
Printed and bound in the United States of America 9 8 7 6 5 4 3

Trademarked names may appear in this book. Rather than use a trademark symbol with every occurrence of a trademarked name, we use the names only in an editorial fashion and to the benefit of the trademark owner, with no intention of infringement of the trademark.

Lead Editor: Ewan Buckingham
Technical Reviewer: Keith Harvey
Editorial Board: Steve Anglin, Dan Appleman, Ewan Buckingham, Gary Cornell, Tony Davis,
    Jason Gilmore, Jonathan Hassell, Chris Mills, Dominic Shakeshaft, Jim Sumser
Production Director and Project Manager: Grace Wong
Copy Edit Manager: Nicole LeClerc
Copy Editor: Kim Wimpsett
Assistant Production Director: Kari Brooks-Copony
Production Editor: Linda Marousek
Compositor: Linda Weidemann, Wolf Creek Press
Proofreader: Patrick Vincent
Indexer: Tim Tate
Artist: Kinetic Publishing Services, LLC
Interior Designer: Van Winkle Design Group
Cover Designer: Kurt Krames
Manufacturing Director: Tom Debolski

Distributed to the book trade worldwide by Springer-Verlag New York, Inc., 233 Spring Street, 6th Floor, New York, NY 10013. Phone 1-800-SPRINGER, fax 201-348-4505, e-mail orders-ny@springer-sbm.com, or visit http://www.springeronline.com.

For information on translations, please contact Apress directly at 2560 Ninth Street, Suite 219, Berkeley, CA 94710. Phone 510-549-5930, fax 510-549-5939, e-mail info@apress.com, or visit http://www.apress.com.

The information in this book is distributed on an "as is" basis, without warranty. Although every precaution has been taken in the preparation of this work, neither the author(s) nor Apress shall have any liability to any person or entity with respect to any loss or damage caused or alleged to be caused directly or indirectly by the information contained in this work.

The source code for this book is available to readers at http://www.apress.com in the Source Code section.

For Sara and Adam
—Ryan Asleson

To Christine, without whom
none of this would matter
—Nathaniel T. Schutta

Contents at a Glance

Contents

About the Authors

 **RYAN ASLESON** is a software developer who lives and works in the Twin Cities area of Minnesota. Ryan has been building Web applications since 1998 and has extensive experience with JavaScript and Web development tools. He helped his organization make the transition from servlet-based content creation to JavaServer Pages and has also maintained a corporate Web application framework based on Java Enterprise Edition. He is the cocreator of the open-source Taconite framework (taconite.sf.net), which greatly simplifies Ajax development. His interests include performance tuning and standards-based development. When not working, Ryan enjoys spending time with his family and outdoor activities such as fishing, hunting, and water sports.

 **NATHANIEL T. SCHUTTA** is a senior software engineer in the Twin Cities area of Minnesota with extensive experience developing Java Enterprise Edition–based Web applications. He has a master's of science degree in software engineering from the University of Minnesota and for the last several years has focused on user interface design. Nathaniel has contributed to corporate interface guidelines and consulted on a variety of Web-based applications. A long-time member of the Association for Computing Machinery's Computer-Human Interaction Special Interest Group and a Sun-certified Web component developer, Nathaniel believes that if the user can't figure out your application, then you've done something wrong. Along with his user interface work, Nathaniel is the cocreator of the open-source Taconite framework, has contributed to two corporate Java frameworks, has developed training material, and has led several study groups. During the brief moments of warm weather found in his home state of Minnesota, he spends as much time on the golf course as his wife will tolerate. He's currently exploring Ruby, Rails, and (after recently making the switch) Mac OS X. For more of his random thoughts, check out his blog at www.ntschutta.com/jat/.

About the Technical Reviewer

■**KEITH HARVEY** is CTO and chief architect for SCOPE iT (www.scopeit.com), which specializes in Web-based project-budgeting applications that quickly and accurately develop IT project estimates, budgets, and plans. SCOPE iT is a Microsoft partner and has ISV/Software Solutions Competency. The SCOPE iT application is built on the latest Microsoft .NET technologies, SQL Server, and Ajax.

Keith is an author and has written numerous articles on Microsoft technologies, databases, Ajax, software project estimation, and more. Keith lives in Northern California with his wife, Tricia, and their daughter, Hanna. His personal Web site is at www.keith-harvey.com.

Acknowledgments

We thank Apress for giving us the opportunity to write this book. We thank Grace Wong for shepherding us through the production process by keeping us focused and on schedule. Keith Harvey and Brent Ashley provided valuable feedback that helped make this a better book. Kim Wimpsett had the misfortune of fixing our multiple spelling and grammatical mistakes, and for this we are forever grateful. We thank Linda Marousek for guiding us through the final production process—we were thrilled to see our work transformed from words in a word processor to a formatted book. Ewan Buckingham eased us into the authoring process by answering our many questions. We appreciate the support that our agent, Laura Lewin, and the staff at Studio B gave us throughout this adventure.

—Ryan Asleson and Nathaniel T. Schutta

I thank the entire Apress team for taking a chance on a rookie author like me. Without their confidence and support, I would not have completed this book. I thank Gary Cornell for his gracious and confidence-inspiring e-mail after I first submitted this book's proposal. I especially thank Chris Mills because he helped me through numerous iterations of the book's outline, from which the final blueprint for this book emerged.

I can't say enough good things about Nate Schutta, my friend, colleague, and coauthor. I appreciate the energy, insight, and dedication he brought to this endeavor—without his help, this book would not have been possible.

Most of all, I thank my wife, Sara, who graciously tolerated my absence for the past few months as I was busy working on this book.

—Ryan Asleson

To my coauthor, Ryan—thanks for letting me help bring your vision to print; it was an honor, my friend. Who would have thought throwing a football around a conference room during breaks would have led to this? As long as I'm on the topic, thanks to Sara and Adam, as well! Of course, I can't go much further without thanking my lovely wife, Christine. You put up with a lot during this adventure, and I couldn't have done it without your love and patience! Many thanks to Nathan Good, who, without your help and advice, I never would have gotten this far. (I'll miss getting coffee with you.)

Without my parent's foresight, I probably wouldn't even be in this field. Many summers ago, they enrolled me in a computer course over the summer and made sure I had the latest hardware from the likes of Commodore. Thanks, Mom and Dad—I don't say it enough! Also, special thanks to Jim Schnepf, Lynn Ziegler, John Miller, Andy Holcy, and Noreen Herzfeld in the computer science department at St. John's University—you were kind enough to accept this former chemistry major and allow me to take a rather, shall we say, unconventional path through the major! I also have to thank the many teachers who shaped my writing voice:

Karen Sweet, Mary Ellen Briel, Michael Youngberg, Peggy Anderson, the late Jim Murphy, and of course Elizabeth Stoltz. I want you all to know that you've enriched my life in ways I will never be able to repay; without your guidance and tutelage, I would not be where I am today. I know I've left some excellent people off this list and for that my heartfelt apologies— I have only so much space! Thanks again to everyone mentioned here and all those who I keep in my heart.

—Nathaniel T. Schutta

Introduction

We thought we had found the Holy Grail of software development when we started building Web applications several years ago. Previously we had been developing thick client applications that required a lengthy installation process every time a new version of the company's application was released. The application was deployed to several hundred users scattered across the country, and much to our dismay we had to watch as the complex and error-prone installation process continually caused headaches and angst for developers and users alike.

Deploying an application through a browser seemed like a much more palatable option because it would eliminate the need to install software on the client computer. So, like many others, our organization moved swiftly to deploying applications on the Web.

Despite the relative ease of deployment, Web applications still had their share of issues. Most notable from a user's perspective was the significant loss of rich interactivity provided by the user interface. Web applications were constrained to the basic set of widgets provided by HTML. Worse yet, interacting with the server required a complete refresh of the page, which was disconcerting to users who were familiar with rich client-server applications.

We always considered this constant need to refresh the page a serious liability of Web applications and often experimented with ways to avoid a page refresh whenever possible; at one point, we even considered writing a Java applet that would handle the communication between the browser and the server. However, it soon became apparent that as more Web applications were deployed, users simply got used to the constant page refreshes, and our zeal for finding alternatives slowly faded.

Fast-forward five years. Even before the term *Ajax* was coined, asynchronous communication between the browser and server using the XMLHttpRequest object was creating a buzz within the developer community thanks to applications such as Google Suggest and Gmail. The XMLHttpRequest object has been available in Internet Explorer for several years, but now that it was being supported by other browsers, it was poised for a breakthrough. We added Ajax functionality to an existing application we happened to be working on at the time, and we were so impressed with the results that we thought, "Hey, somebody should write a book about this." Thus, the seeds for this book were sown.

An Overview of This Book

Foundations of Ajax is written to give you, the developer, all the tools you need to add Ajax techniques to your existing or future applications. Our motto while writing this book was, "Everything you need to know; nothing you don't." We assume that as a reader of this book you are already an experienced Web application developer. Because of this, we focus on the topics that are most likely new to you: Ajax and its associated tools and techniques. We don't spend much time talking about server-side languages because we assume you will develop server-side functionality using the toolset of your choice and that you don't need our help doing it. We don't spend time talking about how to build enterprise-scale applications that just happen to use Ajax. Instead, we focus solely on Ajax and its related tools and techniques.

The examples in this book are deliberately small and tightly focused. They demonstrate one or two important Ajax concepts as succinctly as possible. We assume that as an experienced Web developer you can extrapolate the demonstrated topic into your own environment; thus, we avoid cluttering the examples with information that is of little use to you.

Chapter 1 discusses the themes of Web application development from the past, present, and future. It's easier to see where development techniques are going once you know where they have been.

Chapter 2 introduces the XMLHttpRequest object. This is the Ajax concept with which you're likely the least familiar, so we dedicate an entire chapter to explaining the XMLHttpRequest object's properties and methods. If you're like us, you may not have even been aware of the XMLHttpRequest object until recently, despite the fact that it has been available in Internet Explorer for several years. Therefore, we'll take the time to properly discuss this object and what it can do.

Chapter 3 starts to get into the meat of Ajax. This chapter discusses the various ways in which the XMLHttpRequest object can communicate with the server. We discuss using XML, plain text, and even JavaScript Object Notation (JSON) as the transport medium and discuss the various ways in which you use them in conjunction with the XMLHttpRequest object. By the end of this chapter, you'll be comfortable using the XMLHttpRequest object to communicate with the server without forcing the user to suffer through a complete page refresh.

Too often we, as developers, spend time learning how to use a new technology or technique without learning about how to apply it. Chapter 4 addresses this problem by demonstrating a number of scenarios in which you can use Ajax techniques. As promised, each example is small and focused, enabling you to better understand the topic without having to wade through copious amounts of unnecessary information.

Chapters 5, 6, and 7 are worth their weight in gold to the new Ajax developer. We don't want you to start enhancing your applications with Ajax without being equipped with the proper tools and techniques to do so. Chapter 5 introduces several tools and techniques that you can use to ease the development of Web applications. The tools and techniques described in Chapter 5 will help you produce code that is higher in quality, adheres to industry standards, and is easier to maintain in the future.

Test-driven development (TDD) is changing the way we develop applications. By writing unit tests before you write any code, you can ensure that the code you write is working as expected, greatly increasing the quality of your code. A suite of unit tests also makes future changes easier by ensuring that all code still works as expected after changes are made. There's no reason to exclude Ajax from TDD, and since the benefits of TDD cannot be overstated, we dedicate an entire chapter to it. Since Ajax is primarily a browser-based technology, Chapter 6 demonstrates how to apply TDD to your JavaScript code.

Speaking of JavaScript, if you're going to use Ajax, you're going to have to write at least some JavaScript. Many developers have shied away from JavaScript, claiming it lacks important productivity tools such as debuggers to be truly useful. That is no longer true. Chapter 7 discusses tools and techniques you can use to track down problems when they arise and solve them as quickly and easily as possible. No longer must you avoid JavaScript with the fear that you won't be able to diagnose problems when they arise.

Ajax is a rapidly evolving technology that has grown exponentially during the time we were writing this book. Chapter 8 ties everything together by discussing emerging Ajax development patterns, frameworks, and online resources. Also, the complete example in Chapter 8 shows some advanced Ajax techniques and demonstrates how easy Ajax development can be when using a prebuilt Ajax framework. Using a framework shields you from some of the more mundane tasks of Ajax development, allowing you to focus more on business logic than on the nuances of Ajax.

To cap it all off, Appendix A outlines some quirks and inconsistencies that exist within the W3C DOM and JavaScript implementations that exist across browsers, and ways to overcome these issues. Appendix B summarizes some of the most popular Ajax frameworks and libraries that are available to simplify the adoption of Ajax techniques. The number of frameworks is sure to grow as Ajax becomes more popluar, so stay on the lookout for emerging frameworks and other development tools.

Obtaining This Book's Source Code

All the examples in this book are freely available from the Source Code section of the Apress Web site. Point your browser to www.apress.com, click the Source Code link, and find *Foundations of Ajax* in the list. You can also download the source code as a zip file from this book's home page. The source code is organized by chapter.

Obtaining Updates for This Book

Despite our best efforts, you may find an occasional error or two scattered throughout the book—although we hope not! We apologize for any errors that may be present in the text or source code. A current errata list is available from this book's home page on the Apress Web site (www.apress.com) along with information about how to notify us of any errors you may find.

Contacting Us

We value your questions and comments regarding this book's content and source code examples. Please direct all questions and comments to foundationsofajax@gmail.com. We'll reply to your inquiries as soon as we can; please remember, we (like you!) may not be able to respond immediately.

Thank you for buying this book! We hope you find it a valuable resource and enjoy reading it as much as we enjoyed writing it.

Best regards,
Ryan Asleson and Nathaniel T. Schutta

■■■

CHAPTER 1

Introducing Ajax

The Internet as we know it today has undergone tremendous change. Beginning with simple textual browsers that allowed scientists to exchange research, the Internet is now a hub for commerce and information. Over that time, we've seen a number of new technologies and approaches—from the earliest graphical browsers to podcasts. Today, the Internet has become the leading platform for numerous applications (when was the last time you actually spoke with a travel agent?), but despite the convenience, few would mistake a Web application with its desktop cousin. This chapter will give a brief overview of the evolution of Web applications. Once we have you grounded in the past, we'll introduce you to what we view as the future: Ajax.

A Short History of Web Applications

In the beginning, it was all so simple. Initially connecting a handful of top research institutions in the United States, the original "Internet" was designed to facilitate the sharing of scientific research. Whether you were a librarian, nuclear physicist, or computer scientist, you had quite a complex system to learn—Firefox and Internet Explorer weren't even concepts when J.C.R. Licklider of the Massachusetts Institute of Technology (MIT) first presented his ideas on a "Galactic Network" in 1962.

Licklider went on to head up computer research at the Defense Advanced Research Projects Agency (DARPA), where he preached the importance of his networking ideas. About the same time, Leonard Kleinrock and Lawrence G. Roberts of MIT were working on packet-switching theory, a key concept to networking computers. Roberts went on to create, with Thomas Merrill, the first wide area network in 1965 when he connected a TX-2 in Massachusetts with a Q-32 in California over a dial-up connection.

Roberts took the results of his experiments to DARPA in late 1966 where he designed his plan for the Advanced Research Projects Administration Network (ARPANET). By now, Kleinrock was at the University of California–Los Angeles' Network Measurement Center, which was selected as the first node of ARPANET and where in 1969 Bolt Beranek and Newman (BBN) installed the first packet switches called Interface Message Processors (IMPs). The Stanford Research Center was selected as the second node, and in October 1969 the first host-to-host messages were exchanged. Shortly thereafter, the University of California–Santa Barbara and the University of Utah were added as nodes, beginning what we know today as the Internet.

Minicomputers were just starting to appear: Digital Equipment Corporation created the PDP-1, which was followed by the tremendous success of the PDP-8, the PDP-11, and the VAX-11/780. Computing power was becoming increasingly affordable—no longer were we begging time on a handful of massive mainframe computers. Computing was becoming more democratic; still, we had yet to see the personal computer revolution.

Originally researchers thought Transmission Control Protocol (TCP) would work only with the large systems for which it was designed. However, David Clark's research team at MIT proved that workstations could be networked along with big iron. Clark's research, combined with the personal computing explosion of the 1980s and 1990s, paved the way for the always-on world in which we currently reside.

During the 1980s, a number of changes occurred. As the number of hosts grew from just a few to thousands, they were assigned names so people didn't have to memorize the numeric addresses. This switch, combined with the increasing number of hosts, gave birth to the Domain Name System (DNS). Further, ARPANET was transitioning from using Network Control Protocol (NCP) to Transmission Control Protocol/Internet Protocol (TCP/IP), the standard used by the military. By the mid-1980s, the Internet was established as a platform to connect disparate groups of researchers, and other networks began to appear: National Aeronautics and Space Administration created SPAN, the U.S. Department of Energy established MFENet for research on Magnetic Fusion Energy, and a grant from the National Science Foundation helped create the CSNET for computer science research.

In 1989, Tim Berners-Lee of the European Council for Nuclear Research (CERN) came up with an interesting concept. He thought, rather than merely reference another work, why not actually link to it? While reading one paper, a scientist could simply open a referenced paper. The term *hypertext* was in vogue, and drawing upon his previous work in document and text processing, Berners-Lee invented a subset of Standard Generalized Markup Language (SGML) called HyperText Markup Language (HTML). The beauty of HTML is that it separates the information about how text should be rendered from the actual implementation of the display. Along with creating the simple protocol called HyperText Transfer Protocol (HTTP), Berners-Lee invented the first Web browser, called WorldWideWeb.

Browser History

Until the recent ascent of alternatives such as Firefox, Safari, and Opera, most people associated the Web browser with Microsoft's ubiquitous Internet Explorer. Despite what many newcomers may think, Internet Explorer wasn't even close to being the first browser on the market. In fact, Berners-Lee created the first Web browser (originally called WorldWideWeb but later renamed to Nexus) on and for the NeXT computer, and he released it to personnel at CERN in 1990. Berners-Lee and Jean-Francois Groff ported WorldWideWeb to C, renaming the browser to libwww. The early 1990s saw a number of browsers, including the line-mode browser written by Nicola Pellow (which allowed users of any system from Unix to Microsoft DOS to access the Internet) and Samba, the first browser for the Macintosh.

In February 1993, Marc Andreessen and Eric Bina of the National Center for Supercomputing Applications at the University of Illinois–Urbana-Champaign released Mosaic for Unix. A few months later, Mosaic became the first cross-platform browser when Aleks Totic released a version for the Macintosh. It quickly spread and became the most popular Web browser.[1] The technology was licensed to Spyglass, where it was further licensed to Microsoft for use in Internet Explorer.

---

1. One author recalls his first introduction to Mosaic: "I had just been introduced to Lynx and was, as a freshman chemistry student, amazed I could browse the stacks of Oxford from central Minnesota (albeit via text-based browsing only). After seeing a beta version of Mosaic and noticing how slow and choppy the experience was, I vowed to stick with Lynx, and I'm proud to say I use Firefox today."

Developers at the University of Kansas wrote a text-based browser called Lynx in 1993 that became the standard for character terminals. A team in Oslo, Norway, in 1994 developed Opera, which was made widely available in 1996. In December 1994, Netscape released the 1.0 version of Mozilla, and the first for-profit browser was born. In 2002, an open-source version was released that grew into the popular Firefox browser, released in November 2004.

When Microsoft released Windows 95, it included Internet Explorer 1.0 as part of its Microsoft Plus! pack. Despite its integration with the operating system, most people stuck with Netscape, Lynx, or Opera. Version 2.0 made significant strides by adding support for cookies, Secure Socket Layer (SSL), and other emerging standards. The second version was also available for the Macintosh, making it the first cross-platform browser from Microsoft. Still, most users stuck with what they were using.

However, in the summer of 1996, Microsoft released version 3.0. Virtually overnight, people flocked to Internet Explorer. Of course, it didn't hurt that Netscape charged money for its browser and Microsoft offered Internet Explorer for free. The Internet community was polarized on the issue of browser dominance, as many feared Microsoft would do to the Web what it did to the desktop. Some were concerned about security, and sure enough, nine days after it was released, the first security problem was reported. By 1999's release of Internet Explorer 5, it was the most widely used browser.

The Evolution of Web Applications

At first, all Web pages were static; users requested a resource, and the server returned it. Nothing moved, nothing flashed. Frankly, for a great number of Web sites, this was just fine—Web pages were nothing more than electronic copies of text that was at one point bound and distributed. In the early days of the browser, the static nature of Web pages wasn't an issue; scientists were using the Internet to exchange research papers, and universities were posting class information online. Businesses hadn't yet figured out what to do with this new "channel." In fact, at first, corporate home pages often displayed little more than contact information or some documentation. However, it didn't take long for Web users to want a more dynamic experience. The personal computer was a stalwart of business, and from dorm rooms to home offices more and more computers were starting to appear. With the advent of Windows 95 and the rich experience of thick applications such as Corel Word-Perfect and Microsoft Excel, users' expectations were rising.

CGI

The first solution to making the Web more dynamic was Common Gateway Interface (CGI). Unlike static Web retrieval, CGI allows you to create programs that execute when a user makes a request. Say you want to display items for sale on your Web site—with a CGI script you can access your product database and display the results. Using simple HTML forms and CGI scripts, you can create a simple storefront that allows you to sell products to anyone with a browser. You can write CGI scripts in any number of languages from Perl to Visual Basic, making the scripts available to a wide range of skill sets.

However, CGI is not the safest approach for creating dynamic Web pages. With CGI, you literally let people execute a program on your system. Most of the time this probably isn't a problem, but a user with malicious intent can exploit this and cause your system to run something you didn't intend. Despite that drawback, CGI continues to be used today.

Applets

It was clear that CGI could be improved upon. In May 1995, John Gage of Sun and Andreessen (now of Netscape Communications Corporation) announced the birth of a programming language called Java. Netscape Navigator would offer support for this new language, originally intended for set-top boxes (and you thought Microsoft and Sony were the first companies to fight for control of your living room!). As is often the case when something truly revolutionary happens, Java and the Internet were at the right place at the right time, and within a few months of its release on the Web, thousands of people had downloaded Java. With Netscape's dominant Navigator supporting Java, a new avenue for dynamic Web pages had opened: the era of applets had begun.

Applets allow developers to write small applications that can be embedded on a Web page. As long as they use a Java-aware browser, users can run the applets in the browser's Java Virtual Machine (JVM). While applets can do a number of things, they have some restrictions: they are typically prevented from reading or writing to the file system, they cannot load native libraries, and they may not start programs on the client. In addition to these restrictions, applets run with a sandbox security model that helps protect users from malicious code.

For many people, applets were their first exposure to the Java programming language, and at the time they were an excellent way to create dynamic Web applications. Applets let you create a "thick" client inside your browser, within the security constraints of the platform. In some areas at the time, applets were widely used; however, they never really grabbed the Web community.[2] One problem was familiar to developers of thick clients: you have to deploy the proper Java version to the client. Because applets run in the virtual machine of a browser, developers have to make sure the client has the proper version of Java installed. Though not insurmountable, this issue greatly compromised the adoption of applet technology. It didn't help that poorly written applets caused complications on client machines and made many customers hesitant to use applet-based solutions. For those of you unfamiliar with applets, Figure 1-1 shows a clock applet from Sun.

---

2. The corporate time-tracking software of one author's employer is, believe it or not, an applet.

Figure 1-1. *A clock applet from Sun*

JavaScript

About this same time, Netscape created a scripting language eventually called JavaScript. (It was called Mocha when prototyped and then LiveWire and LiveScript before being released as JavaScript.) JavaScript was designed as a way of making applets easier to develop for Web designers and programmers who weren't familiar with Java. (Of course, Microsoft had its own answer to JavaScript—a scripting language called VBScript.) Netscape hired Brendan Eich to design and implement the new language, and he thought a dynamically typed scripting language was just what was needed. Though it has been much maligned for its lack of development tools, useful error messages, and debuggers, JavaScript is a powerful way to create dynamic Web applications.

Originally, JavaScript was created to help developers dynamically modify the tags on their pages in an effort to provide a richer client experience. It became evident that one could treat the page as an object, and thus was born the Document Object Model (DOM). At first, JavaScript and the DOM were tightly intertwined, but eventually they evolved into separate

constructs. The DOM is a fully object-oriented representation of the page that can be modified with a scripting language such as JavaScript or VBScript.

Eventually, the World Wide Web Consortium (W3C) got involved and standardized the
DOM, while the European Computer Manufacturers Association (ECMA) ratified JavaScript
as the ECMAScript specification. Any page and script written according to these standards
should look and behave identically in any browser that adheres to these guidelines.

A number of factors conspired against JavaScript in its early years. Browser support was
spotty (even today the same script may behave differently across browsers), and clients are
free to turn JavaScript off (some well-publicized security breaches have prompted many users
to do so). The difficulty of developing JavaScript (can you say *alert?*) caused many developers
to shy away from using the language often, while other developers simply ignored JavaScript,
considering it a toy language for graphics designers. Most were content to create simple form-
based applications after experiencing extreme mental fatigue while attempting to use, test,
and debug complex JavaScript.

Servlets and ASPs and PHP . . . Oh My!

Though Web-based, applets still presented many of the issues associated with thick client
applications. In the era of the dial-up connection (still far too prevalent even today), downloading the entire code base for a complex applet could take more time than a user was willing to
invest. Developers also had to worry about the version of Java present on the client, and some
virtual machines left something to be desired.[3] Ideally, you just serve up static Web pages—after
all, that was what the Internet was truly designed to do. Of course, static pages are, well, static,
but if you could *dynamically* generate content on the server and *return* static content, that
would get you somewhere.

Within a year of Java being introduced to the world, Sun introduced servlets. No longer
would your Java code run in the client browser as with applets; it would run on an application
server that you controlled. This would allow developers to leverage existing business applications, and if you needed to upgrade to the latest Java version, you had to worry only about your
server. Java's "write once, run anywhere" nature allowed developers to select best-of-breed
application servers and server environments—yet another advantage of the new technology.
Servlets also served as an alternative to CGI scripts.

Servlets were a huge step forward. They offered full access to the entire set of Java application programming interfaces (APIs) and came with a complete library for handling HTTP.
However, servlets weren't perfect. Interface design with servlets can be hard. In a typical servlet
interaction, you get some information from your user, perform some business logic, and then,
using what amounts to print lines, create the HTML to display for the user. Code like that
shown in Listing 1-1 was common.

---

3. The Microsoft virtual machine never supported Java after the 1.1 specification, greatly hindering
   what applets could do on the Microsoft platform.

Listing 1-1. *Simple Servlet Code*

```
response.setContentType("text/html;charset=UTF-8");
        PrintWriter out = response.getWriter();

        out.println("<html>");
        out.println("<head>");
        out.println("<title>Servlet SimpleServlet</title>");
        out.println("</head>");
        out.println("<body>");
        out.println("<h1>Hello World</h1>");
        out.println("<p>Imagine if this were more complex.</p>");
        out.println("</body>");
        out.println("</html>");

        out.close();
```

This small amount of code produces the rather simple Web page shown in Figure 1-2.

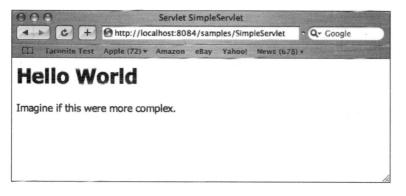

Figure 1-2. *Output from the simple servlet in Listing 1-1*

Besides being error prone and difficult to visualize, servlets had a skill set mismatch. In general, the people writing the server-side code were software developers schooled in algorithms and compilers, not the graphics designers who were crafting elegant corporate Web sites. Business developers were focused not only on writing business logic but also had to worry about creating coherent designs. A separation of presentation and business logic was needed. What we needed were JavaServer Pages (JSPs).

JSPs were, to an extent, a response to Microsoft's Active Server Pages (ASPs). Microsoft learned from the mistakes Sun made with the Servlet specification and created ASPs to simplify creating dynamic pages. Microsoft added excellent tool support and tight integration with its Web server. JSPs and ASPs are similar in that they were designed to separate the business processing from the presentation layout. Some technical differences exist (Sun too learned from Microsoft), but both allow Web designers to focus on the layout while software developers focus on the business logic. Listing 1-2 shows a simple JSP.

Listing 1-2. *Simple JSP*

```jsp
<%@page contentType="text/html"%>
<%@page pageEncoding="UTF-8"%>

<!DOCTYPE HTML PUBLIC "-//W3C//DTD HTML 4.01 Transitional//EN"
    "http://www.w3.org/TR/html4/loose.dtd">

<html>
    <head>
        <meta http-equiv="Content-Type" content="text/html; charset=UTF-8">
        <title>Hello World</title>
    </head>
    <body>

    <h1>Hello World</h1>
    <p>This code is more familiar for Web developers.</p>

    </body>
</html>
```

This code produces the output shown in Figure 1-3.

Figure 1-3. *Output from a simple JSP*

Of course, Microsoft and Sun don't own a monopoly on server-side solutions. A number of other options exist, from PHP to ColdFusion. Amazing tools drive some developers; others are looking for simpler languages. At the end of the day, all these solutions perform the same task—they dynamically generate HTML. Generating content on the server solves the distribution problem; however, the user experience that is possible with raw HTML pales in comparison with what you can do with a thick client or applets. The following sections cover a number of other solutions that were created in an effort to provide a richer user experience.

Flash

Microsoft and Sun weren't the only companies looking to solve the dynamic Web page problem. In the summer of 1996 FutureWave released a product called FutureSplash Animator. Growing out of a Java-based animation player, FutureWave soon sold its company to Macromedia, which rebranded the product as Flash.

Flash allows designers to create amazing applications that are highly dynamic in nature. Companies can deliver highly interactive applications on the Web that are almost indistinguishable from their thick client brethren (see Figure 1-4). Unlike applets, servlets, and CGI scripts, Flash does not require programming skills and is easy to learn. In the go-go days of the late 1990s, this was a significant plus, as many employers scrambled to find employees with the requisite skills. However, this ease of use comes at a cost.

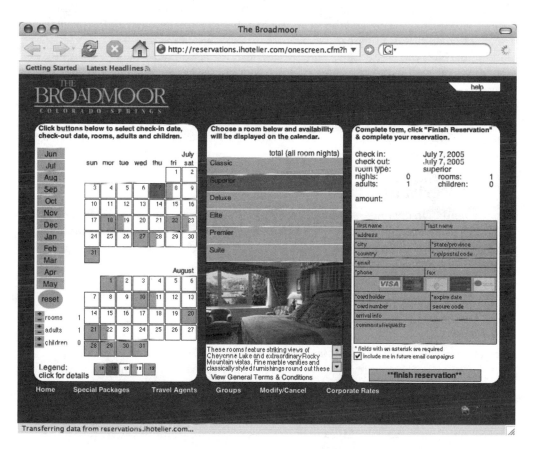

Figure 1-4. *A Flash application*

Like many solutions, Flash requires software on the client. Though the required Shockwave Player plug-in shipped with several popular operating systems and browsers, it was not universal. Despite the free download, fear of viruses caused many users to refuse the install of the software. Flash applications can also require significant amounts of network bandwidth to perform properly, and the lack of widespread broadband connections limited the adoption of

Flash (and thus was born the "skip intro" link). While some sites choose to have multiple versions of their Web application tailored to various connection speeds, many companies could not justify the added development costs of supporting two or three catalog sites.

In sum, creating Flash applications requires proprietary software and browser plug-ins. Unlike applets that can be written with text editors and a free Java Development Kit (JDK), using the complete Flash toolkit costs hundreds of dollars per seat. Though not insurmountable, these factors have slowed the widespread adoption of Flash for dynamic Web applications.

The DHTML Revolution

When Microsoft and Netscape released version 4 of their respective browsers, Web developers had a new option: dynamic HTML (DHTML). Despite what many think, DHTML is not a W3C standard; it's really more of a marketing tool. In reality, it's a combination of HTML, Cascading Style Sheets (CSS), JavaScript, and the DOM. The combination of these technologies allows developers to modify the content and structure of a Web page on the fly.

The initial buzz was very positive for DHTML. However, it required browser versions that weren't yet widely adopted. Though both Internet Explorer and Netscape supported DHTML, their implementations were different, meaning developers had to know which browser their clients were using. Often this meant having lots of code that checked for browser type and version, which further increased the cost of development. Some were hesitant to try this approach because of the lack of an official standard for DHTML. Still, the possibilities were there for something new to come along.

The XML Derivatives

Since its invention in the mid-1990s, the W3C's eXtensible Markup Language (XML) derivative of SGML has been amazingly popular. Seen by many as the answer to all that ails computer development, XML shows up everywhere. In fact, Microsoft has announced that Office 12 will support XML file formats.

Today we have no fewer than four XML derivatives for creating Web applications (and that doesn't count the W3C's XHTML): XUL from Mozilla; XAMJ, an open-source alternative that blends Java into the mix; MXML from Macromedia; and XAML from Microsoft.

> *XUL*: XUL (pronounced "zool") stands for XML User Interface Language and comes from the Mozilla Foundation. The popular Firefox browser and Thunderbird mail client are written in XUL. XUL lets developers build rich applications that can run with or without a connection to the Internet. Designed to be learned quickly by developers familiar with DHTML, XUL provides cross-platform support for standard interface widgets such as windows and buttons. Though not a standard itself, XUL is based on standards such as HTML 4.0, CSS, the DOM, XML, and ECMAScript. XUL applications can be run from a browser or installed on a client machine.
>
> Of course, XUL is not without its drawbacks. XUL requires the Gecko engine, and as of now Internet Explorer has no corresponding plug-in. Though Firefox has certainly captured a respectable share in the browser usage statistics, the lack of Internet Explorer support largely makes XUL unusable for most applications. Several projects are underway to make XUL available to a number of platforms, including Eclipse.

XAML: XAML (pronounced "zammel") is a component of Microsoft's upcoming operating system code-named Vista. XAML is short for eXtensible Application Markup Language and defines the standard for creating user interfaces in Vista. Similar to HTML, XAML uses tags to create standard elements such as buttons and text boxes. Based on top of Microsoft's .NET platform, XAML is compiled into .NET classes.

It should be pretty clear what the limitations of XAML are. As a Microsoft product, you are relegated to a Microsoft operating system. In many cases (especially corporations), this may not be problematic, but no bricks-and-mortar company could justify turning away paying customers simply because they didn't drive a particular model of automobile, for example. Combined with the continually shifting ship date of Vista, XAML isn't much of a player right now. That said, in a few years, we might be whistling a different tune.

MXML: Macromedia created MXML as the markup language for use with its Flex technology; MXML stands for Maximum eXperience Markup Language. MXML is designed to be like HTML, allowing you to design your interface in a declarative manner. Like XUL and XAML, MXML provides a richer set of interface components, such as DataGrid and Tab-Navigator, that allow you to create rich Internet applications. MXML doesn't stand on its own, though; it relies on Flex and the ActionScript programming language to code business logic.

MXML has some of the same limitations that Flash does. It's proprietary and relies on expensive development and deployment environments. Though .NET support is expected in the future, today Flex runs only on top of Java 2 Enterprise Edition (J2EE) application servers such as Tomcat and IBM's WebSphere, further limiting its adoption

XAMJ: Not to be outdone, the open-source community has added an entry to the XML derivative world of interface design. XAMJ was recently introduced as another cross-platform option in the Web application developer's toolkit. This particular derivative is based on Java, which provides the full power of one of the most popular object-oriented languages in use today. XAMJ is essentially an alternative to XAML- or HTML-based applications that seeks to be a more secure option that neither is reliant on a particular framework nor requires a high-speed Internet connection. XAMJ is a compiled language that builds upon a "clientlet" architecture, and though stand-alone applications are possible, in general XAMJ-based programs will be Web based. As of this writing, XAMJ is too new to properly critique; however, it bears watching.

As long as we are talking about "things that start with *X*," let's not forget the W3C XForms specification. XForms is designed to support a richer user interface while decoupling data from presentation. Not surprisingly, XForms data is XML, which allows you to use existing XML technologies such as XPath and XML Schema. XForms can do anything standard HTML can do plus more, including checking field values on the fly and integrating with Web Services. Unlike many W3C specifications, XForms doesn't require a new browser—you can use several existing implementations now. Like most of the XML derivatives, XForms is a fresh approach, so patience may be appropriate.

The Fundamental Problem

Where does that leave you? For all but the most demanding of client applications, the Web has become the platform of choice. While it's obvious that Web-based applications are easy to deploy, the low barrier of entry for users might be their greatest strength. With the ubiquity of the browser and no need to download and install new software, browser-based clients make it simple for users to try a new application. Users are far more likely to simply click a link and try your application than go through the effort of a multiple-megabyte installation. Browser-based applications are also operating system agnostic, which means not only can you reach those people running Linux and OS X, but you don't have to worry about developing and maintaining multiple installation packages.

If Web-based applications are the greatest thing since sliced bread, why did we write this book? If you look to the origins of the Internet, you see a world of scientists and academics exchanging papers and research—a simple request/response paradigm. It had no need for conversational state, and it had no need for a shopping cart; people were simply exchanging documents. While you have long had a number of options for creating dynamic Web-based applications, if you want to truly reach the largest body of users, you have to stay pretty close to the browser, which means you are always held back by the synchronous nature of the request/response underpinnings of the Internet.

Compared to thick client applications such as Microsoft Word or Intuit's Quicken, the Web model was certainly an adjustment for the average user. However, the ease of deployment and the ascent of the browser meant most users learned to adapt. Still, many thought the Web offered applications that were second-class citizens with inferior user experiences. Because the Internet is a synchronous request/response system, the entire page was constantly refreshing in the browser. Originally, it didn't matter how simple the request was—if the user made one or two changes, the entire document had to be sent back to the server and the entire page was repainted. Though usable, this total refresh limitation meant applications were rather crude.

That didn't mean developers simply sat on their hands and accepted the status quo. Microsoft knew a thing or two about interactive applications. Microsoft was never satisfied with the limitations of the standard paradigm, and therefore it introduced the concept of remote scripting. The magic of remote scripting is simple: it allows developers to create pages that interact with the server in an asynchronous manner. For instance, a customer could select their state from a drop-down list, causing a script to run on the server and determine their shipping costs. More important, these costs could then be displayed *without the entire page refreshing*! Of course, Microsoft's solution works with its technology only and requires Java, but this advancement showed that richer browser applications were possible.

Other solutions exist to the synchronous page refresh problem. Brent Ashley developed a platform-neutral answer to Microsoft's remote scripting when he created JavaScript Remote Scripting (JSRS). JSRS relies on a client-side JavaScript library and DHTML to make asynchronous calls to the server. At the same time, many people took advantage of the IFRAME tag to load only portions of the page or make "hidden" calls to the server. Though a workable solution used by many, it certainly wasn't ideal—it was really a bit of a hack.

Ajax

So here we are: clients want a more full-featured application, and developers want to avoid deploying executables to thousands of workstations. We've tried a number of alternatives, but none has been the panacea it was touted as. However, recent developments have added an incredibly powerful tool to our design kit.

Today we have another option, another tool, to create truly rich browser-based applications. Today we have Ajax. Ajax is more of a technique than it is a specific technology, though the aforementioned JavaScript is a primary component. We know you're saying, "JavaScript is not worth it," but with the resurgent interest in the language because of Ajax, application and testing frameworks, combined with better tool support, are easing the burden on developers. With the introduction of Atlas, Microsoft is throwing its weight firmly behind Ajax, while the infamous Rails Web framework comes prebuilt with outstanding Ajax support. In the Java space, Sun has added several Ajax components to its BluePrints Solutions Catalog.

Honestly, Ajax isn't anything new. In fact, the "newest" technology related to the term—the XMLHttpRequest object (XHR)—has been around since Internet Explorer 5 (released in the spring of 1999) as an Active X control. What is new, however, is the level of browser support. Originally, the XHR object was supported in only Internet Explorer (thus limiting its use), but starting with Mozilla 1.0 and Safari 1.2 support is widespread. The little-used object and the basic concepts are even covered in a W3C standard: the DOM Level 3 Load and Save Specification. At this point, especially as applications such as Google Maps, Google Suggest, Gmail, Flickr, Netflix, and A9 proliferate, XHR is becoming a de facto standard.

Unlike many of the approaches mentioned in the previous pages, Ajax works in most modern browsers and doesn't require any proprietary software or hardware. In fact, one of the real strengths of this approach is that developers don't need to learn some new language or scrap their existing investment in server-side technology. Ajax is a client-side approach and can interact with J2EE, .NET, PHP, Ruby, and CGI scripts—it really is server agnostic. Short of a few minor security restrictions, you can start using Ajax right now, leveraging what you already know.

"Who is using Ajax?" you may ask. As mentioned, Google is clearly one of the early adopters, with several examples of the technology, including Google Maps, Google Suggest, and Gmail, to name just a few applications. Yahoo! is beginning to introduce Ajax controls, and Amazon has a neat search tool that uses the technique extensively—moving the sliders for a given facet of a diamond results in dynamically updated results (see Figure 1-5). The page isn't refreshed each time you change your criteria, and the server is queried while you move a slider, allowing you to narrow your options both quickly and easily.

Netflix, the popular DVD rental company, uses Ajax to provide a greater depth of information as users browse for movies. When a customer hovers over the graphic for a movie, the movie ID is sent to their central servers, and a bubble appears that provides more details about the movie (see Figure 1-6). Again, the page is not refreshed, and the specifics for each movie aren't found in hidden form fields. This approach allows Netflix to provide more information about its movies without cluttering its pages. It also makes browsing easier for their customers—they don't have to click the movie and then click back to the list; they simply have to hover over a movie! We want to stress that Ajax isn't limited to "dot-com" darlings; corporate developers are starting to scratch the surface as well, with many using Ajax to solve particularly ugly validation situations or to retrieve data on the fly.

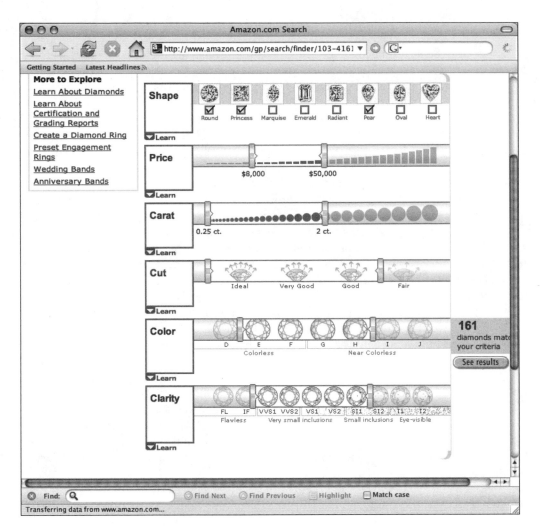

Figure 1-5. *Amazon's diamond search*

If it isn't exactly new, the *approach* that is the meat of Ajax is an important shift in the Internet's default request/response paradigm. Web application developers are now free to interact with the server asynchronously, meaning they can perform many tasks that before were limited to thick clients. For example, when a user enters a zip code, you can validate it and populate other parts of a form with the city and state; or when they select United States, you can populate a state drop-down list. We've been able to mimic these approaches before, but it's much simpler to do with Ajax.

Figure 1-6. *Netflix's browse feature*

So, who invented Ajax? The exact origin involved is a subject of debate; however, Jesse James Garrett of Adaptive Path first coined the term in February 2005. In his essay "Ajax: A New Approach to Web Applications," Garrett discusses how the gap is closing between thick client, or desktop, applications and thin client, or Web, applications. Of course, Google really gave the techniques a high profile when it released Google Maps and Google Suggest in Google Labs; also, there have been numerous articles on the subject. But Garrett gave us a term that wasn't quite as, shall we say, wordy as Asynchronous, XMLHttpRequest, JavaScript, CSS, the DOM, and so on. Though originally considered an acronym for Asynchronous JavaScript + XML, the term is now used simply to encompass all the technologies that allow a browser to communicate with the server without refreshing the current page.

We can hear you saying, "So, what's the big deal?" Well, using XHR and working asynchronously with the server lets you create Web applications that are far more dynamic. For example, say you have a drop-down that is filled based on the input in some other field or drop-down. Ordinarily, you would have to send all the data down to the client when the page first loaded and use JavaScript to populate your drop-down based on the input. It's not hard to do, but it does bloat the size of your page, and depending on just how dynamic that drop-down list is, size could be an issue. With Ajax, when the trigger field changes or the focus is lost, you can make a simple request to the server for only the information you need to update your drop-down.

Imagine the possibilities for validation alone. How many times have you written some JavaScript validation logic? While the edit might be simple in Java or C#, the lack of decent debuggers, combined with JavaScript's weak typing, can make writing them in JavaScript a real pain and error prone. How often do these client-side validation rules duplicate edits on the server? Using XHR, you can make a call to the server and fire *one* set of validation rules. These rules can be far richer and more complex than anything you would write in JavaScript, and you have the full power of debuggers and integrated development environments (IDEs).

We can hear some of you now: "I've been doing that for years with IFRAMES or hidden frames." We've even used this particular technique as a way to post or refresh parts of a page instead of the entire browser, and truth be told, it works. However, many would consider this approach a hack to get around XHR's original lack of cross-browser support. The XHR object that is the heart of Ajax is truly designed to allow asynchronous retrieval of arbitrary data from the server.

As we've discussed, traditional Web applications follow a request/response paradigm. Without Ajax, the entire page (or with IFRAMEs, parts of the page) is reloaded with each request. The previously viewed page is reflected in the browser's history stack (though if IFRAMEs are used, clicking the back button doesn't always result in what the user expects). However, requests made with XHR are *not* recorded in the browser's history. This too can pose an issue if your users are familiar with using the back button to navigate within your Web application.

The Usability Question

While we're talking about user expectations, we should mention usability. The Ajax approach is fairly new—there really aren't any established best practices or heuristics. However, standard Web design principles still apply. As time passes and more people experiment with this approach, we will find the limits and establish guidelines. That said, you should let your users guide you. Depending on how you choose to use Ajax in your application, you may be dynamically changing parts of your page; users who are accustomed to seeing the entire browser refresh may not notice that anything has changed. This issue has led to features such as the Yellow Fade Technique (YFT) popularized by 37signals, as used in the Ajax poster application Basecamp.

In a nutshell, YFT says, "Take the part of the page that changed, and make it yellow." Assuming yellow is not the dominant color of your application, the user is likely to notice this change. Over time, you fade the yellow color until it returns to the original background color. Obviously, you could choose any color you want; all you are doing is drawing attention to what has changed.

Perhaps YTF isn't right for your application; instead, you may choose to alert your users in a less obvious though no less useful manner. Gmail shows a red flashing "Loading" sign in the upper-right corner to indicate that it is fetching data (see Figure 1-7).

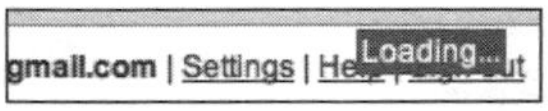

gmail.com | Settings | He[Loading...]ut

Figure 1-7. *Gmail's "Loading" sign*

Whether you need to use YFT or a similar technique is really up to your users. The simplest approach is to test it with a group of representative users. You could do this using paper-based or Web-based prototypes depending on where you are in the design process, but however you test it, you should get some user feedback before simply introducing complex Ajax usage.

You should also start small. Your first attempt at using Ajax shouldn't be to create a dynamic portal site with adjustable columns. Rather, begin by moving client-side validation to the server. Once you get the hang of it, begin to venture into more dynamic uses, such as populating a drop-down list or setting some default text.

However you choose to apply Ajax, remember to not do anything wacky. We know that this is not scientific advice. However, at this point, there aren't any hard-and-fast rules. Listen to your users, test before you deploy, and remember how quickly we all learned to hit the "skip intro" link.

You should be aware of a few common mistakes when using Ajax. We've already discussed providing visual clues to your users when something changes, but Ajax changes the standard Web approach in other ways. First, unlike IFRAMES and hidden frames, making a request via XHR does not modify the history stack of your browser. In many cases, this won't matter (how often have you clicked the back arrow only to discover that nothing has changed?), but if your users are expecting the back button to work, you will have some issues.

Unlike other browser-based approaches, Ajax won't modify the link displayed in the address bar, meaning you cannot easily bookmark a page or send a link to a friend. For many applications this may be desirable, but if your site provides driving directions or something similar, you will need a solution to this problem.

It's important to not go overboard with Ajax. Remember, JavaScript is running on your client's browser, and having thousands of lines of JavaScript can severely slow down your users' experiences. Poorly coded scripts can quickly spiral out of control, especially as volume increases.

Ajax allows you to perform operations asynchronously, which is both its greatest strength and one of its major weaknesses. We've trained users that our Web applications perform in a request/response paradigm, but with Ajax, we no longer have that limitation. We might be modifying a part of the page, and if the users aren't expecting that, they may be confused. So, you need to be careful to keep things obvious to your users—don't try to be too clever. Remember, when in doubt, test with representative users!

The Skill Set

If you've picked up this book, you probably have most of the skills necessary to implement Ajax in your application. Once again, we want to emphasize that Ajax is a client-side technique—it will work with whatever server-side technology you are currently using, whether it's Java, .NET, Ruby, PHP, or CGI. In fact, in this book, we will be pretty agnostic to the server side and assume you know best how to work with the server-side technology you use in your day-to-day work. What we will focus on over the course of the next few hundred pages is the client-side techniques and technology you'll need to create rich browser-based applications.

While you can use any server-side technology you want, using Ajax involves a bit of a shift. In a typical Web application, server-side code renders an entire page and involves an entire unit of work. With Ajax, you might return only a small bit of text and might involve only a small subset of a business application. For most experienced Web developers, this won't be much of an issue, but it's something you need to keep in mind.

Emerging frameworks will help shield developers from some of the ins and outs of Ajax; however, you will need some familiarity with JavaScript. We know that JavaScript can be a real pain to use. Sorry, there's really no getting around it. Most of us learned to use "alerts" as a type of system out for debugging purposes, and sadly this technique is still widely used. However, we have new hammers in our toolkit.

Along with JavaScript, you will need some familiarity with other presentation-related technologies such as HTML, the DOM, and CSS. You don't need to be an expert, but you need to know the basics. We'll cover most of what you need to know in this book and supplement the text with various Web resources.

For the test driven among us (you do write unit tests, right?), we will cover JsUnit and Selenium (see Figure 1-8). These tools allow you to develop your JavaScript test first and check for browser compatibility testing. It is widely expected that the next generation of developer environments will feature improved support for JavaScript, and other Ajax-related technologies will further ease the burden on developers. Scripts and frameworks are being introduced regularly that also make development simpler.

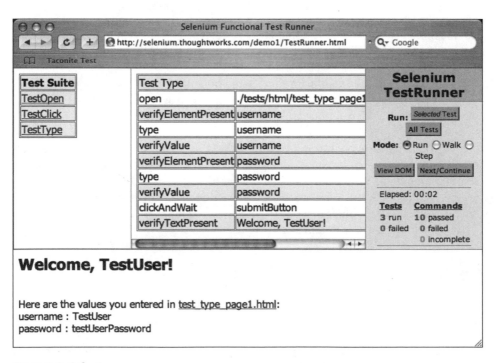

Figure 1-8. *Selenium*

Usage

Now that we've piqued your interest, it's important to know when you should and when you shouldn't use Ajax techniques. First, don't be afraid to try an approach on your applications. We believe almost every Web application can benefit from Ajax techniques; just don't go overboard until you have a good feel for where it makes sense. Validation is a perfect place to start, but don't limit yourself. Though you certainly can post data using Ajax, it probably shouldn't be the primary approach.

Second, browser issues are the only factor that should slow you down in your implementation of Ajax. If a large number of your users (or if particularly important users) are still using older browsers—anything before Internet Explorer 5, Safari 1.2, or Mozilla 1.0—these techniques won't work. If this is an important class of users, you will need to use cross-browser alternatives that work for your target audience, forgo Ajax altogether, or develop a site that will degrade gracefully. Browser support probably isn't a significant factor, because Netscape Navigator 4 usage is fractional; however, you should consult your Web logs to see what applies to your applications.

As we've stated, validation and form population are prime candidates for Ajax. You can also make truly dynamic portal sites using the DOM's drag technique shown in Google's personalized home page (see Figure 1-9).

Figure 1-9. *Google's personalized home page*

As you can see, Ajax creates a whole new set of opportunities for Web application development. No longer are you hindered by proprietary techniques and disappointing compromises. With Ajax, the line between thick and thin is blurred, and the real winners are your users!

Design Considerations

Now that you have some ideas on where to use Ajax, we'll take a minute to cover some design considerations for applying Ajax. Many of these principles are no different from what you would normally do in a Web application, but they still bear mentioning. Strive to minimize the traffic between the client and server. Applied well, Ajax will make your application more responsive, but if you are trying to send an encyclopedia's worth of data back and forth every time your user navigates off a field, your users will not be amused. When in doubt, follow standard conventions. If most applications do XYZ, then you probably should too. When in doubt, look at the standards for Web desktop applications. Some patterns have been established, and more are sure to follow (www.ajaxpatterns.org).

When you first start using Ajax techniques, the way your application works may not be clear to your users. We've trained users over the years that Web applications work in a certain way, and Ajax adds an asynchronous component that may throw them. Put simply, don't surprise your users. If your pre-Ajax application didn't save the form when they tabbed off the last field, your post-Ajax application probably shouldn't either.

The most important issue to consider when implementing Ajax is simple: it's all about the user, stupid. Always remember the user, and don't practice "résumé-driven design." The desire to pass your next employer's buzzword filter is not a good enough reason to add Ajax to your application; if using Ajax benefits your user by providing a richer experience, by all means, get it out there. But don't forget—just because you can, doesn't mean you should. Be smart, think of your users first, and you should be fine.

We'll talk more about security later, but we want to point out that Ajax has some security considerations. Remember that source is viewable in a browser, meaning that anyone can figure out how you created your snappy widget. Since you have to include uniform resource locators (URLs) when you set up your XHR objects, it is possible that someone with malicious intent could hack your site and run their own code. Applying Ajax judiciously can mitigate this risk.

Summary

The Internet has certainly evolved from its early origins as a way for researchers to connect and share information. The Internet began with simple textual browsers and static pages, but it is now hard to find a company that doesn't have a polished Web site. In its early days, who could have possibly imagined that people would one day flock to the Internet to research that new car or buy the latest Stephen King novel?

Developers fed up with the difficulty of deploying thick client applications to thousands of users looked to the Web to ease their burden. Several Web application technologies have been developed over the years—some proprietary, others requiring significant programming abilities. Though some provided a richer user experience than others, no one would confuse a thin client application with its desktop-based cousin. Still, the ease of deployment, the ability to reach a wider customer base, and the lower cost of maintenance means that despite the limitations of browsers, they are still the target platform of choice for many applications.

Developers have used hacks to circumvent some of the most troublesome restrictions the Internet places on developers. Various remote scripting options and HTML elements let developers work asynchronously with the server, but it wasn't until the major browsers added support for the XMLHttpRequest object that a true cross-browser method was possible. With companies such as Google, Yahoo, and Amazon leading the way, we are finally seeing browser-based applications that rival thick clients. With Ajax, you get the best of both worlds—your code sits on a server that you control, and any customer with a browser can access an application that provides a full, rich user experience.

CHAPTER 2

■ ■ ■

Using the XMLHttpRequest Object

Now that we've discussed the history of dynamic Web applications and introduced Ajax, it's time to cover the heart of the matter: how to use the XMLHttpRequest object. While Ajax is more of a technique than a technology, without widespread support for XMLHttpRequest, Google Suggest and Ta-da List wouldn't exist as we currently know them. And you wouldn't be reading this book!

XMLHttpRequest was originally implemented in Internet Explorer 5 as an ActiveX component. That it worked only in Internet Explorer kept most developers from using XMLHttpRequest until its recent adoption as a de facto standard in Mozilla 1.0 and Safari 1.2. It's important to note that XMLHttpRequest is *not* a W3C standard, though much of the functionality is covered in a new proposal: the DOM Level 3 Load and Save Specification. Because it is not a standard, its behavior may differ slightly from browser to browser, though most methods and properties are widely supported. Currently, Firefox, Safari, Opera, Konqueror, and Internet Explorer all implement the behavior of the XMLHttpRequest object similarly.

That said, if a significant number of your users still access your site or application with older browsers, you will need to consider your options. As we discussed in Chapter 1, if you are going to use Ajax techniques, you need to either develop an alternative site or allow your application to degrade gracefully. With most usage statistics indicating that only a small fraction of browsers in use today lack XMLHttpRequest support, the chances of this being a problem are slim. However, you need to check your Web logs and determine what clients your customers are using to access your sites.

Overview of the XMLHttpRequest Object

You must first create an XMLHttpRequest object using JavaScript before you can use the object to send requests and process responses. Since XMLHttpRequest is not a W3C standard, you can use JavaScript in a couple of ways to create an instance of XMLHttpRequest. Internet Explorer implements XMLHttpRequest as an ActiveX object, and other browsers such as Firefox, Safari, and Opera implement it as a native JavaScript object. Because of these differences, the JavaScript code must contain logic to create an instance of XMLHttpRequest using the ActiveX technique or using the native JavaScript object technique.

The previous statement might send shivers down the spines of those who remember the days when the implementation of JavaScript and the DOM varied widely among browsers. Fortunately, in this case you don't need elaborate code to identify the browser type to know how to create an instance of the XMLHttpRequest object. All you need to do is check the browser's support of ActiveX objects. If the browser supports ActiveX objects, then you create the XMLHttpRequest object using ActiveX. Otherwise, you create it using the native JavaScript object technique. Listing 2-1 demonstrates the simplicity of creating cross-browser JavaScript code that creates an instance of the XMLHttpRequest object.

Listing 2-1. *Creating an Instance of the XMLHttpRequest Object*

```
var xmlHttp;

function createXMLHttpRequest() {
    if (window.ActiveXObject) {
        xmlHttp = new ActiveXObject("Microsoft.XMLHTTP");
    }
    else if (window.XMLHttpRequest) {
        xmlHttp = new XMLHttpRequest();
    }
}
```

As you can see, creating the XMLHttpRequest object is rather trivial. First, you create a globally scoped variable named `xmlHttp` to hold the reference to the object. The `createXMLHttpRequest` method does the work of actually creating an instance of XMLHttpRequest. The method contains simple branching logic that determines how to go about creating the object. The call to `window.ActiveXObject` will return an object or `null`, which is evaluated by the `if` statement as true or false, thus indicating whether the browser supports ActiveX controls and thus is Internet Explorer. If so, then the XMLHttpRequest object is created by instantiating a new instance of ActiveXObject, passing a string indicating the type of ActiveX object you want to create. In this instance, you provide `Microsoft.XMLHTTP` to the constructor, indicating your desire to create an instance of XMLHttpRequest.

If the call to `window.ActiveXObject` fails, then the JavaScript branches to the `else` statement, which determines whether the browser implements XMLHttpRequest as a native JavaScript object. If `window.XMLHttpRequest` exists, then an instance of XMLHttpRequest is created.

Thanks to JavaScript's dynamically typed nature and that XMLHttpRequest implementations are compatible across various browsers, you can access the properties and methods of an instance of XMLHttpRequest identically, regardless of the method used to create the instance. This greatly simplifies the development process and keeps the JavaScript free of browser-specific logic.

Methods and Properties

Table 2-1 shows some typical methods on the XMLHttpRequest object. Don't worry; we'll talk about these methods in greater detail in a moment.

Table 2-1. *Standard XMLHttpRequest Operations*

Method	Description
abort()	Aborts the current request.
getAllResponseHeaders()	Returns all the response headers for the HTTP request as key/value pairs.
getResponseHeader("header")	Returns the string value of the specified header.
open("method", "url")	Sets the stage for a call to the server. The method argument can be either GET, POST, or PUT. The url argument can be relative or absolute. This method includes three optional arguments.
send(content)	Sends the request to the server.
setRequestHeader("header", "value")	Sets the specified header to the supplied value. open() must be called before attempting to set any headers.

Let's take a closer look at these methods.

void open(string method, string url, boolean asynch, string username, string password): This method sets up your call to the server. This method is meant to be the script-only method of initializing a request. It has two required arguments and three optional arguments. You are required to supply the specific method you are invoking (GET, POST, or PUT) and the URL of the resource you are calling. You may optionally pass a Boolean indicating whether this call is meant to be asynchronous—the default is true, which means the request is asynchronous in nature. If you pass a false, processing waits until the response returns from the server. Since making calls asynchronously is one of the main benefits of using Ajax, setting this parameter to false somewhat defeats the purpose of using the XMLHttpRequest object. That said, you may find it useful in certain circumstances such as validating user input before allowing the page to be persisted. The last two parameters are self-explanatory, allowing you to include a specific username and password.

void send(content): This method actually makes the request to the server. If the request was declared as asynchronous, this method returns immediately, otherwise it waits until the response is received. The optional argument can be an instance of a DOM object, an input stream, or a string. The content passed to this method is sent as part of the request body.

void setRequestHeader(string header, string value): This method sets a value for a given header value in the HTTP request. It takes a string representing the header to set and a string representing the value to place in the header. Note that it must be called after a call to open(). Of all these methods, the two you will use the most are open() and send(). The XMLHttpRequest object has a number of properties that prove themselves quite useful while designing Ajax interactions.

void abort(): This method is really quite self-explanatory—it stops the request.

string getAllResponseHeaders(): The core functionality of this method should be familiar to Web application developers—it returns a string containing response headers from the HTTP request. Headers include Content-Length, Date, and URI.

string getResponseHeader(string header): This method is a companion to getAllResponseHeaders() except it takes an argument representing the specific header value you want, returning this value as a string.

In addition to these standard methods, the XMLHttpRequest object exposes the properties listed in Table 2-2. You'll use these properties extensively when working with XMLHttpRequest.

Table 2-2. *Standard XMLHttpRequest Properties*

Property	Description
onreadystatechange	The event handler that fires at every state change, typically a call to a JavaScript function.
readyState	The state of the request. The five possible values are 0 = uninitialized, 1 = loading, 2 = loaded, 3 = interactive, and 4 = complete.
responseText	The response from the server as a string.
responseXML	The response from the server as XML. This object can be parsed and examined as a DOM object.
status	The HTTP status code from the server (that is, 200 for OK, 404 for Not Found, and so on).
statusText	The text version of the HTTP status code (that is, OK or Not Found, and so on).

An Example Interaction

At this point, you might be wondering what a typical Ajax interaction looks like. Figure 2-1 shows the standard interaction paradigm in an Ajax application.

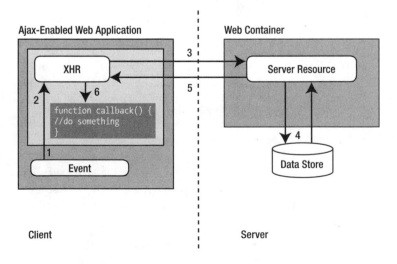

Figure 2-1. *Standard Ajax interaction*

Unlike the standard request/response approach found in a standard Web client, an Ajax application does things a little bit differently.

1. A client-side event triggers an Ajax event. Any number of things can trigger this, from a simple onchange event to some specific user action. You might have code like this:

```
<input type="text"id="email" name="email" onblur="validateEmail()";>
```

2. An instance of the XMLHttpRequest object is created. Using the open() method, the call is set up—the URL is set along with the desired HTTP method, typically GET or POST. The request is actually triggered via a call to the send() method. This code might look something like this:

```
var xmlHttp;
function validateEmail() {
  var email = document.getElementById("email");
  var url = "validate?email=" + escape(email.value);
  if (window.ActiveXObject) {
    xmlHttp = new ActiveXObject("Microsoft.XMLHTTP");
  }
  else if (window.XMLHttpRequest) {
    xmlHttp = new XMLHttpRequest();
  }
  xmlHttp.open("GET", url);
  xmlHttp.onreadystatechange = callback;
  xmlHttp.send(null);
}
```

3. A request is made to the server. This might be a call to a servlet, a CGI script, or any server-side technique.

4. The server can do anything you can think of, including accessing a data store or even another system.

5. The request is returned to the browser. The Content-Type is set to text/xml—the XMLHttpRequest object can process results only of the text/html type. In more complex instances, the response might be quite involved and include JavaScript, DOM manipulation, or other related technologies. Note that you also need to set the headers so that the browser will not cache the results locally. You do this with the following code:

```
response.setHeader("Cache-Control", "no-cache");
response.setHeader("Pragma", "no-cache");[1]
```

---

1. Pragma and Cache-Control...don't they do the same thing? Yes, they do, but Pragma is defined for backward compatibility.

6. In this example, you configure the XMLHttpRequest object to call the function `callback()` when the processing returns. This function checks the `readyState` property on the XMLHttpRequest object and then looks at the status code returned from the server. Provided everything is as expected, the `callback()` function does something interesting on the client. A typical callback method looks something like this:

```
function callback() {
  if (xmlHttp.readyState == 4) {
    if (xmlHttp.status == 200) {
        //do something interesting here
    }
  }
}
```

As you can see, this is different from the normal request/response paradigm but not in a way that is foreign to Web developers. Obviously, you have a bit more going on when you create and set up an XMLHttpRequest object and when the "callback" has some checks for states and statuses. Typically, you will wrap these standard calls into a library that you will use throughout your application, or you will use one that is available on the Web. This field is new, but a considerable amount of activity is happening in the open-source community.

In general, the various frameworks and toolkits available on the Web take care of the basic wiring and the browser abstractions, and some add user interface components. Some are purely client based; others require work on the server. Many of these frameworks have just begun development or are in the early phases of release; the landscape is constantly changing, with new libraries and versions coming out regularly. As the field matures, the best ones will become apparent. Some of the more mature libraries include libXmlRequest, RSLite, sarissa, JavaScript Object Notation (JSON), JSRS, Direct Web Remoting (DWR), and Ruby on Rails. This is a dynamic space, so keep your RSS aggregator tuned to those sites dedicated to posting about all things Ajax!

GET vs. POST

You might be wondering what the difference is between GET and POST and when you should use one or the other. In theory, use GET when the request is idempotent, meaning that multiple requests will return the same result. In truth, if your corresponding server method modifies state in some way, it's unlikely this is actually true. That said, it is the standard. The more practical difference comes in terms of payload size—in many cases, browsers and servers will limit the length of the URL used to send data to the server. In general, use GET to retrieve data from the server; in other words, avoid changing state on the server with a GET call.

In general, use POST methods anytime you are changing the state on the server. Unlike GET, you are required to set the Content-Type header on the XMLHttpRequest object like this:

```
xmlHttp.setRequestHeader("Content-Type", "application/x-www-form-urlencoded");
```

Unlike GET, POST does not restrict the size of the payload that is sent to the server, and POST requests are not guaranteed to be idempotent.

Chances are, most of the requests you will make will be GET requests; however, POST is there if you need to use it.

Remote Scripting

Now that we've introduced Ajax, we want to briefly touch on remote scripting. Many of you might be thinking, "What's the big deal with Ajax? I've been doing that same thing with IFRAMEs for years." In fact, we have used this approach too. What we've done in the past is typically referred to as *remote scripting* and is thought of by many as a hack. However, it does provide a mechanism to avoid page refreshes.

Overview of Remote Scripting

Essentially, remote scripting is a type of remote procedure call. You are interacting with your server just like a normal Web application, but you don't refresh the entire page. Just as with Ajax, you can call any server-side technology that can receive requests, process those requests, and return a meaningful result. Just as on the server side, you have a number of options on the client side when implementing remote scripting. You can imbed a Flash animation, a Java applet, or an ActiveX component into your application. You can even go so far as using XML-RPC, but the complexity of this approach makes it less than ideal unless you are experienced with the techniques. Common implementations of remote scripting include combining scripting with an IFRAME (hidden or otherwise) and having the server return JavaScript, which is then run within the browser.

Microsoft has its own solution for remote scripting, cleverly called Microsoft Remote Scripting (MSRS), that allows you to call server scripts as if they were local. A Java applet is embedded in the page to facilitate the communication with the server, an .asp page is used to house the server-side scripts, and an .htm file manages the client side of the arrangement. You can use Microsoft's solution in Netscape and Internet Explorer versions 4.0 and greater. Calls can be made both synchronously and asynchronously. However, this solution requires Java, which may mean an additional installation routine, and it expects Internet Information Services (IIS), which limits your server-side options.

Brent Ashley has created two free cross-platform libraries for remote scripting. JSRS is a client-side JavaScript library that takes advantage of DHTML to make remote calls to the server. It works on a wide variety of operating systems and browsers. With common and popular server-side implementations (including PHP, Python, and Perl CGI), it is likely you can get JSRS up and running on your site. Ashley provides JSRS free of charge and makes the source code available on his Web site at www.ashleyit.com/rs/main.htm.

If JSRS is too heavyweight for your tastes, Ashley has also created RSLite, which uses cookies. It is limited to small amounts of data and single calls but is supported in most browsers.

A Remote Scripting Example

For comparison, we'll show you an example of how Ajax-like techniques are implemented using IFRAMEs. It's pretty straightforward, and we have used this approach in the past (before XMLHttpRequest came on the scene). This example won't actually call the server, but it gives you an idea of how to use IFRAMEs for remote scripting.

This example involves two files: iframe.html (see Listing 2-2) and server.html (see Listing 2-3). The server.html mimics the response that would actually be returned from a server.

Listing 2-2. *The* iframe.html *File*

```html
<html>
  <head>
    <title>Example of remote scripting in an IFRAME</title>
  </head>
  <script type="text/javascript">
    function handleResponse() {
      alert('this function is called from server.html');
    }
  </script>
  <body>
  <h1>Remote Scripting with an IFRAME</h1>

  <iframe id="beforexhr"
  name="beforexhr"
  style="width:0px; height:0px; border: 0px"
  src="blank.html"></iframe>

  <a href="server.html" target="beforexhr">call the server</a>

  </body>
</html>
```

Listing 2-3. *The* server.html *File*

```html
<html>
  <head>
    <title>the server</title>
  </head>
  <script type="text/javascript">
    window.parent.handleResponse();
  </script>
  <body>
  </body>
</html>
```

Figure 2-2 shows the original page. Running this code produces a result like the one shown in Figure 2-3.

Figure 2-2. *The original page*

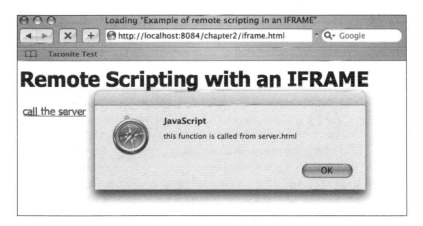

Figure 2-3. *The page after calling the "server"*

How to Send a Simple Request

You're now ready to start using the XMLHttpRequest object. We've just discussed how to create the object, so now we can show how to send requests to the server and process the server's response.

The simplest request you can make is the one where you don't send any information to the server in the form of query parameters or posted form data. In practice, you'll almost always want to send some information to the server.

The basic steps for sending a request using the XMLHttpRequest object are as follows:

1. Obtain a reference to an instance of XMLHttpRequest, either by creating a new one or accessing a variable that already holds an instance of XMLHttpRequest.

2. Tell the XMLHttpRequest object about the function that will handle changes in the XMLHttpRequest object's state. You accomplish this by setting the object's onreadystatechange property with a pointer to a JavaScript function.

3. Assign the properties of the request. The XMLHttpRequest object's open() method assigns the impending request. The open() method takes three parameters: a string indicating the method (usually either GET or POST), a string representing the URL of the destination resource, and a Boolean indicating whether the request should be made asynchronously.

4. Send the request to the server. The XMLHttpRequest object's send() method transmits the request to the indicated destination resource. The send() method accepts one parameter, which is typically a string or a DOM object. This parameter is transmitted to the destination URL as part of the request body. When providing a parameter to the send() method, be sure the method assigned in the open() method is POST. Use null when there is no data to be sent as part of the request body.

These steps are intuitive: you need an instance of the XMLHttpRequest object, you need to tell it what to do when it undergoes changes in state, you need to tell it where and how to send the request, and finally you need to direct XMLHttpRequest to transmit the request. However, unless you're experienced with C or C++, the notion of a *function pointer* may be foreign to you.

A function pointer is just like any variable, except that instead of pointing to data like a string or number or even an instance of an object, it points to a function. In JavaScript, all functions are addressed in memory and can be referenced using the function name. This gives you the flexibility of passing function pointers as parameters to other functions or storing a function pointer in an object's properties.

In the case of the XMLHttpRequest object, the onreadystatechange property stores the pointer to the callback function. The callback function is called when the XMLHttpRequest object's internal state changes. When an asynchronous call is made, the request is transmitted, and the script continues processing immediately—the script doesn't have to wait for the request to complete before continuing. Once the request is sent, the object's readyState property undergoes numerous changes. While you could base processing on any state, typically you are most interested in the one that indicates the server is finished sending the response. By setting the callback function, you are effectively telling the XMLHttpRequest object, "Call this function to handle the response whenever it arrives."

A Simple Request Example

This first example is simple. It's a small HTML page with a single button. Clicking the button initiates an asynchronous request to the server. The server will respond by sending a simple static text file. The response is handled by displaying the contents of the static text file in an alert window. Listing 2-4 shows the HTML page and associated JavaScript.

Listing 2-4. *The* simpleRequest.html *Page*

```
<!DOCTYPE html PUBLIC "-//W3C//DTD XHTML 1.0 Strict//EN"
  "http://www.w3.org/TR/xhtml1/DTD/xhtml1-strict.dtd">
<html xmlns="http://www.w3.org/1999/xhtml">
<head>
<title>Simple XMLHttpRequest</title>
```

```
<script type="text/javascript">
var xmlHttp;

function createXMLHttpRequest() {
    if (window.ActiveXObject) {
        xmlHttp = new ActiveXObject("Microsoft.XMLHTTP");
    }
    else if (window.XMLHttpRequest) {
        xmlHttp = new XMLHttpRequest();
    }
}

function startRequest() {
    createXMLHttpRequest();
    xmlHttp.onreadystatechange = handleStateChange;
    xmlHttp.open("GET", "simpleResponse.xml", true);
    xmlHttp.send(null);
}

function handleStateChange() {
    if(xmlHttp.readyState == 4) {
        if(xmlHttp.status == 200) {
            alert("The server replied with: " + xmlHttp.responseText);
        }
    }
}
</script>
</head>

<body>
    <form action="#">
        <input type="button" value="Start Basic Asynchronous Request"
                onclick="startRequest();"/>
    </form>
</body>
</html>
```

The server's response file, simpleResponse.xml, contains only a single line of text.
Clicking the button on the HTML page should produce an alert box with the contents of
the simpleResponse.xml file. Figure 2-4 displays the identical alert boxes that contain the
server's response in both Internet Explorer and Firefox.

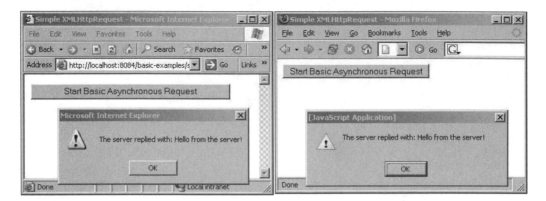

Figure 2-4. *The first simple asynchronous request*

The request to the server was sent asynchronously, allowing the browser to continue responding to user input while awaiting the server's response in the background. If a synchronous operation was chosen and if the server's response had taken several seconds to arrive, the browser would have been unresponsive to user input during the waiting time. The asynchronous behavior, while subtle, can measurably improve the end user's experience by avoiding the appearance that the browser has frozen and is failing to respond to user input. This allows the user to continue working while the server works on the previous request in the background.

The ability to communicate with the server without interrupting the user's workflow opens a wide variety of techniques for improving the user experience. One application, for example, is for validating user input. While a user is filling out the fields on an input form, the browser could periodically send the form values to the server for validation, without interrupting the user filling in the remaining form fields. If a validation rule fails, the user could be notified immediately, before the form is actually sent to the server for processing, saving the user time and reducing the load on the server, as the form's contents don't have to be rebuilt after an unsuccessful form submission.

A Word About Security

Any discussion of browser-based technologies wouldn't be complete without mentioning security. The XMLHttpRequest object is subjected to the browser's security "sandbox." Any resources requested by the XMLHttpRequest object must reside within the same domain from which the calling script originated. This security restriction prevents the XMLHttpRequest object from requesting resources outside the domain from which the script was originally served.

The strength of this security restriction varies by browser (see Figure 2-5). Internet Explorer shows an alert stating that a potential security risk exists but gives the user a choice of whether to continue with the request. Firefox simply stops the request and shows an error message in the JavaScript console.

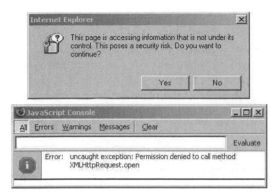

Figure 2-5. *Internet Explorer's and Firefox's responses to potential security threats*

Firefox does provide some JavaScript tricks to allow XMLHttpRequest to request resources from an outside URL. However, since these techniques are specific to the browser, it's best to not use them and to avoid attempting to access outside URLs using XMLHttpRequest.

DOM Level 3 Load and Save

So far, none of the solutions we've discussed is a standard. Though XMLHttpRequest enjoys widespread support, you've already seen how the process of creating it differs from browser to browser. Many people mistakenly believe Ajax has W3C backing; however, it does not. The W3C has addressed this and other shortcomings in a new standard with a rather lengthy name: the DOM Level 3 Load and Save Specification. This specification is designed to be a platform- and language-independent way to modify the content of a DOM document with XML content. The 1.0 version was recommended in April 2004, but currently no browser has implemented it.

When will Load and Save replace Ajax? Your bet is as good as ours. Considering how many browsers don't fully support existing standards, it's hard to say, but as more sites and applications take advantage of Ajax techniques, expect to see support in future releases. However, based on the length of time it took for earlier DOM versions to be adopted, don't hold your breath. In an interview, DOM Activity Lead Philippe Le Hégaret said it will take "significant time" to see widespread adoption. Some support exists for DOM Level 3—Opera's XMLHttpRequest implementation is based on its work in supporting DOM Level 3, and the Java API for XML Processing (JAXP) version 1.3 supports it. However, the emergence of a W3C specification signals the importance of Ajax techniques.

Load and Save is the culmination of an effort that began in August 1997 as a way of solving the incompatibilities in the browsers of the day. You may notice that the title says *Level 3*—what were Levels 1 and 2 all about? Level 1 was finished in October 1998 and gave us HTML 4.0 and XML 1.0. Today, Level 1 is widely supported. In November 2000, Level 2 was completed, though its adoption has been slow. CSS was part of Level 2.

What will developers gain from the Load and Save specification? Ideally, it will solve many of the cross-browser issues we currently encounter. Though Ajax is pretty straightforward, you'll recall that just to create an instance of the XMLHttpRequest object you need to check the browser type. A true W3C specification would alleviate those types of coding hacks. Basically,

Load and Save will provide Web developers with a common API to access and modify the DOM in a language- and platform-independent way. In other words, it won't matter if you're on Windows or Linux, and it won't matter if you're developing in VBScript or JavaScript. You will also be able to save a DOM tree as an XML document or take an XML document and load it into the DOM. The specification also provides support for XML 1.1, XML Schema 1.0, and SOAP 1.2. Once available, it is expected to be widely used by developers.

The DOM

We keep talking about the DOM, and if you haven't done a lot of work on the client side, you might not know what the DOM is. The DOM is a W3C specification for a platform- and language-independent way of accessing and modifying the content and structure of a document. In other words, it's a common way to represent and manipulate an HTML or XML document.

It's important to note that the design of the DOM is based on specifications from the Object Management Group, which allows it to be used with any programming language. It was originally conceived as a way of making JavaScript portable across browsers, though it has expanded beyond that limited application.

The DOM really is an object model in the object-oriented sense. The DOM defines the objects needed to represent and modify documents, the behavior and attributes of these objects, and the relationship between these objects. You can think of the DOM as a tree representation of the data and structure on a page, though of course it may not actually be implemented that way. Say you have a Web page that looks something like Listing 2-5.

Listing 2-5. *Simple Table*

```
<table>
  <tbody>
    <tr>
        <td>Foo</td>
        <td>Bar</td>
    </tr>
  </tbody>
</table>
```

You can picture the DOM of this simple table as something like Figure 2-6.

The beauty of the DOM specification is that it gives you a standard way to interact with your documents. Without the DOM, the most interesting aspects of Ajax wouldn't be possible. Since the DOM allows you to not only traverse but also edit the content, you can make highly dynamic pages.

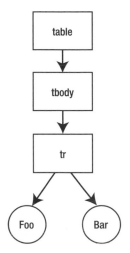

Figure 2-6. *Simple DOM*

Summary

While Ajaxesque techniques have been used for many years, the recent adoption of the XMLHttpRequest object by modern browsers has ushered in a new era of developing rich Web applications. In this chapter, we established the basics of working with the heart of Ajax, the XMLHttpRequest object. At this point, you know the methods and properties of the XMLHttpRequest object, and we've shown you some simple examples of their use. As you can see, the object is pretty straightforward and hides much of its complexity from you. Combined with a healthy dose of JavaScript and some basic DOM manipulation, Ajax allows for a level of interactivity previously unmatched on the Web.

As mentioned in Chapter 1, with XMLHttpRequest you are no longer limited to complete page refreshes and synchronous conversations with your server. In the upcoming chapters, we'll show you how to combine your existing expertise of server-side technologies with the unique capabilities of XMLHttpRequest to provide highly interactive Web applications.

■ ■ ■

CHAPTER 3

Communicating with the Server: Sending Requests and Processing Responses

Now the real fun begins! It's time to put your newfound knowledge of the XMLHttpRequest object to work. By showing some simple examples, we'll demonstrate how the XMLHttpRequest object sends requests to the server and how to process the server response with JavaScript.

■Note The examples in this chapter do not use a dynamic server to process the response and provide a real-time response. Instead, the examples use simple text files to mimic the server's response. Doing so removes complexity, allowing you to focus on what's happening in the browser.

Processing the Server Response

The XMLHttpRequest object provides two properties that provide access to the server response. The first property, responseText, simply provides the response as a string. The second property, responseXML, provides the response as an XML object. Retrieving the response as simple text is fine for simple use cases, such as when the response is displayed in an alert box or the response is a simple one-word phrase indicating success or failure.

The previous example in Chapter 2 accessed the server response using the responseText property and displayed it in an alert box.

Using the innerHTML Property to Create Dynamic Content

Accessing the server response as simple text doesn't provide much flexibility. Simple text lacks structure and is difficult to parse logically with JavaScript. It also makes it more difficult to dynamically generate page content.

The responseText property becomes useful if you utilize it in conjunction with the innerHTML property of HTML elements. The innerHTML property is a nonstandard property first implemented by Internet Explorer and later by many other popular browsers. It is a simple string that represents the content between a set of start and end tags.

By using responseText and innerHTML together, the server can produce HTML content that is consumed by the browser using the innerHTML property. The following example illustrates search functionality using the XMLHttpRequest object, its responseText property, and the innerHTML property of HTML elements. Clicking the search button initiates a "search" on the server. The server responds by generating a table of results. The browser processes the response by setting the innerHTML property of a div element to the value of the XMLHttpRequest object's responseText property. Figure 3-1 shows the browser window after the search button has been clicked and the results table has been added to the window content.

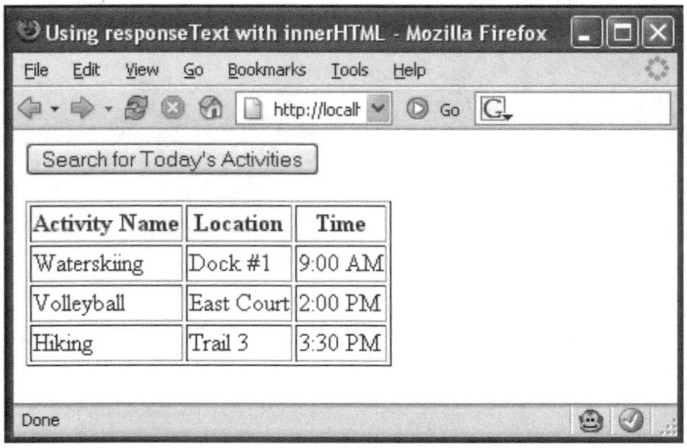

Figure 3-1. *The browser window showing the search results retrieved using XMLHttpRequest and processed using* innerHTML

The code for this example is similar to the example from Chapter 2 that simply displayed the server response in an alert box. The steps are as follows:

1. Clicking the search button calls the startRequest function, which first calls the createXMLHttpRequest function to initialize a new instance of the XMLHttpRequest object.

2. The startRequest function sets the callback function to be the handleStateChange function.

3. The startRequest function continues by using the open() method to set the request's method (GET) and its destination and to perform the request asynchronously.

4. The request is then sent using the send() method of the XMLHttpRequest object.

5. Each time the XMLHttpRequest object's internal state changes, the handleStateChange function is called. Once the response has been received (indicated by the readyState property having a value of 4), the innerHTML property of the div element is set using the responseText property of XMLHttpRequest.

Listing 3-1 shows innerHTML.html, and Listing 3-2 shows innerHTML.xml, which represents the content produced by the search.

Listing 3-1. innerHTML.html

```
<!DOCTYPE html PUBLIC "-//W3C//DTD XHTML 1.0 Strict//EN"
  "http://www.w3.org/TR/xhtml1/DTD/xhtml1-strict.dtd">
 <html xmlns="http://www.w3.org/1999/xhtml">
<head>
<title>Using responseText with innerHTML</title>

<script type="text/javascript">
var xmlHttp;

function createXMLHttpRequest() {
    if (window.ActiveXObject) {
        xmlHttp = new ActiveXObject("Microsoft.XMLHTTP");
    }
    else if (window.XMLHttpRequest) {
        xmlHttp = new XMLHttpRequest();
    }
}

function startRequest() {
    createXMLHttpRequest();
    xmlHttp.onreadystatechange = handleStateChange;
    xmlHttp.open("GET", "innerHTML.xml", true);
    xmlHttp.send(null);
}

function handleStateChange() {
    if(xmlHttp.readyState == 4) {
        if(xmlHttp.status == 200) {
            document.getElementById("results").innerHTML = xmlHttp.responseText;
        }
    }
}
</script>
</head>

<body>
    <form action="#">
        <input type="button" value="Search for Today's Activities"
                onclick="startRequest();"/>
    </form>
    <div id="results"></div>
</body>
</html>
```

Listing 3-2. `innerHTML.xml`

```
<table border="1">
    <tbody>
        <tr>
            <th>Activity Name</th>
            <th>Location</th>
            <th>Time</th>
        </tr>
        <tr>
            <td>Waterskiing</td>
            <td>Dock #1</td>
            <td>9:00 AM</td>
        </tr>
        <tr>
            <td>Volleyball</td>
            <td>East Court</td>
            <td>2:00 PM</td>
        </tr>
        <tr>
            <td>Hiking</td>
            <td>Trail 3</td>
            <td>3:30 PM</td>
        </tr>
    </tbody>
</table>
```

Using `responseText` and `innerHTML` greatly simplifies adding dynamic content to the page. Unfortunately, the approach has its drawbacks. As mentioned, the `innerHTML` property is not a standard property of HTML elements, making its implementation by standards-compliant browsers optional. Most modern browsers, however, support the `innerHTML` property. Ironically, Internet Explorer, the browser that pioneered the use of `innerHTML`, has the most limited implementation of it. Many of today's modern browsers expose the `innerHTML` property as a read/write property on all HTML elements. Internet Explorer, on the other hand, restricts the `innerHTML` property to read-only on HTML elements such as tables and table rows, somewhat limiting its usefulness.

Parsing the Response As XML

You have already seen that the server doesn't necessarily need to send the response in XML format. It's perfectly legal to send the response as simple text as long as the `Content-Type` response header is set to text/plain, as opposed to text/xml for XML. Complex data structures are good candidates to be sent in XML format. Modern browsers have consistently good support for navigating an XML document and also for modifying the XML document's structure and contents.

How exactly does the browser handle XML returned by the server? Modern browsers treat the XML as an XML document in accordance with the W3C DOM. The W3C DOM specifies a rich set of APIs for searching and manipulating XML documents. DOM-compliant browsers are required to implement these APIs and exhibit the prescribed behavior, maximizing the portability of scripts between browsers.

The W3C Document Object Model

What exactly is the W3C DOM? The W3C Web page provides this clear definition:

> *The Document Object Model is a platform- and language-neutral interface that will allow programs and scripts to dynamically access and update the content, structure, and style of documents. The document can be further processed, and the results of that processing can be incorporated back into the presented page.*

Furthermore, the W3C explains the motivation behind defining a standard DOM. The W3C received numerous requests from its members regarding the method by which the object model of XML and HTML documents should be exposed to scripts. The submissions do not propose any new tags or style sheet technology but rather attempt to ensure that interoperable and scripting language–neutral solutions are agreed upon and embraced by the community. In short, the W3C DOM standard intends to help avoid the scripting nightmares of the late 1990s when competing browsers had their own proprietary, often incompatible object models, which made cross-platform scripting exceedingly difficult.

The W3C DOM and JavaScript

It's easy to confuse the W3C DOM with JavaScript. The DOM is an API for HTML and XML documents that provides a structural representation of the document and defines how the document structure is accessed through script. JavaScript is a language that is *used* to access and manipulate the DOM. Without the DOM, JavaScript would not have any notion of Web pages and the elements that make up the pages. Every element within the document is part of the DOM, making the element's properties and methods available to JavaScript.

The DOM is independent of any programming language. Typically the DOM is accessed through JavaScript, although this is not a requirement. You can use any scripting language to access the DOM, thanks to its single, consistent API. Table 3-1 lists useful properties of DOM elements, and Table 3-2 lists useful methods.

Table 3-1. *Properties of DOM Elements Useful for Processing XML Documents*

Property Name	Description
childNodes	Returns an array of the current element's children
firstChild	Returns the first direct child of the current element
lastChild	Returns the last child of the current element
nextSibling	Returns the element immediately following the current element
nodeValue	Specifies the read/write property representing the element's value
parentNode	Returns the element's parent node
previousSibling	Returns the element immediately preceding the current element

Table 3-2. *Methods of DOM Elements Useful for Traversing XML Documents*

Method Name	Description
getElementById(id) (document)	Retrieves the element in the document that has the specified unique ID attribute value
getElementsByTagName(name)	Returns an array of the current element's children that have the specified tag name
hasChildNodes()	Returns a Boolean indicating whether the element has any child elements
getAttribute(name)	Returns the value of the element's attribute specified by name

Thanks to the W3C DOM, you can harness the power and flexibility of XML as the communication medium between the browser and server by writing simple, cross-browser scripts.

The following example demonstrates how easily you can read an XML document using W3C DOM-compliant JavaScript. Listing 3-3 shows the content of the XML document returned by the server to the browser. It's a simple list of U.S. states where the states are broken down by region.

Listing 3-3. *List of U.S. States Returned by the Server*

```
<?xml version="1.0" encoding="UTF-8"?>
<states>
    <north>
        <state>Minnesota</state>
        <state>Iowa</state>
        <state>North Dakota</state>
    </north>
    <south>
        <state>Texas</state>
        <state>Oklahoma</state>
        <state>Louisiana</state>
    </south>
    <east>
        <state>New York</state>
        <state>North Carolina</state>
        <state>Massachusetts</state>
    </east>
    <west>
        <state>California</state>
        <state>Oregon</state>
        <state>Nevada</state>
    </west>
</states>
```

In the browser, this yields a simple HTML page with two buttons. Clicking the first button loads the XML document from the server and then displays in an alert box all the states listed in the document. Clicking the second button loads the XML document from the server and displays just the northern states in an alert box (see Figure 3-2).

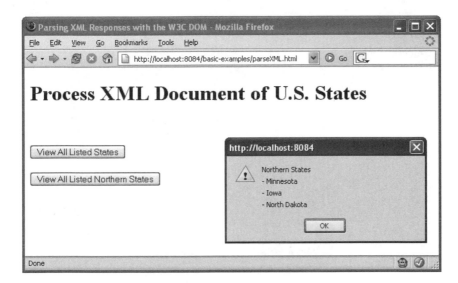

Figure 3-2. *Clicking either of the buttons on the page loads the XML document from the server and displays the appropriate results in an alert box.*

Listing 3-4 shows parseXML.html.

Listing 3-4. parseXML.html

```
<!DOCTYPE html PUBLIC "-//W3C//DTD XHTML 1.0 Strict//EN"
  "http://www.w3.org/TR/xhtml1/DTD/xhtml1-strict.dtd">
<html xmlns="http://www.w3.org/1999/xhtml">
<head>
<title>Parsing XML Responses with the W3C DOM</title>

<script type="text/javascript">
var xmlHttp;
var requestType = "";

function createXMLHttpRequest() {
    if (window.ActiveXObject) {
        xmlHttp = new ActiveXObject("Microsoft.XMLHTTP");
    }
    else if (window.XMLHttpRequest) {
        xmlHttp = new XMLHttpRequest();
    }
}
```

```
function startRequest(requestedList) {
    requestType = requestedList;
    createXMLHttpRequest();
    xmlHttp.onreadystatechange = handleStateChange;
    xmlHttp.open("GET", "parseXML.xml", true);
    xmlHttp.send(null);
}

function handleStateChange() {
    if(xmlHttp.readyState == 4) {
        if(xmlHttp.status == 200) {
            if(requestType == "north") {
                listNorthStates();
            }
            else if(requestType == "all") {
                listAllStates();
            }
        }
    }
}

function listNorthStates() {
    var xmlDoc = xmlHttp.responseXML;
    var northNode = xmlDoc.getElementsByTagName("north")[0];

    var out = "Northern States";
    var northStates = northNode.getElementsByTagName("state");

    outputList("Northern States", northStates);
}

function listAllStates() {
    var xmlDoc = xmlHttp.responseXML;
    var allStates = xmlDoc.getElementsByTagName("state");

    outputList("All States in Document", allStates);
}

function outputList(title, states) {
    var out = title;
    var currentState = null;
    for(var i = 0; i < states.length; i++) {
        currentState = states[i];
        out = out + "\n- " + currentState.childNodes[0].nodeValue;
    }
```

```
        alert(out);
}
</script>
</head>

<body>
    <h1>Process XML Document of U.S. States</h1>
    <br/><br/>
    <form action="#">
        <input type="button" value="View All Listed States"
                onclick="startRequest('all');"/>
        <br/><br/>
        <input type="button" value="View All Listed Northern States"
                onclick="startRequest('north');"/>
    </form>
</body>
</html>
```

The scripting to retrieve the XML document from the server and process it is similar to the examples you saw previously when processing the response as simple text. The key differences lie in the listNorthStates and listAllStates functions. The previous examples retrieved the server response from the XMLHttpRequest object as text by using the object's responseText property. The listNorthStates and listAllStates functions instead use the XMLHttpRequest object's responseXML property to retrieve the results as an XML document, and doing so allows you to use the W3C DOM methods to traverse the XML document.

Study the listAllStates function. The first thing it does is create a local variable named xmlDoc and initialize it to the XML document returned by the server using the XMLHttpRequest object's responseXML property. You utilize the getElementsByTagName method of the XML document to retrieve all the elements in the document that have a tag name of state. The getElementsByTagName method returns an array of all the state elements that is assigned to the local variable named allStates.

After retrieving all the state elements from the XML document, the listAllStates function calls the outputList function to display the state elements in an alert box. The listAllStates method iterates over the array of state elements and for each element appends the state name to the string that is eventually displayed in the alert box.

One particular item to note is *how* the state name is retrieved from the state element. You might expect that the state element simply provides a property or method to retrieve the element's text. This is not the case.

The text representing the state's name is actually a child element of the state element. In an XML document, text is considered a node unto itself and must be the child of some other element. Since the text representing the state's name is actually a child element of the state element, it must be retrieved by first retrieving the text element from the state element and then asking the text element for its textual content.

The outputList function does just that. It iterates through all the elements in the array, assigning the current element to the currentState variable. Because the text element representing the state name is always the first child of the state element, you use the childNodes property to retrieve the text element. Once you have the actual text element, the nodeValue property returns the text content representing the state's name.

The `listNorthStates` function is similar to `listAllStates` except with an added twist. You want only the states that are in the northern region, not all the states. To do this, you first retrieve the `north` tag using the `getElementsByTagName` method to retrieve the `north` element from the XML document. Because the document contains only one `north` element and because the `getElementsByTagName` method always returns an array, you use the `[0]` notation to extract the `state` element since it's in the first (and only) position in the array returned by the `getElementsByTagName` method. Now that you have the `north` element, you can retrieve the `state` elements that are children of the `north` element by calling the `getElementsByTag-Name` method on the `north` element. Once you have an array of all the `state` elements that are children of the `north` element, you can again use the `outputList` method to display the states in an alert box.

Dynamically Editing Page Content with the W3C DOM

The Web has evolved from a medium for distributing static text documents to an application development platform in its own right. Legacy enterprise systems often deployed through text-only terminals or as client-server applications are being replaced by systems that are deployed completely through a Web browser.

As end users become more accustomed to using Web-based applications, they are beginning to demand a richer user experience. No longer are they satisfied with a complete page refresh every time they edit some data on the page. They want to see the results *right now* without waiting for an entire round-trip to the server.

You've now seen how simple it is to parse XML messages sent by the server. The W3C DOM provides properties and methods that allow you to traverse the XML structure and extract the desired data.

The previous example didn't do anything useful with the XML response sent by the server. Displaying the values of the XML document in an alert box doesn't provide much real-world value. What you really want to do is bring a rich client feel to the user by avoiding the constant page refreshing found in typical Web applications. Not only is the constant page refreshing annoying to the user, but also it wastes precious processor cycles on the server by rebuilding the entire page's content and needlessly using network bandwidth to carry the refreshed page.

The best solution, of course, is to change the existing content on the page on an as-needed basis. Instead of refreshing the entire page when most of the data on the page probably hasn't changed, we prefer to simply change the parts of the page where information has changed.

Traditionally this has been difficult to do within the confines of the Web browser. The browser is really just a tool that interprets special markup tags (HTML) and displays them according to a set of predefined rules. The Web, and thus Web browsers, was originally intended to display static information—information that didn't change without requesting new data from the server in the form of a new page.

With some exceptions, modern browsers represent the contents of a Web page using the W3C DOM. Doing so ensures that Web pages will be rendered identically among different browsers and that scripts intended for modifying the contents of the page will behave identically across browsers. The continuing maturity of the W3C DOM and JavaScript implementations by Web browsers has greatly simplified the task of creating content dynamically on the browser. Extensive hacks to work around the incompatibilities among browsers have largely evaporated. Table 3-3 lists the useful DOM properties and methods for creating content dynamically.

Table 3-3. *W3C DOM Properties and Methods Useful When Creating Content Dynamically*

Property/Method	Description
document.createElement(tagName)	The createElement method on the document object creates the element specified by tagName. Providing the string div as the method parameter produces a div element.
document.createTextNode(text)	This document object's createTextNode method creates a node containing static text.
<element>.appendChild(childNode)	The appendChild method adds the specified node to the current element's list of child nodes. For example, you can add an option element as a child node of a select element.
<element>.getAttribute(name) <element>.setAttribute(name, value)	These methods, respectively, get and set the value of the attribute name of the element.
<element>.insertBefore(newNode, targetNode)	This inserts the node newNode before the element targetNode as a child of the current element.
<element>.removeAttribute(name)	This removes the attribute name from the element.
<element>.removeChild(childNode)	This removes the element childNode from the element.
<element>.replaceChild(newNode, oldNode)	This method replaces the node oldNode with the node newNode.
<element>.hasChildnodes()	This method returns a Boolean indicating whether the element has any child elements.

A WORD ABOUT BROWSER INCOMPATIBILITIES

Despite the continually improving implementation of the W3C DOM and JavaScript in modern Web browsers, some quirks and incompatibilities still cause headaches when developing with the DOM and JavaScript.

Internet Explorer has the most limited implementation of the W3C DOM and JavaScript. In the early 2000s, Internet Explorer by some accounts held more than 95 percent of the total browser market, and with no competition in sight, Microsoft chose not to completely implement the various Web standards.

You can work around most of these quirks, although doing so makes the scripting messier and nonstandard. For example, a <tr> element added directly to a <table> using appendChild will not appear in Internet Explorer, but it does in other browsers. The workaround is to add the <tr> element to the table's <tbody> element. This workaround performs correctly in all browsers.

Internet Explorer also has trouble with the setAttribute method. Internet Explorer won't correctly set the class attribute using setAttribute. The cross-browser workaround is to use both setAttribute("class", "newClassName") and setAttribute("className", "newClassName"). Also, you cannot set the style attribute using setAttribute in Internet Explorer. Instead of using <element>.setAttribute("style, "font-weight:bold;"), the most browser-compatible technique is <element>.style.cssText = "font-weight:bold;";.

The examples in this book will adhere as closely as possible to the W3C DOM and JavaScript standards but will stray from the standards when necessary to ensure compatibility with most modern browsers.

The following example demonstrates how you can use the W3C DOM and JavaScript to dynamically create content. The example is a fictional search engine for real estate listings. Clicking the Search button on the form will retrieve the results in XML format using the XMLHttpRequest object. The response XML will be processed using JavaScript to produce a table that lists the results of the search (see Figure 3-3).

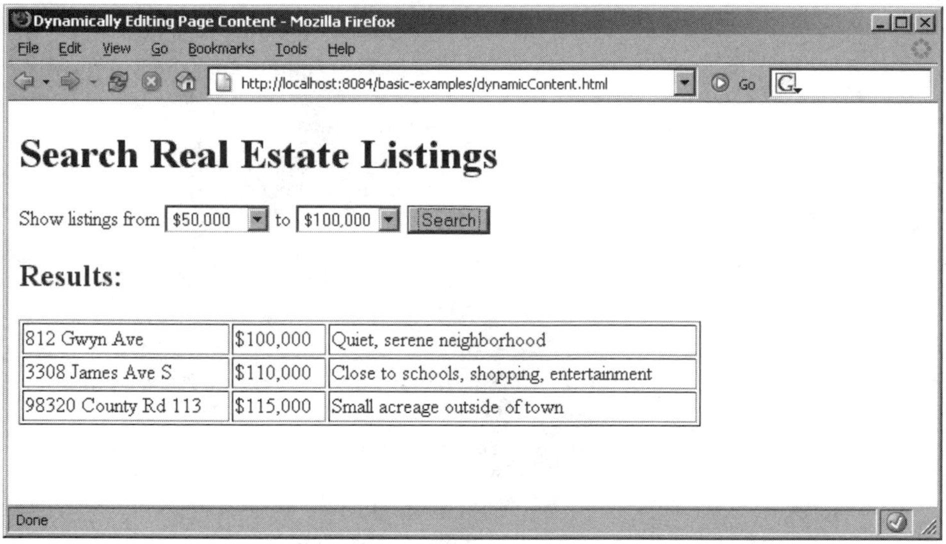

Figure 3-3. *The results of the search were created dynamically using W3C DOM methods and JavaScript.*

The XML returned by the server is simple (see Listing 3-5). The root `properties` node contains all the resulting property elements. Each `property` element contains three child elements: `address`, `price`, and `comments`.

Listing 3-5. dynamicContent.xml

```xml
<?xml version="1.0" encoding="UTF-8"?>
<properties>
    <property>
        <address>812 Gwyn Ave</address>
        <price>$100,000</price>
        <comments>Quiet, serene neighborhood</comments>
    </property>
    <property>
        <address>3308 James Ave S</address>
        <price>$110,000</price>
        <comments>Close to schools, shopping, entertainment</comments>
    </property>
```

```
        <property>
            <address>98320 County Rd 113</address>
            <price>$115,000</price>
            <comments>Small acreage outside of town</comments>
        </property>
</properties>
```

The JavaScript for actually sending the request to the server and responding to its response is the same as previous examples. The differences begin in the handleReadyStateChange function. Assuming the request completes successfully, the first thing that happens is that the content created by any previous searches is deleted by calling the clearPreviousResults function.

The clearPreviousResults function performs two tasks: removing the "Results" header text that appears at the top and clearing any rows from the results table. The header text is removed by first checking to see whether the span that surrounds the header text has any children by using the hasChildNodes method. You know that the header text exists if the hasChildNodes method returns true; if it does, delete the first (and only) child node of the span element, as that child node represents the header text.

The next task in clearPreviousResults is to delete any rows that may already be in the table displaying the search results. Any result rows are child nodes of the tbody node, so you start by obtaining a reference to that node using the document.getElementById method. Once you have the tbody node, you iterate for as long as the tbody node has child nodes, where the child nodes are tr elements. During each iteration the first child node in the childNodes collection is removed from the table body. The iteration ends once no more rows are left in the table body.

The table of search results is built in the parseResults function. This function starts by creating a local variable named results, which is the XML document retrieved from the XMLHttpRequest object's responseXML property.

You use the getElementsByTagName method to retrieve all the property elements in the XML document as an array and assign the array to the local variable properties. Once you have the array of property elements, you can iterate over each element in the array and retrieve the property's address, price, and comments.

```
var properties = results.getElementsByTagName("property");
for(var i = 0; i < properties.length; i++) {
    property = properties[i];
    address = property.getElementsByTagName("address")[0].firstChild.nodeValue;
    price = property.getElementsByTagName("price")[0].firstChild.nodeValue;
    comments = property.getElementsByTagName("comments")[0].firstChild.nodeValue;

    addTableRow(address, price, comments);
}
```

Let's examine this iteration closely, as this is the heart of the parseResults function. Within the for loop the first thing that happens is you get the next element in the array and assign it to the local property named property. Then, for each of the child elements in which you're interested—address, price, and comments—you retrieve their respective node values.

Consider the `address` element, which is a child of the `property` element. You first get the single `address` element by calling the `getElementsByTagName` method on the `property` element. The `getElementsByTagName` method returns an array, but since you know that one and only one `address` element exists, you can reference it using the `[0]` notation.

Continuing your way down the XML structure, you now have a reference to the `address` tag, and you now need to get its textual content. Remembering that text is actually a child node of the parent element, you can access the text node of the `address` element by using the `firstChild` property. Now that you have the text node, you can retrieve the text by referring to the `nodeValue` property of the text node.

You use the same process to retrieve the values of the `price` and `comments` elements, and each value is assigned to the `price` and `comments` local variables, respectively. The `address`, `price`, and `comments` are then passed to a helper function named `addTableRow` that actually builds a table row with the results data.

The `addTableRow` function uses W3C DOM methods and JavaScript to build a table row. A row object is created by using the `document.createElement` method. After creating the `row` object, a `cell` object is created for each of the `address`, `price`, and `comments` values using a helper function named `createCellWithText`. The `createCellWithText` function creates and returns a `cell` object with the specified text as the cell's contents.

The `createCellWithText` function starts by creating a `td` element by using the `document.createElement` method. A text node containing the desired text is then created using the `document.createTextNode` method, and the resulting text node is appended to the `td` element. The function then returns the newly created `td` element to the calling function.

The `addTableRow` function repeats a call to the `createCellWithText` function for the `address`, `price`, and `comments` value, each time appending the newly created `td` element to the `tr` element. Once all the cells have been added to the row, the row is added to the table's `tbody` element.

That's all! You've successfully read the XML document returned by the server and dynamically created a table of results. Listing 3-6 shows the complete JavaScript and eXtensible HTML (XHTML) code for this example.

Listing 3-6. `dynamicContent.html`

```
<!DOCTYPE html PUBLIC "-//W3C//DTD XHTML 1.0 Strict//EN"
  "http://www.w3.org/TR/xhtml1/DTD/xhtml1-strict.dtd">
<html xmlns="http://www.w3.org/1999/xhtml">
<head>
<title>Dynamically Editing Page Content</title>

<script type="text/javascript">
var xmlHttp;

function createXMLHttpRequest() {
    if (window.ActiveXObject) {
        xmlHttp = new ActiveXObject("Microsoft.XMLHTTP");
    }
    else if (window.XMLHttpRequest) {
        xmlHttp = new XMLHttpRequest();
    }
}
```

```
function doSearch() {
    createXMLHttpRequest();
    xmlHttp.onreadystatechange = handleStateChange;
    xmlHttp.open("GET", "dynamicContent.xml", true);
    xmlHttp.send(null);
}

function handleStateChange() {
    if(xmlHttp.readyState == 4) {
        if(xmlHttp.status == 200) {
            clearPreviousResults();
            parseResults();
        }
    }
}

function clearPreviousResults() {
    var header = document.getElementById("header");
    if(header.hasChildNodes()) {
        header.removeChild(header.childNodes[0]);
    }

    var tableBody = document.getElementById("resultsBody");
    while(tableBody.childNodes.length > 0) {
        tableBody.removeChild(tableBody.childNodes[0]);
    }
}

function parseResults() {
    var results = xmlHttp.responseXML;

    var property = null;
    var address = "";
    var price = "";
    var comments = "";

    var properties = results.getElementsByTagName("property");
    for(var i = 0; i < properties.length; i++) {
        property = properties[i];
        address = property.getElementsByTagName("address")[0].firstChild.nodeValue;
        price = property.getElementsByTagName("price")[0].firstChild.nodeValue;
        comments = property.getElementsByTagName("comments")[0]
                                                    .firstChild.nodeValue;

        addTableRow(address, price, comments);
    }
```

```
        var header = document.createElement("h2");
        var headerText = document.createTextNode("Results:");
        header.appendChild(headerText);
        document.getElementById("header").appendChild(header);

        document.getElementById("resultsTable").setAttribute("border", "1");
    }


    function addTableRow(address, price, comments) {
        var row = document.createElement("tr");
        var cell = createCellWithText(address);
        row.appendChild(cell);

        cell = createCellWithText(price);
        row.appendChild(cell);

        cell = createCellWithText(comments);
        row.appendChild(cell);

        document.getElementById("resultsBody").appendChild(row);
    }

    function createCellWithText(text) {
        var cell = document.createElement("td");
        var textNode = document.createTextNode(text);
        cell.appendChild(textNode);

        return cell;
    }
</script>
</head>

<body>
    <h1>Search Real Estate Listings</h1>

    <form action="#">
        Show listings from
            <select>
                <option value="50000">$50,000</option>
                <option value="100000">$100,000</option>
                <option value="150000">$150,000</option>
            </select>
            to
```

```
        <select>
            <option value="100000">$100,000</option>
            <option value="150000">$150,000</option>
            <option value="200000">$200,000</option>
        </select>
    <input type="button" value="Search" onclick="doSearch();"/>
  </form>



  <span id="header">

  </span>

  <table id="resultsTable" width="75%" border="0">
    <tbody id="resultsBody">
    </tbody>
  </table>
</body>
</html>
```

Sending Request Parameters

So far you've seen how you can use Ajax techniques to send requests to the server and the various ways the client can parse the server's response. The only thing missing in the previous examples is that you're not sending any data as part of the request to the server. For the most part, sending a request to the server without any request parameters doesn't do much good. Without any request parameters, the server has no contextual data by which to create a "personalized" response for the client, and in essence the server will send the identical response to every client.

Unlocking the real power of Ajax techniques requires that you send some contextual data to the server. Imagine an input form that includes a section for entering mailing addresses. You can use Ajax techniques to prepopulate the name of the city that corresponds to the ZIP code entered by the user. Of course, to look up the ZIP code's city, the server needs to know the ZIP code entered by the user.

Somehow you need to pass the ZIP code value entered by the user to the server. Fortunately, the XMLHttpRequest object works much the same as the old HTTP techniques you're used to working with: GET and POST.

The GET method passes the value as name/value pairs as part of the request URL. The end of the resource URL ends with a question mark (?), and after the question mark are the name/value pairs. The name/value pairs are in the form name=value, and they are separated by an ampersand (&).

The following line is an example of a GET request. The request is sending two parameters, firstName and middleName, to the application named yourApp on the server named localhost.

Note that the resource URL and the parameters set are separated by a question mark, and `firstName` and `middleName` are separated by an ampersand:

`http://localhost/yourApp?firstName=Adam&middleName=Christopher`

The server knows how to retrieve the named parameters in the URL. Most modern server-side programming environments provide simple APIs, allowing easy access to the named parameters.

The `POST` method of sending named parameters to the server is nearly identical to the `GET` method. The `POST` method, like the `GET` method, encodes the parameters as name/value pairs in the form `name=value`, with each name/value pair separated by an ampersand. The main difference between the two is that the `POST` method sends the parameter string within the request body rather than appending it to the URL the way the `GET` method does.

The HTML usage specification technically recommends that you use the `GET` method when the data processing does not change a data model's state, effectively meaning that you should use the `GET` method when retrieving data. The `POST` method is recommended for operations that change a data model's state, perhaps by storing or updating data or by sending an e-mail.

Each method has its subtle advantages. Since the parameters of a `GET` request are encoded in the request URL, you can bookmark the URL in a browser and easily repeat the request later. In the context of asynchronous requests, though, this doesn't provide much usefulness. The `POST` request is more flexible in terms of the amount of data that can be sent to the server. The amount of data that can be sent using a `GET` request is typically a fixed amount that varies among different browsers, while the `POST` method can send any amount of data.

The HTML `form` element allows you to dictate the desired method by setting the element's method attribute to `GET` or `POST`. The `form` element automatically encodes the data of its input elements according to its method attribute's rules when the form is submitted. The XMLHttpRequest object does not have such built-in behavior. Instead, the developer is responsible for creating the query string containing the data to be sent to the server as part of the request using JavaScript. The techniques for creating the query string are identical regardless of whether you use a `GET` or `POST` request. The only difference is that when sending the request using `GET`, the query string will be appended to the request URL, while with `POST` the query string is sent when calling the XMLHttpRequest object's `send()` method.

Figure 3-4 shows a sample page that demonstrates how to send request parameters to the server. It's a simple input form asking for a first name, middle name, and birthday. The form has two buttons. Each button sends the first name, middle name, and birthday data to the server, one using the `GET` method and one using the `POST` method. The server responds by echoing the input data. The cycle completes when the browser prints the server's response on the page.

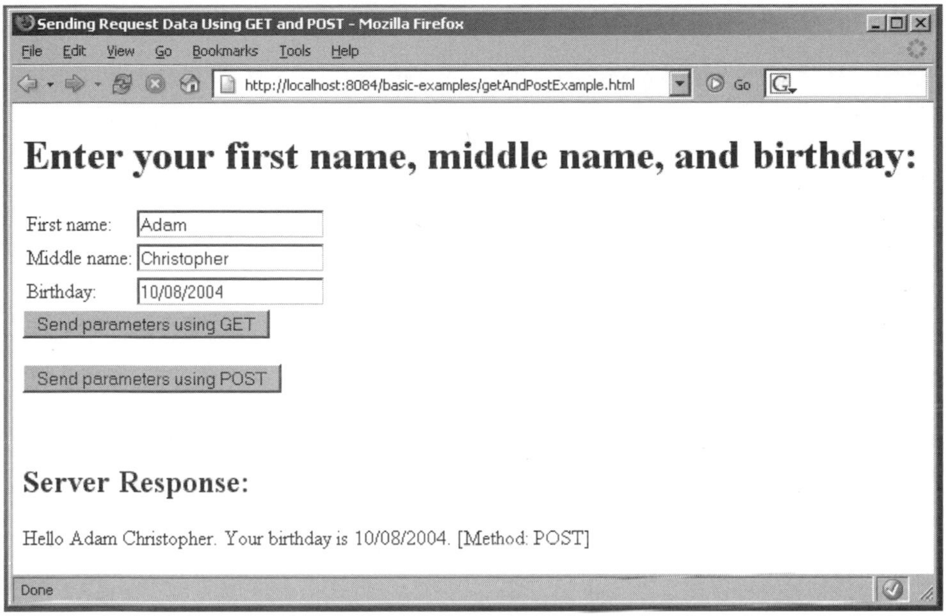

Figure 3-4. *The browser sends the input data using either a* GET *or a* POST *method, and the server responds by echoing the input data.*

Listing 3-7 shows getAndPostExample.html, and Listing 3-8 shows the Java servlet that echoes the first name, middle name, and birthday back to the browser.

Listing 3-7. getAndPostExample.html

```
<!DOCTYPE html PUBLIC "-//W3C//DTD XHTML 1.0 Strict//EN"
  "http://www.w3.org/TR/xhtml1/DTD/xhtml1-strict.dtd">
<html xmlns="http://www.w3.org/1999/xhtml">
<head>
<title>Sending Request Data Using GET and POST</title>

<script type="text/javascript">
var xmlHttp;

function createXMLHttpRequest() {
    if (window.ActiveXObject) {
        xmlHttp = new ActiveXObject("Microsoft.XMLHTTP");
    }
    else if (window.XMLHttpRequest) {
        xmlHttp = new XMLHttpRequest();
    }
}
```

```
function createQueryString() {
    var firstName = document.getElementById("firstName").value;
    var middleName = document.getElementById("middleName").value;
    var birthday = document.getElementById("birthday").value;

    var queryString = "firstName=" + firstName + "&middleName=" + middleName
        + "&birthday=" + birthday;

    return queryString;
}

function doRequestUsingGET() {
    createXMLHttpRequest();

    var queryString = "GetAndPostExample?";
    queryString = queryString + createQueryString()
        + "&timeStamp=" + new Date().getTime();
    xmlHttp.onreadystatechange = handleStateChange;
    xmlHttp.open("GET", queryString, true);
    xmlHttp.send(null);
}

function doRequestUsingPOST() {
    createXMLHttpRequest();

    var url = "GetAndPostExample?timeStamp=" + new Date().getTime();
    var queryString = createQueryString();

    xmlHttp.open("POST", url, true);
    xmlHttp.onreadystatechange = handleStateChange;
    xmlHttp.setRequestHeader("Content-Type",
                "application/x-www-form-urlencoded");
    xmlHttp.send(queryString);
}

function handleStateChange() {
    if(xmlHttp.readyState == 4) {
        if(xmlHttp.status == 200) {
            parseResults();
        }
    }
}

function parseResults() {
    var responseDiv = document.getElementById("serverResponse");
    if(responseDiv.hasChildNodes()) {
        responseDiv.removeChild(responseDiv.childNodes[0]);
    }
```

```
        var responseText = document.createTextNode(xmlHttp.responseText);
        responseDiv.appendChild(responseText);
}

</script>
</head>

<body>
  <h1>Enter your first name, middle name, and birthday:</h1>

  <table>
    <tbody>
        <tr>
            <td>First name:</td>
            <td><input type="text" id="firstName"/>
        </tr>
        <tr>
            <td>Middle name:</td>
            <td><input type="text" id="middleName"/>
        </tr>
        <tr>
            <td>Birthday:</td>
            <td><input type="text" id="birthday"/>
        </tr>
    </tbody>

  </table>

  <form action="#">
    <input type="button" value="Send parameters using GET"
            onclick="doRequestUsingGET();"/>

    <br/><br/>
    <input type="button" value="Send parameters using POST"
            onclick="doRequestUsingPOST();"/>
  </form>

  <br/>
  <h2>Server Response:</h2>

  <div id="serverResponse"></div>

</body>
</html>
```

Listing 3-8. *Echoing the First Name, Middle Name, and Birthday Back to the Browser*

```java
package ajaxbook.chap3;

import java.io.*;
import java.net.*;
import javax.servlet.*;
import javax.servlet.http.*;

public class GetAndPostExample extends HttpServlet {

    protected void processRequest(HttpServletRequest request,
            HttpServletResponse response, String method)
    throws ServletException, IOException {

        //Set content type of the response to text/xml
        response.setContentType("text/xml");

        //Get the user's input
        String firstName = request.getParameter("firstName");
        String middleName = request.getParameter("middleName");
        String birthday = request.getParameter("birthday");

        //Create the response text
        String responseText = "Hello " + firstName + " " + middleName
                + ". Your birthday is " + birthday + "."
                + " [Method: " + method + "]";

        //Write the response back to the browser
        PrintWriter out = response.getWriter();
        out.println(responseText);

        //Close the writer
        out.close();
    }

    protected void doGet(HttpServletRequest request, HttpServletResponse response)
    throws ServletException, IOException {
        //Process the request in method processRequest
        processRequest(request, response, "GET");
    }

    protected void doPost(HttpServletRequest request, HttpServletResponse response)
    throws ServletException, IOException {
        //Process the request in method processRequest
        processRequest(request, response, "POST");
    }
}
```

Let's examine the server-side code first. This example uses a Java servlet to handle the request, although you can use any server-side technology such as PHP, CGI, or .NET. Java servlets must define a doGet method and a doPost method, with each method being called according to the request method. In this example, both doGet and doPost will call the same method, processRequest, to handle the request.

The processRequest method starts by setting the content type of the response to text/xml, even though in this example XML isn't actually used. The three input fields are retrieved from the request object by using the getParameter method. A simple sentence is built using the first name, middle name, and birthday, along with the type of request method. The sentence is then written to the response output stream, and finally the response output stream is closed.

The browser-side JavaScript is again similar to previous examples but with a few added twists. A utility function named createQueryString is responsible for encoding the input parameters as a query string. The createQueryString function simply retrieves the input values for the first name, middle name, and birthday and appends them as name/value pairs. Each name/value pair is separated by an ampersand. This function returns the query string, allowing it to be reused by both the GET and POST operations.

Clicking the Send Parameters Using GET button calls the doRequestUsingGET function. This function, like many of the previous examples, starts by calling the function that creates an instance of the XMLHttpRequest object. Next, the query string that encodes the input values is created.

The request endpoint for this example is the servlet named GetAndPostExample. The query string is created by concatenating the query string returned by the createQueryString function to the request endpoint, separated by a question mark.

The JavaScript continues as you've seen before. The XMLHttpRequest object's onreadystatechange property is set to use the handleStateChange function. The open() method specifies that this is a GET request and the endpoint URL, which in this case contains the encoded parameters. The send() method sends the request to the server, and the handleStateChange function handles the server response.

The handleStateChange function calls the parseResults function upon successful completion of the request. The parseResults function retrieves the div element that contains the server's response and stores it in a local variable named responseDiv. Any previous server results are first removed from responseDiv by using its removeChild method. Finally, a new text node is created containing the server's response and is appended to responseDiv.

The techniques for using the POST method instead of GET are identical except for how the request parameters are sent to the server. Recall that when using GET, the name/value pairs are appended to the destination URL. The POST method sends the same query string as part of the request body.

Clicking the Send Parameters Using POST button calls the doRequestUsingPOST function. Like the doRequestUsingGET function, it starts by creating an instance of the XMLHttpRequest object. The script continues by creating the query string that contains the parameters to be sent to the server. Note that the query string is not concatenated with the destination URL.

The XMLHttpRequest object's open() method is invoked, this time specifying POST as the request method in addition to specifying the "bare" destination URL. The onreadystatechange property is set to the handleStateChange function, allowing the response to be processed in the same way as the GET method. To ensure that the server knows that the request parameters can be found within the request body, the setRequestHeader is called, setting the Content-Type value to `application/x-www-form-urlencoded`. Lastly, the `send()` method is invoked by passing the query string as the method parameter.

The output of clicking the two buttons is identical. A string echoing the specified first name, middle name, and birthday is displayed on the page along with the type of request method that was used.

WHY IS THE TIMESTAMP APPENDED TO THE DESTINATION URL?

Under some conditions, some browsers cache the results of multiple XMLHttpRequest requests to the same URL. This can cause undesirable results if the response could be different for each request. Appending the current timestamp to the end of the URL ensures the uniqueness of the URL and thus prevents browsers from caching the results.

Sending Request Parameters As XML

Compatibility of JavaScript amongst today's modern browsers is light years ahead of where it was even a few years ago. Combined with the increasing sophistication of JavaScript development tools and techniques, you may decide to begin using the Web browser as a development platform. Instead of merely relying on the browser to serve as the View in the Model-View-Controller pattern, you may decide to implement part of the business model in JavaScript. You can use Ajax techniques to persist changes in the model to the backend server. If the model is kept on the browser, then changes to the model can be communicated to the server en masse, reducing the number of remote calls made to the server and possibly increasing performance.

A simple query string consisting of name/value pairs is probably not robust enough to communicate a large number of possibly complex model changes to the server. A better solution might be to send changes to the model as XML to the server. How can you send XML to the server?

You can send XML to the server as part of the request body, much like the query string is sent as part of the request body during a `POST` request. The server can read XML from the request body and work with it from there.

The following example demonstrates how you can send XML to the server during an Ajax request. Figure 3-5 shows the page, which is a simple select box in which the user selects the types of pets the user has. It's a simplistic example, but it shows how you can send XML to the server.

Figure 3-5. *The items selected in the select box are sent to the server as XML.*

Listing 3-9 shows postingXML.html.

Listing 3-9. postingXML.html

```
<!DOCTYPE html PUBLIC "-//W3C//DTD XHTML 1.0 Strict//EN"
   "http://www.w3.org/TR/xhtml1/DTD/xhtml1-strict.dtd">
<html xmlns="http://www.w3.org/1999/xhtml">
<head>
<title>Sending an XML Request</title>

<script type="text/javascript">

var xmlHttp;

function createXMLHttpRequest() {
    if (window.ActiveXObject) {
        xmlHttp = new ActiveXObject("Microsoft.XMLHTTP");
    }
    else if (window.XMLHttpRequest) {
        xmlHttp = new XMLHttpRequest();
    }
}

function createXML() {
    var xml = "<pets>";
```

```
    var options = document.getElementById("petTypes").childNodes;
    var option = null;
    for(var i = 0; i < options.length; i++) {
        option = options[i];
        if(option.selected) {
            xml = xml + "<type>" + option.value + "<\/type>";
        }
    }

    xml = xml + "<\/pets>";
    return xml;
}

function sendPetTypes() {
    createXMLHttpRequest();

    var xml = createXML();
    var url = "PostingXMLExample?timeStamp=" + new Date().getTime();

    xmlHttp.open("POST", url, true);
    xmlHttp.onreadystatechange = handleStateChange;
    xmlHttp.setRequestHeader("Content-Type", "application/x-www-form-urlencoded");
    xmlHttp.send(xml);
}

function handleStateChange() {
    if(xmlHttp.readyState == 4) {
        if(xmlHttp.status == 200) {
            parseResults();
        }
    }
}

function parseResults() {
    var responseDiv = document.getElementById("serverResponse");
    if(responseDiv.hasChildNodes()) {
        responseDiv.removeChild(responseDiv.childNodes[0]);
    }

    var responseText = document.createTextNode(xmlHttp.responseText);
    responseDiv.appendChild(responseText);
}


</script>
</head>
```

```
<body>
  <h1>Select the types of pets in your home:</h1>

  <form action="#">
    <select id="petTypes" size="6" multiple="true">
        <option value="cats">Cats</option>
        <option value="dogs">Dogs</option>
        <option value="fish">Fish</option>
        <option value="birds">Birds</option>
        <option value="hamsters">Hamsters</option>
        <option value="rabbits">Rabbits</option>
    </select>

    <br/><br/>
    <input type="button" value="Submit Pets" onclick="sendPetTypes();"/>
  </form>

  <h2>Server Response:</h2>

  <div id="serverResponse"></div>

</body>
</html>
```

This example works much the same as the earlier POST example. The difference is that instead of a query string composed of name/value pairs being sent, an XML string is sent to the server.

Clicking the Submit Pets button on the form invokes the sendPetTypes function. Like previous examples, this function first creates an instance of the XMLHttpRequest object. It then calls a helper function named createXML that builds the XML string of the selected pet types.

The function createXML retrieves a reference to the select element using the document.getElementById method. It then iterates over all its child option elements and for each selected option creates the XML tag for the selected pet type and appends it to the rest of the XML. At the end of the iteration, the closing pets tag is appended to the XML string before it's returned to the calling function.

Once it has obtained the XML string, the sendPetTypes function continues by preparing XMLHttpObject for the request and then sends the XML to the server by specifying the XML string as the parameter to the send() method.

IN THE CREATEXML METHOD, WHY DOES A BACKSLASH PRECEDE THE FORWARD SLASH IN THE CLOSE TAGS?

Thanks to a quirk in the SGML specification from which HTML is derived, end tags are recognized within script elements, but other content such as start tags and comments are not. The backslash prevents the string from being parsed from markup. Most browsers will safely handle the instances where a backslash is omitted, but to stick to the strict XHTML standard, use a backslash.

The astute reader will notice that according to the documentation for the XMLHttpRequest object, the send() method can take both a string and an instance of an XML document object. Why, then, does this example use string concatenation to create the XML instead of creating document and element objects? Unfortunately, at this time no cross-browser technique exists for building a document object from scratch. Internet Explorer exposes this functionality through ActiveX objects, Mozilla browsers expose it through native JavaScript objects, and other browsers either don't support it at all or support it via other means.

The server-side code to read the XML, shown in Listing 3-10, is a bit more complicated. This example uses a Java servlet to read the request and parse the XML string, although you could also use other server-side technologies.

The servlet's doPost method is invoked upon receipt of the XMLHttpRequest object's request. The doPost method uses a helper method named readXMLFromRequestBody to extract the XML from the body of the request. The doPost method then converts the XML string into a Document object using the JAXP interfaces.

Note that the Document object is an instance of the Document interface specified by the W3C. As such, it has the same methods as the browser's document object such as getElementsByTagName. You use this method to get a list of all the type elements in the document. For each type element in the document, the text value is obtained (remember that the text value is the first child node of the type element) and appended to a string. After all the type elements have been consumed, the response string is written back to the browser.

Listing 3-10. PostingXMLExample.java

```
package ajaxbook.chap3;

import java.io.*;
import javax.servlet.*;
import javax.servlet.http.*;
import javax.xml.parsers.DocumentBuilderFactory;
import javax.xml.parsers.ParserConfigurationException;
import org.w3c.dom.Document;
import org.w3c.dom.NodeList;
import org.xml.sax.SAXException;

public class PostingXMLExample extends HttpServlet {

    protected void doPost(HttpServletRequest request, HttpServletResponse response)
    throws ServletException, IOException {

        String xml = readXMLFromRequestBody(request);
        Document xmlDoc = null;
        try {
            xmlDoc =
                    DocumentBuilderFactory.newInstance().newDocumentBuilder()
                    .parse(new ByteArrayInputStream(xml.getBytes()));
        }
```

```java
            catch(ParserConfigurationException e) {
                System.out.println("ParserConfigurationException: " + e);
            }
            catch(SAXException e) {
                System.out.println("SAXException: " + e);
            }

            /* Note how the Java implementation of the W3C DOM has the same methods
             * as the JavaScript implementation, such as getElementsByTagName and
             * getNodeValue.
             */
            NodeList selectedPetTypes = xmlDoc.getElementsByTagName("type");
            String type = null;
            String responseText = "Selected Pets: ";
            for(int i = 0; i < selectedPetTypes.getLength(); i++) {
                type = selectedPetTypes.item(i).getFirstChild().getNodeValue();
                responseText = responseText + " " + type;
            }

            response.setContentType("text/xml");
            response.getWriter().print(responseText);
        }

    private String readXMLFromRequestBody(HttpServletRequest request){
        StringBuffer xml = new StringBuffer();
        String line = null;
        try {
            BufferedReader reader = request.getReader();
            while((line = reader.readLine()) != null) {
                xml.append(line);
            }
        }
        catch(Exception e) {
            System.out.println("Error reading XML: " + e.toString());
        }
        return xml.toString();
    }
}
```

Sending Data to the Server Using JSON

Now that you've been working with JavaScript a little more, you may be thinking to yourself that you want to keep more model information on the browser. However, after seeing the previous example that uses XML to send complex data structures to the server, you may be less inclined to do so. Creating XML strings by string concatenation is not an appealing or robust technique for generating or modifying XML data structures.

Overview of JSON

An alternative to XML is JSON, which you can find at `www.json.org`. JSON is a text format that is language independent but that uses conventions similar to the C family of languages such as C, C#, JavaScript, and others. JSON is built on the following two data structures that are supported by virtually all modern programming languages:

- A collection of name/value pairs. In modern programming languages these are realized as an object, record, or dictionary.

- An ordered list of values, which is usually realized as an array.

Since these structures are supported by so many programming languages, JSON is an ideal choice as a data interchange format between disparate systems. Additionally, since JSON is based on a subset of standard JavaScript, it should be compatible in all modern Web browsers.

A JSON object is an unordered set of name/value pairs. The object begins with a { and ends with a }. A colon separates the name/value pairs. A JSON array is an ordered collection of values that begins with a [and ends with a]. A comma separates the values of the array. A value can be a string (enclosed in double quotes), a number, a `true` or `false`, an object, or an array. This allows structures to be nested. Figure 3-6 is a good visual guide for describing the makeup of a JSON object.

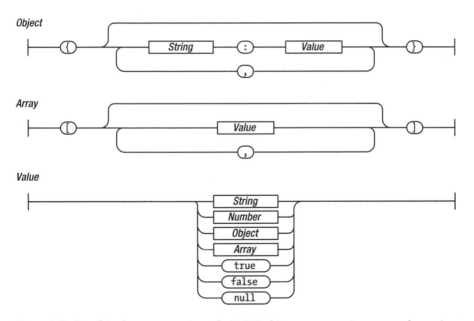

Figure 3-6. *Graphical representation of a JSON object structure (courtesy of* `www.json.org`*)*

Consider the simple example of an `Employee` object. An `Employee` object might consist of data such as a first name, last name, employee number, and title. Using JSON, you represent an instance of the `Employee` object like this:

```
var employee = {
    "firstName" : John
    , "lastName" : Doe
    , "employeeNumber" : 123
    , "title" : "Accountant"
}
```

You can then use the object's properties using the standard dot notation, like so:

```
var lastName = employee.lastName;   //Access the last name
var title = employee.title;         //Access the title
employee.employeeNumber = 456;      //Change the employee number
```

JSON prides itself on being a lightweight data interchange format. The same Employee object described as XML might look like this:

```
<employee>
    <firstName>John</firstName>
    <lastName>Doe</lastName>
    <employeeNumber>123</employeeNumber>
    <title>Accountant</title>
</employee>
```

Clearly, the JSON encoding is smaller than the XML encoding. The smaller size of the JSON encoding could potentially make a big performance difference when sending large amounts of data over a network.

The Web site at www.json.org lists at least 14 bindings to other programming languages, meaning no matter what technology you use on the server, you should be able to communicate with the browser through JSON.

Example Using JSON

The following example is a simple demonstration of how to use JSON to translate JavaScript objects to a string format and send the string to the server using Ajax techniques; the server will then create an object based on the string. The example has no business logic and little user interaction, as it focuses on the JSON techniques both on the client side and on the server side. Figure 3-7 shows a "stringified" Car object.

Because this example is nearly identical to the previous POST examples, we'll focus on the JSON-specific techniques. Clicking the form button invokes the doJSON function. This function first asks the getCarObject function to return a new instance of a Car object. You then use the JSON JavaScript library (freely available from www.json.org) to translate the Car object into a JSON string that is then displayed in an alert box. The JSON-encoded Car object is then sent to the server using the XMLHttpRequest object.

Thanks to the freely available JSON-to-Java library, coding the Java servlet that services the JSON request is simple. Better yet, since JSON bindings are available for every flavor of server technology, you can easily implement this example using any server-side technology.

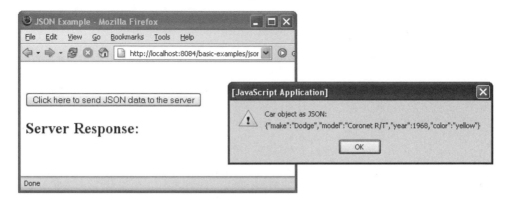

Figure 3-7. *The "stringified"* `Car` *object*

The `JSONExample` servlet's `doPost` method services the JSON request. It first asks the `readJSONStringFromRequestBody` method to obtain the JSON string from the request body. It then creates an instance of `JSONObject`, supplying the JSON string to the object constructor. The `JSONObject` automatically parses the JSON string at object creation time. Once `JSONObject` is created, you can use the various `get` methods to retrieve the object properties in which you're interested.

You use the `getString` and `getInt` methods to retrieve the year, make, model, and color properties. These properties are concatenated to form the string that is returned to the browser and displayed on the page. Figure 3-8 shows the response from the server after reading the JSON object.

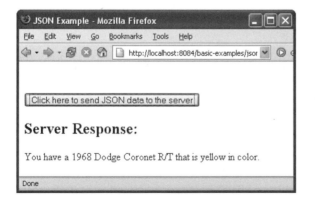

Figure 3-8. *The response from the server after reading the JSON string*

Listing 3-11 shows `jsonExample.html`, and Listing 3-12 shows `JSONExample.java`.

Listing 3-11. jsonExample.html

```
<!DOCTYPE html PUBLIC "-//W3C//DTD XHTML 1.0 Strict//EN"
  "http://www.w3.org/TR/xhtml1/DTD/xhtml1-strict.dtd">
<html xmlns="http://www.w3.org/1999/xhtml">
<head>
<title>JSON Example</title>

<script type="text/javascript" src="json.js"></script>
<script type="text/javascript">

var xmlHttp;

function createXMLHttpRequest() {
    if (window.ActiveXObject) {
        xmlHttp = new ActiveXObject("Microsoft.XMLHTTP");
    }
    else if (window.XMLHttpRequest) {
        xmlHttp = new XMLHttpRequest();
    }
}

function doJSON() {
    var car = getCarObject();

    //Use the JSON JavaScript library to stringify the Car object
    var carAsJSON = JSON.stringify(car);
    alert("Car object as JSON:\n " + carAsJSON);

    var url = "JSONExample?timeStamp=" + new Date().getTime();

    createXMLHttpRequest();
    xmlHttp.open("POST", url, true);
    xmlHttp.onreadystatechange = handleStateChange;
    xmlHtlp.setRequestHeader("Content-Type",
                "application/x-www-form-urlencoded");
    xmlHttp.send(carAsJSON);
}

function handleStateChange() {
    if(xmlHttp.readyState == 4) {
        if(xmlHttp.status == 200) {
            parseResults();
        }
    }
}
```

```
function parseResults() {
    var responseDiv = document.getElementById("serverResponse");
    if(responseDiv.hasChildNodes()) {
        responseDiv.removeChild(responseDiv.childNodes[0]);
    }

    var responseText = document.createTextNode(xmlHttp.responseText);
    responseDiv.appendChild(responseText);
}

function getCarObject() {
    return new Car("Dodge", "Coronet R/T", 1968, "yellow");
}

function Car(make, model, year, color) {
    this.make = make;
    this.model = model;
    this.year = year;
    this.color = color;
}

</script>
</head>

<body>

  <br/><br/>
  <form action="#">
      <input type="button" value="Click here to send JSON data to the server"
        onclick="doJSON();"/>
  </form>

  <h2>Server Response:</h2>

  <div id="serverResponse"></div>

</body>
</html>
```

Listing 3-12. JSONExample.java

```
package ajaxbook.chap3;

import java.io.*;
import java.net.*;
import java.text.ParseException;
import javax.servlet.*;
import javax.servlet.http.*;
import org.json.JSONObject;
```

```java
public class JSONExample extends HttpServlet {

    protected void doPost(HttpServletRequest request, HttpServletResponse response)
    throws ServletException, IOException {
        String json = readJSONStringFromRequestBody(request);

        //Use the JSON-Java binding library to create a JSON object in Java
        JSONObject jsonObject = null;
        try {
            jsonObject = new JSONObject(json);
        }
        catch(ParseException pe) {
            System.out.println("ParseException: " + pe.toString());
        }

        String responseText = "You have a " + jsonObject.getInt("year") + " "
            + jsonObject.getString("make") + " " + jsonObject.getString("model")
            + " " + " that is " + jsonObject.getString("color") + " in color.";

        response.setContentType("text/xml");
        response.getWriter().print(responseText);
    }

    private String readJSONStringFromRequestBody(HttpServletRequest request){
        StringBuffer json = new StringBuffer();
        String line = null;
        try {
            BufferedReader reader = request.getReader();
            while((line = reader.readLine()) != null) {
                json.append(line);
            }
        }
        catch(Exception e) {
            System.out.println("Error reading JSON string: " + e.toString());
        }
        return json.toString();
    }
}
```

Summary

In this chapter, you explored the myriad methods by which the XMLHttpRequest object and server can communicate with each other. The XMLHttpRequest object can send requests using either the HTTP GET or POST methods, while the request data can be sent as a query string, XML, or JSON data. After handling the request, the server will typically respond by sending simple text, XML data, or even JSON data. Each format may be best suited for certain situations.

Ajax wouldn't be particularly useful if you had no way to dynamically update the page's contents based on the results of a request. Today's modern browsers expose the contents of a Web page as an object model in accordance with the W3C DOM standards. This object model allows scripting languages such as JavaScript to add, update, and remove content on the page without the need for a round-trip to the server. While some quirks still exist, most Web pages written according to W3C standards and modified using standard JavaScript will behave identically in any standards-compliant browser. Most of today's modern browsers also support the nonstandard `innerHTML` property, which can be used to update the elements on a Web page.

You are now familiar with the XMLHttpRequest object and how you can use it to seamlessly communicate with the server. You also know how to update the Web page's contents dynamically. What's next?

Chapter 4 offers a glimpse into the endless possibilities now afforded by Ajax. It's one thing to know how to use Ajax, but it's a completely different thing to apply it in a useful setting. The next chapter introduces situations common to Web applications that are prime candidates for Ajax techniques.

CHAPTER 4

■ ■ ■

Implementing Basic Ajax Techniques

You've been introduced to Ajax technology, you know how to use the XMLHttpRequest object, and you want to put it all together. But how? To what sorts of scenarios should you apply Ajax technology? Of course, its potential uses are nearly limitless. This chapter will demonstrate some situations where you can use Ajax techniques to really turbocharge your application. Some are obvious, and some aren't, but either way, as you gain more experience with Ajax you'll discover your own ways in which it can improve your application. While most of these examples use Java servlets for the server-side component, every example could just as easily have been written using .NET, Ruby, Perl, PHP, or any server-side technology.

Performing Validation

A central tenant of usability says you should prevent errors from occurring, but barring that, you should inform your users of errors as soon as possible. Before Ajax, Web-based applications had to post the entire page to validate the data or rely on complex JavaScript to check the form. While some checks are fairly simple to write in JavaScript, others just plain can't be done. Of course, every validation routine you write on the client has to be rewritten on the server anyway since it's possible a user has JavaScript turned off.

With Ajax, you no longer have to confine yourself to simple client-side validations and duplicated logic. Now when you want to provide a more responsive experience for your users, you can simply call the validation routine you wrote for the server. In most cases, this logic will be simpler to write and easier to test, and it's likely you can rely on existing frameworks.

When we're asked where people should start using Ajax in their applications, we typically recommend starting with validation. Chances are pretty good you've got some JavaScript you'd like to get rid of, and you can probably easily tie into some existing server-side logic. In this section, we'll show an example of one of the most common validations: dates.

The HTML for this example is pretty straightforward (see Listing 4-1). You have a standard input box with an onchange() event (of course, you could use whatever event you think is appropriate) that triggers the validation method. You can see that you're calling the standard createXMLHttpRequest() method and then sending the input value to the ValidationServlet servlet. The callback() function gets the results from the server and then delegates to the setMessage() method, which looks at the values to determine in which color the message should be displayed.

Listing 4-1. `validation.html`

```
<!DOCTYPE HTML PUBLIC "-//W3C//DTD HTML 4.01 Transitional//EN" >

<html>
  <head>
    <title>Using Ajax for validation</title>

    <script type="text/javascript">
        var xmlHttp;

        function createXMLHttpRequest() {
            if (window.ActiveXObject) {
                xmlHttp = new ActiveXObject("Microsoft.XMLHTTP");
            }
            else if (window.XMLHttpRequest) {
                xmlHttp = new XMLHttpRequest();
            }
        }

        function validate() {
            createXMLHttpRequest();
            var date = document.getElementById("birthDate");
            var url = "ValidationServlet?birthDate=" + escape(date.value);
            xmlHttp.open("GET", url, true);
            xmlHttp.onreadystatechange = callback;
            xmlHttp.send(null);
        }

        function callback() {
            if (xmlHttp.readyState == 4) {
                if (xmlHttp.status == 200) {
                    var mes =
                        xmlHttp.responseXML
                            .getElementsByTagName("message")[0].firstChild.data;
                    var val =
                        xmlHttp.responseXML
                                .getElementsByTagName("passed")[0].firstChild.data;
                    setMessage(mes, val);
                }
            }
        }

        function setMessage(message, isValid) {
            var messageArea = document.getElementById("dateMessage");
            var fontColor = "red";
```

```
                    if (isValid == "true") {
                        fontColor = "green";
                    }
                    messageArea.innerHTML = "<font color=" + fontColor + ">" ➥
                        + message + " </font>";
                }

        </script>
    </head>
    <body>
        <h1>Ajax Validation Example</h1>
        Birth date: <input type="text" size="10" id="birthDate" onchange="validate();"/>
        <div id="dateMessage"></div>
    </body>
</html>
```

The server-side code is equally straightforward (see Listing 4-2). For simplicity, place the validation code in the servlet—in a production environment, you would probably delegate this to a validation service.

Listing 4-2. ValidationServlet.java

```
package ajaxbook.chap4;

import java.io.*;
import java.text.ParseException;
import java.text.SimpleDateFormat;

import javax.servlet.*;
import javax.servlet.http.*;

public class ValidationServlet extends HttpServlet {

    /** Handles the HTTP <code>GET</code> method.
     * @param request servlet request
     * @param response servlet response
     */
    protected void doGet(HttpServletRequest request, HttpServletResponse response)
    throws ServletException, IOException {
        PrintWriter out = response.getWriter();

        boolean passed = validateDate(request.getParameter("birthDate"));
        response.setContentType("text/xml");
        response.setHeader("Cache-Control", "no-cache");
        String message = "You have entered an invalid date.";
```

```java
        if (passed) {
            message = "You have entered a valid date.";
        }
        out.println("<response>");
        out.println("<passed>" + Boolean.toString(passed) + "</passed>");
        out.println("<message>" + message + "</message>");
        out.println("</response>");
        out.close();
    }

    /**
     * Checks to see whether the argument is a valid date.
     * A null date is considered invalid. This method
     * used the default data formatter and lenient
     * parsing.
     *
     * @param date a String representing the date to check
     * @return message a String representing the outcome of the check
     */
    private boolean validateDate(String date) {

        boolean isValid = true;
        if(date != null) {
            SimpleDateFormat formatter= new SimpleDateFormat("MM/dd/yyyy");
            try {
                formatter.parse(date);
            } catch (ParseException pe) {
                System.out.println(pe.toString());
                isValid = false;
            }
        } else {
            isValid = false;
        }
        return isValid;
    }
}
```

Running this example gives the results shown in Figure 4-1 and Figure 4-2.

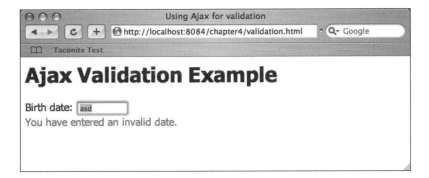

Figure 4-1. *Entering an invalid date*

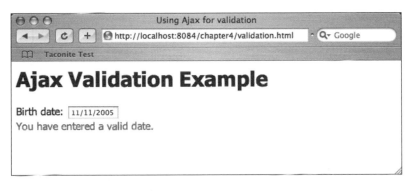

Figure 4-2. *Entering a valid date*

Reading Response Headers

Sometimes you won't need to retrieve any content from the server, for instance, in the case where you just want to "ping" the server to verify that it is operational. You may want to simply read the response headers sent by the server and ignore the content. By reading the response headers, you can find out the Content-Type, the Content-Length, or even the Last-Modified date.

The standard way to perform a request where you're interested only in the response headers is to use a HEAD request, as opposed to a GET or POST request as discussed earlier. When a server responds to a HEAD request, it sends only the response headers, omitting the content even if the requested content could be returned to the browser. By omitting the content, the response to a HEAD request is much smaller than a GET or POST response.

Listing 4-3 demonstrates the various ways in which you can retrieve the response headers from the XMLHttpRequest object and use them for practical purposes. The page has four links on it that exercise various methods on the XMLHttpRequest object to read the response headers.

Listing 4-3. readingResponseHeaders.html

```
<!DOCTYPE html PUBLIC "-//W3C//DTD XHTML 1.0 Strict//EN"
  "http://www.w3.org/TR/xhtml1/DTD/xhtml1-strict.dtd">
<html xmlns="http://www.w3.org/1999/xhtml">
<head>
<title>Reading Response Headers</title>

<script type="text/javascript">
var xmlHttp;
var requestType = "";

function createXMLHttpRequest() {
    if (window.ActiveXObject) {
        xmlHttp = new ActiveXObject("Microsoft.XMLHTTP");
    }
    else if (window.XMLHttpRequest) {
        xmlHttp = new XMLHttpRequest();
    }
}

function doHeadRequest(request, url) {
    requestType = request;
    createXMLHttpRequest();
    xmlHttp.onreadystatechange = handleStateChange;
    xmlHttp.open("HEAD", url, true);
    xmlHttp.send(null);
}

function handleStateChange() {
    if(xmlHttp.readyState == 4) {
        if(requestType == "allResponseHeaders") {
            getAllResponseHeaders();
        }
        else if(requestType == "lastModified") {
            getLastModified();
        }
        else if(requestType == "isResourceAvailable") {
            getIsResourceAvailable();
        }
    }
}

function getAllResponseHeaders() {
    alert(xmlHttp.getAllResponseHeaders());
}

function getLastModified() {
    alert("Last Modified: " + xmlHttp.getResponseHeader("Last-Modified"));
}
```

```
function getIsResourceAvailable() {
    if(xmlHttp.status == 200) {
        alert("Successful response");
    }
    else if(xmlHttp.status == 404) {
        alert("Resource is unavailable");
    }
    else {
        alert("Unexpected response status: " + xmlHttp.status);
    }
}

</script>
</head>

<body>
  <h1>Reading Response Headers</h1>

  <a href="javascript:doHeadRequest('allResponseHeaders',
              'readingResponseHeaders.xml');">Read All Response Headers</a>

  <br/>
  <a href="javascript:doHeadRequest('lastModified',
              'readingResponseHeaders.xml');">Get Last Modified Date</a>

  <br/>
  <a href="javascript:doHeadRequest('isResourceAvailable',
                  'readingResponseHeaders.xml');">Read Available Resource</a>

  <br/>
  <a href="javascript:doHeadRequest('isResourceAvailable',
                  'not-available.xml');">Read Unavailable Resource</a>

</body>
</html>
```

The first link on the page demonstrates the XMLHttpRequest object's getAllResponseHeaders() method. This method simply retrieves all the response headers as a string. In this example, the response headers are displayed in an alert box. The getAllResponseHeaders() method may be of limited value because it returns all the response headers together as a string. Retrieving a single response header using the getAllResponseHeaders() method requires parsing the returned string to find the single response header in which you're interested.

The getResponseHeader method solves this problem by returning the value for a single response header. This method takes a single string argument representing the name of the response header for which the value is desired. This example uses the getResponseHeader method to display the Last-Modified header in an alert box. A real-world application of the getResponseHeader method would be to poll a server resource at certain intervals. The browser would try to update its content from the server resource only if the Last-Modified response header had changed from the last time the server resource was polled.

The last two links on the page utilize the XMLHttpRequest object's ability to inspect the HTTP status code returned by the server. The XMLHttpRequest object's status method returns the HTTP status code as an integer. A status code of 200 indicates a normal, successful server response. A status code of 500, conversely, indicates that some kind of internal error occurred while the server was attempting to fulfill the request.

This example uses the HTTP status code to determine whether a server resource is available. The HTTP status code 404 indicates that the requested resource is not available. The "Read Available Resource" link on the page requests a simple XML file residing on the server. Because the file is available, the HTTP status code is 200, indicating a successful response. The last link on the page, labeled "Read Unavailable Resource," requests a file that does not reside on the server. The server responds with an HTTP status code of 404. The JavaScript event handler inspects the server response, sees the 404 status code, and displays an alert box indicating that the requested resource is not available.

Listing 4-4 shows `readingResponseHeaders.xml`.

Listing 4-4. `readingResponseHeaders.xml`

```
<?xml version="1.0" encoding="UTF-8"?>

<readingResponseHeaders>

</readingResponseHeaders>
```

Figure 4-3 shows the result of displaying all the response headers, Figure 4-4 shows the result of reading the `Last-Modified` header, and Figure 4-5 shows the result of determining whether a Web resource is available.

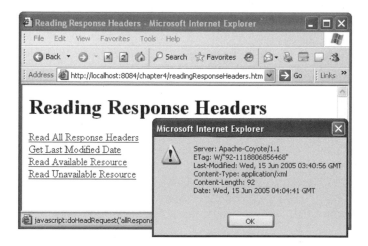

Figure 4-3. *Displaying all the response headers*

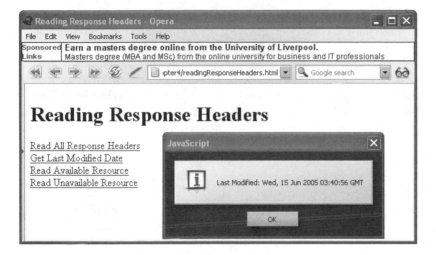

Figure 4-4. *Reading a single response header, in this case* `Last-Modified`

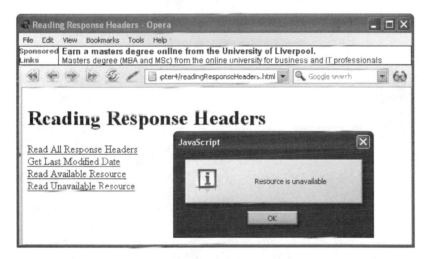

Figure 4-5. *Determining whether a Web resource is available*

Dynamically Loading List Boxes

Web applications are often built using the "wizard" design philosophy, where each screen asks the user for small bits of input and each successive page's data is built from the previous screen's input. This design pattern is quite useful for certain types of scenarios such as when the user is performing a task that is best completed in a step-by-step, ordered manner. Unfortunately, too many Web applications use this approach because they *have* to do so. Before Ajax techniques were available, it was difficult if not impossible to update a page dynamically without refreshing the entire page when certain parts of the page needed to change based on user input.

One technique to avoid constant page refreshes is to hide data on the page and display it as needed. In the situation where the values in select box B are populated depending on the selected value in select box A, the available values for select box B can be held in hidden select boxes. When the selected value in select box A changes, JavaScript can determine which hidden select should be displayed. That select box can then be made visible and the previous select box hidden. Another variation is to dynamically populate the option elements of select box B with the elements from a hidden list box. These techniques are useful, but their use is limited to scenarios where the changes to the page are restricted to a finite set of choices based on the user's input, and even then the set choices must be relatively small.

Say you're building an online classified ads service for automobiles. Potential buyers search for their desired autos by specifying a car's model year, make, and model. To avoid typographical errors on a user's part and reduce the number of dynamic validations required, you've decided that the model year, make, and model input fields should all be select boxes and that the ads should go back 25 model years. Changing the selection in the model year select box or the manufacturer select box must change the list of available models for that model year and manufacturer.

Remember that with each model year the number of available makes changes as new nameplates are introduced and old ones are retired. Also keep in mind that the models available from each manufacturer vary from year to year. With dozens of manufacturers and several models available per manufacturer per model year, the number of combinations of model year, make, and model is staggering. That is far too many combinations to populate the select boxes using JavaScript alone.

You can solve this problem easily using Ajax techniques. Each time the selection in the model year or manufacturer select boxes changes, an asynchronous request is sent to the server requesting the list of models available for that particular manufacturer in that particular model year. The server is responsible for determining the list of models for the make and model year requested by the browser. The server will most likely employ a high-speed data lookup component, possibly implemented as a relational database, to perform the actual work of finding the available models. Once the available models are found, the server packages them in an XML file and returns them to the browser.

The browser is responsible for parsing the server's XML response and populating the model select box with the available models for the specified make and model year. In this case, notice how well the view of the data is separated from the raw data. The browser is solely responsible for rendering the view of the data. The server is responsible for mining the raw data that must be rendered into a view on the browser.

Listing 4-5 demonstrates how you can use Ajax techniques to dynamically create the contents of one select box based on the values of two other list boxes. The example's use case is the classified ads scenario described, where the selected values in a model year select box and a manufacturer select box determine the contents of the model select box. This example uses only four model years, three manufacturers, and four models available from a certain manufacturer for a certain model year. Still, this makes 48 combinations of model year, make, and model! This example would be impossible to do by hiding the list of models for every model year and manufacturer combination and showing the appropriate list depending on the selected manufacturer and model year values.

Listing 4-5. dynamicLists.html

```
<!DOCTYPE html PUBLIC "-//W3C//DTD XHTML 1.0 Strict//EN"
  "http://www.w3.org/TR/xhtml1/DTD/xhtml1-strict.dtd">
<html xmlns="http://www.w3.org/1999/xhtml">
<head>
<title>Dynamically Filling Lists</title>

<script type="text/javascript">
var xmlHttp;

function createXMLHttpRequest() {
    if (window.ActiveXObject) {
        xmlHttp = new ActiveXObject("Microsoft.XMLHTTP");
    }
    else if (window.XMLHttpRequest) {
        xmlHttp = new XMLHttpRequest();
    }
}

function refreshModelList() {
    var make = document.getElementById("make").value;
    var modelYear = document.getElementById("modelYear").value;

    if(make == "" || modelYear == "") {
        clearModelsList();
        return;
    }

    var url = "RefreshModelList?"
        + createQueryString(make, modelYear) + "&ts=" + new Date().getTime();

    createXMLHttpRequest();
    xmlHttp.onreadystatechange = handleStateChange;
    xmlHttp.open("GET", url, true);
    xmlHttp.send(null);
}

function createQueryString(make, modelYear) {
    var queryString = "make=" + make + "&modelYear=" + modelYear;
    return queryString;
}
```

```
function handleStateChange() {
    if(xmlHttp.readyState == 4) {
        if(xmlHttp.status == 200) {
            updateModelsList();
        }
    }
}

function updateModelsList() {
    clearModelsList();

    var models = document.getElementById("models");
    var results = xmlHttp.responseXML.getElementsByTagName("model");
    var option = null;
    for(var i = 0; i < results.length; i++) {
        option = document.createElement("option");
        option.appendChild
                    (document.createTextNode(results[i].firstChild.nodeValue));
        models.appendChild(option);
    }
}

function clearModelsList() {
    var models = document.getElementById("models");
    while(models.childNodes.length > 0) {
        models.removeChild(models.childNodes[0]);
    }
}
</script>
</head>

<body>
  <h1>Select Model Year and Make</h1>

  <form action="#">
    <span style="font-weight:bold;">Model Year:</span>
    <select id="modelYear" onchange="refreshModelList();">
        <option value="">Select One</option>
        <option value="2006">2006</option>
        <option value="1995">1995</option>
        <option value="1985">1985</option>
        <option value="1970">1970</option>
    </select>
```

```
<br/><br/>
<span style="font-weight:bold;">Make:</span>
<select id="make" onchange="refreshModelList();">
    <option value="">Select One</option>
    <option value="Chevrolet">Chevrolet</option>
    <option value="Dodge">Dodge</option>
    <option value="Pontiac">Pontiac</option>
</select>

<br/><br/>
<span style="font-weight:bold;">Models:</span>
<br/>
<select id="models" size="6" style="width:300px;">

</select>

    </form>

</body>
</html>
```

The update of the page is driven by the onchange event of the make and model year select boxes. Whenever the selected value in either of the select boxes changes, the browser sends an asynchronous request to the server. The request is sent with a query string containing the values of the selected make and model year.

The RefreshModelList servlet accepts the request from the browser and determines the list of models for the specified make and model year. The servlet first parses the query string to determine the requested make and model year. Once the requested make and model year have been determined, the servlet iterates over a collection of objects representing the available model year, manufacturer, and model combinations. If a particular object's model year and manufacturer properties match the requested model year and manufacturer, then the object's model property is added to the response XML string. Once all the models for the specified make and model year have been found, the response XML is written back to the browser.

Please note that in a real-world implementation the server-side piece would almost certainly not rely on hard-coded values to populate the select box. The most likely implementation would involve searching a high-speed database for the models available for the requested model year and manufacturer.

Listing 4-6 shows RefreshModelListServlet.java.

Listing 4-6. RefreshModelListServlet.java

```
package ajaxbook.chap4;

import java.io.*;
import java.util.ArrayList;
import java.util.Iterator;
import java.util.List;
```

```java
import javax.servlet.*;
import javax.servlet.http.*;

public class RefreshModelListServlet extends HttpServlet {

    private static List availableModels = new ArrayList();

    protected void processRequest(HttpServletRequest request
                                                    , HttpServletResponse response)
    throws ServletException, IOException {
        response.setContentType("text/html;charset=UTF-8");

        int modelYear = Integer.parseInt(request.getParameter("modelYear"));
        String make = request.getParameter("make");

        StringBuffer results = new StringBuffer("<models>");
        MakeModelYear availableModel = null;
        for(Iterator it = availableModels.iterator(); it.hasNext();) {
            availableModel = (MakeModelYear)it.next();
            if(availableModel.modelYear == modelYear) {
                if(availableModel.make.equals(make)) {
                    results.append("<model>");
                    results.append(availableModel.model);
                    results.append("</model>");
                }
            }
        }
        results.append("</models>");

        response.setContentType("text/xml");
        response.getWriter().write(results.toString());
    }

    protected void doGet(HttpServletRequest request, HttpServletResponse response)
    throws ServletException, IOException {
        processRequest(request, response);
    }

    public void init() throws ServletException {
        availableModels.add(new MakeModelYear(2006, "Dodge", "Charger"));
        availableModels.add(new MakeModelYear(2006, "Dodge", "Magnum"));
        availableModels.add(new MakeModelYear(2006, "Dodge", "Ram"));
        availableModels.add(new MakeModelYear(2006, "Dodge", "Viper"));
        availableModels.add(new MakeModelYear(1995, "Dodge", "Avenger"));
        availableModels.add(new MakeModelYear(1995, "Dodge", "Intrepid"));
        availableModels.add(new MakeModelYear(1995, "Dodge", "Neon"));
        availableModels.add(new MakeModelYear(1995, "Dodge", "Spirit"));
```

```
        availableModels.add(new MakeModelYear(1985, "Dodge", "Aries"));
        availableModels.add(new MakeModelYear(1985, "Dodge", "Daytona"));
        availableModels.add(new MakeModelYear(1985, "Dodge", "Diplomat"));
        availableModels.add(new MakeModelYear(1985, "Dodge", "Omni"));
        availableModels.add(new MakeModelYear(1970, "Dodge", "Challenger"));
        availableModels.add(new MakeModelYear(1970, "Dodge", "Charger"));
        availableModels.add(new MakeModelYear(1970, "Dodge", "Coronet"));
        availableModels.add(new MakeModelYear(1970, "Dodge", "Dart"));

        availableModels.add(new MakeModelYear(2006, "Chevrolet", "Colorado"));
        availableModels.add(new MakeModelYear(2006, "Chevrolet", "Corvette"));
        availableModels.add(new MakeModelYear(2006, "Chevrolet", "Equinox"));
        availableModels.add(new MakeModelYear(2006, "Chevrolet", "Monte Carlo"));
        availableModels.add(new MakeModelYear(1995, "Chevrolet", "Beretta"));
        availableModels.add(new MakeModelYear(1995, "Chevrolet", "Camaro"));
        availableModels.add(new MakeModelYear(1995, "Chevrolet", "Cavalier"));
        availableModels.add(new MakeModelYear(1995, "Chevrolet", "Lumina"));
        availableModels.add(new MakeModelYear(1985, "Chevrolet", "Cavalier"));
        availableModels.add(new MakeModelYear(1985, "Chevrolet", "Chevette"));
        availableModels.add(new MakeModelYear(1985, "Chevrolet", "Celebrity"));
        availableModels.add(new MakeModelYear(1985, "Chevrolet", "Citation II"));
        availableModels.add(new MakeModelYear(1970, "Chevrolet", "Bel Air"));
        availableModels.add(new MakeModelYear(1970, "Chevrolet", "Caprice"));
        availableModels.add(new MakeModelYear(1970, "Chevrolet", "Chevelle"));
        availableModels.add(new MakeModelYear(1970, "Chevrolet", "Monte Carlo"));

        availableModels.add(new MakeModelYear(2006, "Pontiac", "G6"));
        availableModels.add(new MakeModelYear(2006, "Pontiac", "Grand Prix"));
        availableModels.add(new MakeModelYear(2006, "Pontiac", "Solstice"));
        availableModels.add(new MakeModelYear(2006, "Pontiac", "Vibe"));
        availableModels.add(new MakeModelYear(1995, "Pontiac", "Bonneville"));
        availableModels.add(new MakeModelYear(1995, "Pontiac", "Grand Am"));
        availableModels.add(new MakeModelYear(1995, "Pontiac", "Grand Prix"));
        availableModels.add(new MakeModelYear(1995, "Pontiac", "Firebird"));
        availableModels.add(new MakeModelYear(1985, "Pontiac", "6000"));
        availableModels.add(new MakeModelYear(1985, "Pontiac", "Fiero"));
        availableModels.add(new MakeModelYear(1985, "Pontiac", "Grand Prix"));
        availableModels.add(new MakeModelYear(1985, "Pontiac", "Parisienne"));
        availableModels.add(new MakeModelYear(1970, "Pontiac", "Catalina"));
        availableModels.add(new MakeModelYear(1970, "Pontiac", "GTO"));
        availableModels.add(new MakeModelYear(1970, "Pontiac", "LeMans"));
        availableModels.add(new MakeModelYear(1970, "Pontiac", "Tempest"));
    }
```

```
private static class MakeModelYear {
    private int modelYear;
    private String make;
    private String model;

    public MakeModelYear(int modelYear, String make, String model) {
        this.modelYear = modelYear;
        this.make = make;
        this.model = model;
    }
}
}
```

Figure 4-6 shows that selecting a different value in either select box updates the model list.

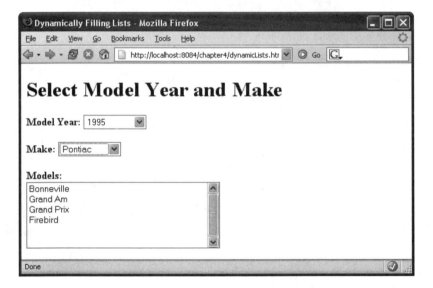

Figure 4-6. *Selecting a different value in either select box updates the model list.*

Creating an Autorefreshing Page

Stock tickers, weather data, headline news—all of these represent data that changes frequently but really doesn't justify a full *manual* refresh of the page. While sites such as CNN.com do reload at intervals, it can be jarring to see the entire page repainted to change one or two headlines and a couple of images. Of course, with the entire page refreshed, it can be difficult to figure out what is actually new!

Using Ajax, you can save your users from repeatedly clicking the refresh button. One site that uses this technique is the technology news site Digg (http://digg.com/spy). Digg combines the autorefresh approach to constantly update its page with the helpful color-fade technique to visually let the user know which headlines are new (see Figure 4-7).

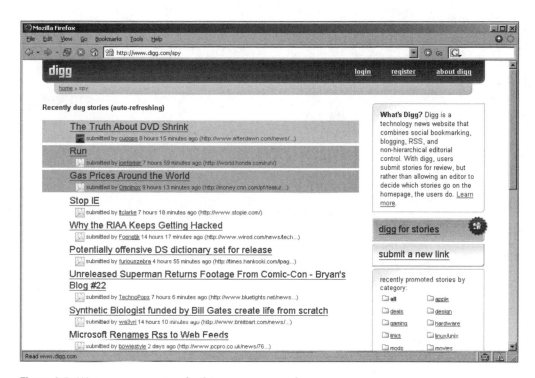

Figure 4-7. *Digg.com, an autorefreshing page example*

If you track Apple news, you may have followed Steve Jobs's keynote speech from Apple's 2005 Worldwide Developers Conference, where he revealed Apple would begin moving to Intel processors. The team at MacRumors.com (`http://www.macrumors.com/`) used Ajax to deliver this information in a timely fashion while reducing the strain on its servers. More recently, Apple's iTunes site (`http://www.apple.com/itunes/`) is using Ajax to dynamically update its count to 500 million downloads (see Figure 4-8).

Refreshing a page automatically is actually pretty straight-forward. For the example shown in Listing 4-7, you use a button to start the polling, though in a real-world application this would probably be replaced with an `onload` event. The `doStart()` method kicks things off, but the really interesting part is the `setTimeout()` method in the `pollCallback()` method, which allows a given method to be evaluated at a set time interval expressed in milliseconds. The `createRow()` method is just a helper function that takes advantage of DOM methods for creating content on the fly, and `refreshTime()` just moves the timer value.

Figure 4-8. *Apple iTunes Ajax-based counter*

Listing 4-7. dynamicUpdate.html

```html
<!DOCTYPE HTML PUBLIC "-//W3C//DTD HTML 4.01 Transitional//EN">

<html>
  <head>
    <title>Ajax Dynamic Update</title>
    <script type="text/javascript">
        var xmlHttp;

        function createXMLHttpRequest() {
            if (window.ActiveXObject) {
                xmlHttp = new ActiveXObject("Microsoft.XMLHTTP");
            }
            else if (window.XMLHttpRequest) {
                xmlHttp = new XMLHttpRequest();
            }
        }

        function doStart() {
            createXMLHttpRequest();
            var url = "DynamicUpdateServlet?task=reset";
            xmlHttp.open("GET", url, true);
            xmlHttp.onreadystatechange = startCallback;
            xmlHttp.send(null);
        }

        function startCallback() {
            if (xmlHttp.readyState == 4) {
                if (xmlHttp.status == 200) {
                    setTimeout("pollServer()", 5000);
                    refreshTime();
                }
            }
        }

        function pollServer() {
            createXMLHttpRequest();
            var url = "DynamicUpdateServlet?task=foo";
            xmlHttp.open("GET", url, true);
            xmlHttp.onreadystatechange = pollCallback;
            xmlHttp.send(null);
        }

        function refreshTime(){
            var time_span = document.getElementById("time");
            var time_val = time_span.innerHTML;
```

```
            var int_val = parseInt(time_val);
            var new_int_val = int_val - 1;

            if (new_int_val > -1) {
                setTimeout("refreshTime()", 1000);
                time_span.innerHTML = new_int_val;
            } else {
                time_span.innerHTML = 5;
            }
        }

        function pollCallback() {
            if (xmlHttp.readyState == 4) {
                if (xmlHttp.status == 200) {
                    var message =
                        xmlHttp.responseXML
                            .getElementsByTagName("message")[0].firstChild.data;

                    if (message != "done") {
                        var new_row = createRow(message);
                        var table = document.getElementById("dynamicUpdateArea");
                        var table_body =
                                    table.getElementsByTagName("tbody").item(0);
                        var first_row =
                                    table_body.getElementsByTagName("tr").item(1);
                        table_body.insertBefore(new_row, first_row);
                        setTimeout("pollServer()", 5000);
                        refreshTime();
                    }
                }
            }
        }

        function createRow(message) {
            var row = document.createElement("tr");
            var cell = document.createElement("td");
            var cell_data = document.createTextNode(message);
            cell.appendChild(cell_data);
            row.appendChild(cell);
            return row;
        }
    </script>
</head>
```

```
  <body>
    <h1>Ajax Dynamic Update Example</h1>
    This page will automatically update itself:
        <input type="button" value="Launch" id="go" onclick="doStart();"/>
    <p>
    Page will refresh in <span id="time">5</span> seconds.
    <p>
    <table id="dynamicUpdateArea" align="left">
        <tbody>
            <tr id="row0"><td></td></tr>
        </tbody>
    </table>
  </body>
</html>
```

The server code is pretty straightforward; it simply returns a chunk of information based on a simple counter (see Listing 4-8).

Listing 4-8. DynamicUpdateServlet.java

```java
package ajaxbook.chap4;

import java.io.*;
import java.net.*;

import javax.servlet.*;
import javax.servlet.http.*;

public class DynamicUpdateServlet extends HttpServlet {
    private int counter = 1;

    /** Handles the HTTP <code>GET</code> method.
     * @param request servlet request
     * @param response servlet response
     */
    protected void doGet(HttpServletRequest request, HttpServletResponse response)
    throws ServletException, IOException {
        String res = "";
        String task = request.getParameter("task");
        String message = "";

        if (task.equals("reset")) {
            counter = 1;
        } else {
            switch (counter) {
                case 1: message = "Steve walks on stage"; break;
                case 2: message = "iPods rock"; break;
                case 3: message = "Steve says Macs rule"; break;
```

```
                 case 4: message = "Change is coming"; break;
                 case 5: message = "Yes, OS X runs on Intel - has for years"; break;
                 case 6: message = "Macs will soon have Intel chips"; break;
                 case 7: message = "done"; break;
            }
            counter++;
        }

        res = "<message>" + message + "</message>";

        PrintWriter out = response.getWriter();
        response.setContentType("text/xml");
        response.setHeader("Cache-Control", "no-cache");
        out.println("<response>");
        out.println(res);
        out.println("</response>");
        out.close();
    }
}
```

Figure 4-9 shows the dynamic update example in a browser.

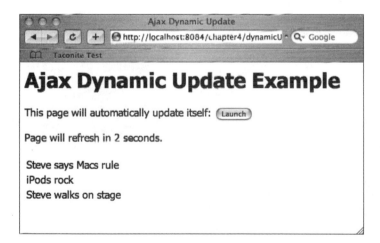

Figure 4-9. *Dynamic update example*

Displaying a Progress Bar

Almost without exception, every application will from time to time invoke a long-running transaction. If you are concerned about the usability of your system, you can make sure your users
can easily see the status of your systems. With a thick client, the solution to the long-running
transaction problem is simple: you just display a progress bar so that your users have an idea

of where they stand. However, before Ajax, this option wasn't so easy with a Web application. In this section, you'll investigate how you can use Ajax to build a progress bar for a Web application.

Once again, in the example shown in Listing 4-9, you use setTimeout() in the pollCallback() method to continually call the server every two seconds. In the processResult() method, you just look for the first digit of the percent completed from the server to figure out which blocks need to be colored in the progress bar area.

Listing 4-9. progressBar.html

```html
<!DOCTYPE HTML PUBLIC "-//W3C//DTD HTML 4.01 Transitional//EN">

<html>
  <head>
    <title>Ajax Progress Bar</title>
    <script type="text/javascript">
        var xmlHttp;
        var key;
        var bar_color = 'gray';
        var span_id = "block";
        var clear = "   "

        function createXMLHttpRequest() {
            if (window.ActiveXObject) {
                xmlHttp = new ActiveXObject("Microsoft.XMLHTTP");
            }
            else if (window.XMLHttpRequest) {
                xmlHttp = new XMLHttpRequest();
            }
        }

        function go() {
            createXMLHttpRequest();
            checkDiv();
            var url = "ProgressBarServlet?task=create";
            var button = document.getElementById("go");
            button.disabled = true;
            xmlHttp.open("GET", url, true);
            xmlHttp.onreadystatechange = goCallback;
            xmlHttp.send(null);
        }

        function goCallback() {
            if (xmlHttp.readyState == 4) {
                if (xmlHttp.status == 200) {
                    setTimeout("pollServer()", 2000);
                }
            }
        }
```

```
function pollServer() {
    createXMLHttpRequest();
    var url = "ProgressBarServlet?task=poll&key=" + key;
    xmlHttp.open("GET", url, true);
    xmlHttp.onreadystatechange = pollCallback;
    xmlHttp.send(null);
}

function pollCallback() {
    if (xmlHttp.readyState == 4) {
        if (xmlHttp.status == 200) {
            var percent_complete =
                    xmlHttp.responseXML
                        .getElementsByTagName("percent")[0].firstChild.data;

            var index = processResult(percent_complete);
            for (var i = 1; i <= index; i++) {
                var elem = document.getElementById("block" + i);
                elem.innerHTML = clear;

                elem.style.backgroundColor = bar_color;
                var next_cell = i + 1;
                if (next_cell > index && next_cell <= 9) {
                    document.getElementById("block" + next_cell)
                        .innerHTML =
                                percent_complete + "%";
                }
            }
            if (index < 9) {
                setTimeout("pollServer()", 2000);
            } else {
                document.getElementById("complete").innerHTML = "Complete!";
                document.getElementById("go").disabled = false;
            }
        }
    }
}

function processResult(percent_complete) {
    var ind;
    if (percent_complete.length == 1) {
        ind = 1;
    } else if (percent_complete.length == 2) {
        ind = percent_complete.substring(0, 1);
    } else {
        ind = 9;
    }
    return ind;
}
```

```
        function checkDiv() {
            var progress_bar = document.getElementById("progressBar");
            if (progress_bar.style.visibility == "visible") {
                clearBar();
                document.getElementById("complete").innerHTML = "";
            } else {
                progress_bar.style.visibility = "visible"
            }
        }

        function clearBar() {
            for (var i = 1; i < 10; i++) {
                var elem = document.getElementById("block" + i);
                elem.innerHTML = clear;
                elem.style.backgroundColor = "white";
            }
        }
    </script>
  </head>
  <body>
    <h1>Ajax Progress Bar Example</h1>
    Launch long-running process:
            <input type="button" value="Launch" id="go" onclick="go();"/>
    <p>
    <table align="center">
        <tbody>
            <tr><td>
                <div id="progressBar"
                    style="padding:2px;border:solid black 2px;visibility:hidden">
                    <span id="block1">   </span>
                    <span id="block2">   </span>
                    <span id="block3">   </span>
                    <span id="block4">   </span>
                    <span id="block5">   </span>
                    <span id="block6">   </span>
                    <span id="block7">   </span>
                    <span id="block8">   </span>
                    <span id="block9">   </span>
                </div>
            </td></tr>
            <tr><td align="center" id="complete"></td></tr>
        </tbody>
    </table>
  </body>
</html>
```

The server code for this example "fakes" a long-running transaction (see Listing 4-10). In a production environment, you would be creating new instances and registering them, and your client would have to ask about a specific item. For simplicity sake, we've omitted this and any threading code.

Listing 4-10. ProgressBarServlet.java

```java
package ajaxbook.chap4;

import java.io.*;

import javax.servlet.*;
import javax.servlet.http.*;

public class ProgressBarServlet extends HttpServlet {
    private int counter = 1;

    /** Handles the HTTP <code>GET</code> method.
     * @param request servlet request
     * @param response servlet response
     */
    protected void doGet(HttpServletRequest request, HttpServletResponse response)
    throws ServletException, IOException {
        String task = request.getParameter("task");
        String res = "";

        if (task.equals("create")) {
            res = "<key>1</key>";
            counter = 1;
        }
        else {
            String percent = "";
            switch (counter) {
                case 1: percent = "10"; break;
                case 2: percent = "23"; break;
                case 3: percent = "35"; break;
                case 4: percent = "51"; break;
                case 5: percent = "64"; break;
                case 6: percent = "73"; break;
                case 7: percent = "89"; break;
                case 8: percent = "100"; break;
            }
            counter++;

            res = "<percent>" + percent + "</percent>";
        }
```

```
        PrintWriter out = response.getWriter();
        response.setContentType("text/xml");
        response.setHeader("Cache-Control", "no-cache");
        out.println("<response>");
        out.println(res);
        out.println("</response>");
        out.close();
    }
}
```

Figure 4-10 shows the progress bar in action, and Figure 4-11 shows it on completion.

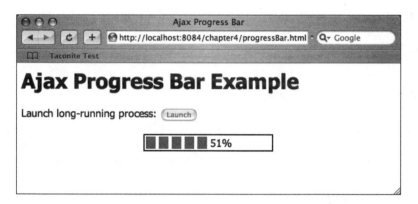

Figure 4-10. *Progress bar example*

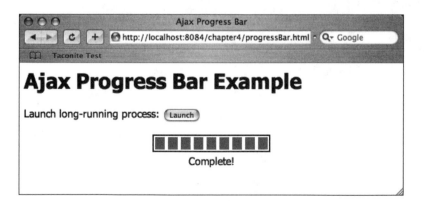

Figure 4-11. *Progress bar finished*

Creating Tooltips

One of the most interesting uses of Ajax that we've seen so far involves the DVD rental service Netflix. When you browse the selections at Netflix, you are presented with graphics and text for recent films in numerous categories; however, when you hover over a given movie's graphic, you see additional information (see Figure 4-12). While this effect could have been achieved without Ajax, the initial fetch of the page would be bloated with a tremendous amount of information that might never be used. By using Ajax, you send only the information that is needed when it is needed.

Figure 4-12. *Netflix browse feature*

While we won't show how to do anything quite this fancy, we will show you how you can provide your own dynamic tooltip-like information. The client-side code is pretty straightforward (see Listing 4-11). The interesting bits here involve the `calculateOffset()` method. In an ideal world, you could rely on the offset attributes of the elements in question; however, this doesn't work perfectly across browsers. However, you can walk the DOM to generate a precise offset that you can then use to place your dynamic area. This example takes a simple table of famous golf courses and displays additional information when the user hovers over the cell in the table.

Listing 4-11. `toolTip.html`

```html
<!DOCTYPE HTML PUBLIC "-//W3C//DTD HTML 4.01 Transitional//EN">

<html>
  <head>
    <title>Ajax Tool Tip</title>
    <script type="text/javascript">
        var xmlHttp;
        var dataDiv;
        var dataTable;
        var dataTableBody;
        var offsetEl;

        function createXMLHttpRequest() {
            if (window.ActiveXObject) {
                xmlHttp = new ActiveXObject("Microsoft.XMLHTTP");
            }
            else if (window.XMLHttpRequest) {
                xmlHttp = new XMLHttpRequest();
            }
        }

        function initVars() {
            dataTableBody = document.getElementById("courseDataBody");
            dataTable = document.getElementById("courseData");
            dataDiv = document.getElementById("popup");
        }

        function getCourseData(element) {
            initVars();
            createXMLHttpRequest();
            offsetEl = element;
            var url = "ToolTipServlet?key=" + escape(element.id);

            xmlHttp.open("GET", url, true);
            xmlHttp.onreadystatechange = callback;
            xmlHttp.send(null);
        }
```

```
function callback() {
    if (xmlHttp.readyState == 4) {
        if (xmlHttp.status == 200) {
            setData(xmlHttp.responseXML);
        }
    }
}

function setData(courseData) {
    clearData();
    setOffsets();
    var length =
            courseData.getElementsByTagName("length")[0].firstChild.data;
    var par = courseData.getElementsByTagName("par")[0].firstChild.data;

    var row, row2;
    var parData = "Par: " + par
    var lengthData = "Length: " + length;

    row = createRow(parData);
    row2 = createRow(lengthData);

    dataTableBody.appendChild(row);
    dataTableBody.appendChild(row2);
}

function createRow(data) {
    var row, cell, txtNode;
    row = document.createElement("tr");
    cell = document.createElement("td");

    cell.setAttribute("bgcolor", "#FFFAFA");
    cell.setAttribute("border", "0");

    txtNode = document.createTextNode(data);
    cell.appendChild(txtNode);
    row.appendChild(cell);

    return row;
}

function setOffsets() {
    var end = offsetEl.offsetWidth;
    var top = calculateOffsetTop(offsetEl);
    dataDiv.style.border = "black 1px solid";
    dataDiv.style.left = end + 15 + "px";
    dataDiv.style.top = top + "px";
}
```

```
        function calculateOffsetTop(field) {
          return calculateOffset(field, "offsetTop");
        }

        function calculateOffset(field, attr) {
          var offset = 0;
          while(field) {
            offset += field[attr];
            field = field.offsetParent;
          }
          return offset;
        }

        function clearData() {
            var ind = dataTableBody.childNodes.length;
            for (var i = ind - 1; i >= 0 ; i--) {
                dataTableBody.removeChild(dataTableBody.childNodes[i]);
            }
            dataDiv.style.border = "none";
        }
    </script>
  </head>
  <body>
    <h1>Ajax Tool Tip Example</h1>
    <h3>Golf Courses</h3>
    <table id="courses" bgcolor="#FFFAFA" border="1"
                                        cellspacing="0" cellpadding="2"/>
        <tbody>
            <tr><td id="1" onmouseover="getCourseData(this);"
                        onmouseout="clearData();">Augusta National</td></tr>
            <tr><td id="2" onmouseover="getCourseData(this);"
                        onmouseout="clearData();">Pinehurst No. 2</td></tr>
            <tr><td id="3" onmouseover="getCourseData(this);"
                        onmouseout="clearData();">
                        St. Andrews Links</td></tr>
            <tr><td id="4" onmouseover="getCourseData(this);"
                       onmouseout="clearData();">Baltusrol Golf Club</td></tr>
        </tbody>
    </table>
    <div style="position:absolute;" id="popup">
        <table id="courseData" bgcolor="#FFFAFA" border="0"
                                        cellspacing="2" cellpadding="2"/>
            <tbody id="courseDataBody"></tbody>
        </table>
    </div>

  </body>
</html>
```

Keep in mind that in a production environment you would most likely retrieve the extra information from a data store of some sort, and you probably wouldn't have an inner class in the servlet! Listing 4-12 shows ToolTipServlet.java.

Listing 4-12. ToolTipServlet.java

```java
package ajaxbook.chap4;

import java.io.*;
import java.util.HashMap;
import java.util.Map;

import javax.servlet.*;
import javax.servlet.http.*;

public class ToolTipServlet extends HttpServlet {

    private Map courses = new HashMap();

    public void init(ServletConfig config) throws ServletException {
        CourseData augusta = new CourseData(72, 7290);
        CourseData pinehurst = new CourseData(70, 7214);
        CourseData standrews = new CourseData(72, 6566);
        CourseData baltusrol = new CourseData(70, 7392);
        courses.put(new Integer(1), augusta);
        courses.put(new Integer(2), pinehurst);
        courses.put(new Integer(3), standrews);
        courses.put(new Integer(4), baltusrol);
    }

    /** Handles the HTTP <code>GET</code> method.
     * @param request servlet request
     * @param response servlet response
     */
    protected void doGet(HttpServletRequest request, HttpServletResponse response)
    throws ServletException, IOException {
        Integer key = Integer.valueOf(request.getParameter("key"));
        CourseData data = (CourseData) courses.get(key);

        PrintWriter out = response.getWriter();

        response.setContentType("text/xml");
        response.setHeader("Cache-Control", "no-cache");

        out.println("<response>");
        out.println("<par>" + data.getPar() + "</par>");
        out.println("<length>" + data.getLength() + "</length>");
        out.println("</response>");
        out.close();
    }
}
```

```
private class CourseData {
        private int par;
        private int length;

        public CourseData(int par, int length) {
            this.par = par;
            this.length = length;
        }

        public int getPar() {
            return this.par;
        }

        public int getLength() {
            return this.length;
        }
    }
}
```

Figure 4-13 shows the tooltip in action.

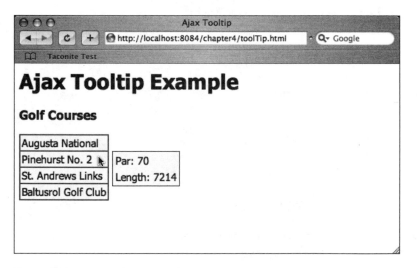

Figure 4-13. *Ajax tooltip example*

Dynamically Updating a Web Page

As discussed previously, Ajax techniques are best applied when only a small portion of the page needs to change. In other words, use cases that were previously implemented using a complete page refresh to update a small portion of the page are fabulous candidates for applying Ajax techniques.

Consider the use case involving a single page into which the user enters information that is added to a list. In this example, you'll see a Web page that lists the employees in an organization. The top of the page has three input boxes that accept the employee's name, position, and department. Clicking the Add button submits the name, position, and department data to the server, where the employee information is added to the database.

Using traditional Web application techniques, the server would respond by re-creating the entire page, with the only difference from the previous page being that the new employee information is added to the list. In this example, you'll use Ajax techniques to asynchronously submit the employee data to the server and insert the data into the database. The server will respond to the browser by sending a status code indicating the success or failure of the database operation. Assuming a successful database insert, the browser will use JavaScript DOM operations to dynamically update the page content with the new employee information. This example also creates a Delete button so employee information can be deleted from the database.

Listing 4-13 shows the source code for the HTML Web page. The page has two sections: the first section consists of the input boxes that accept the employee name, title, and department and the Add button that initiates the database insert. The second section lists all the employees in the database, with each record having its own Delete button so the information can be deleted from the database.

Listing 4-13. employeeList.html

```
<!DOCTYPE html PUBLIC "-//W3C//DTD XHTML 1.0 Strict//EN"
  "http://www.w3.org/TR/xhtml1/DTD/xhtml1-strict.dtd">
<html xmlns="http://www.w3.org/1999/xhtml">
<head>
<title>Employee List</title>

<script type="text/javascript">
var xmlHttp;
var name;
var title;
var department;
var deleteID;
var EMP_PREFIX = "emp-";

function createXMLHttpRequest() {
    if (window.ActiveXObject) {
        xmlHttp = new ActiveXObject("Microsoft.XMLHTTP");
    }
    else if (window.XMLHttpRequest) {
        xmlHttp = new XMLHttpRequest();
    }
}

function addEmployee() {
    name = document.getElementById("name").value;
    title = document.getElementById("title").value;
    department = document.getElementById("dept").value;
    action = "add";
```

```
    if(name == "" || title == "" || department == "") {
        return;
    }

    var url = "EmployeeList?"
        + createAddQueryString(name, title, department, "add")
        + "&ts=" + new Date().getTime();

    createXMLHttpRequest();
    xmlHttp.onreadystatechange = handleAddStateChange;
    xmlHttp.open("GET", url, true);
    xmlHttp.send(null);
}

function createAddQueryString(name, title, department, action) {
    var queryString = "name=" + name
        + "&title=" + title
        + "&department=" + department
        + "&action=" + action;
    return queryString;
}

function handleAddStateChange() {
    if(xmlHttp.readyState == 4) {
        if(xmlHttp.status == 200) {
            updateEmployeeList();
            clearInputBoxes();
        }
        else {
            alert("Error while adding employee.");
        }
    }
}

function clearInputBoxes() {
    document.getElementById("name").value = "";
    document.getElementById("title").value = "";
    document.getElementById("dept").value = "";
}

function deleteEmployee(id) {
    deleteID = id;

    var url = "EmployeeList?"
        + "action=delete"
        + "&id=" + id
        + "&ts=" + new Date().getTime();
```

```javascript
        createXMLHttpRequest();
        xmlHttp.onreadystatechange = handleDeleteStateChange;
        xmlHttp.open("GET", url, true);
        xmlHttp.send(null);
    }

    function updateEmployeeList() {
        var responseXML = xmlHttp.responseXML;

        var status = responseXML.getElementsByTagName("status")
                                            .item(0).firstChild.nodeValue;
        status = parseInt(status);
        if(status != 1) {
            return;
        }


        var row = document.createElement("tr");
        var uniqueID = responseXML.getElementsByTagName("uniqueID")[0]
                                            .firstChild.nodeValue;
        row.setAttribute("id", EMP_PREFIX + uniqueID);

        row.appendChild(createCellWithText(name));
        row.appendChild(createCellWithText(title));
        row.appendChild(createCellWithText(department));

        var deleteButton = document.createElement("input");
        deleteButton.setAttribute("type", "button");
        deleteButton.setAttribute("value", "Delete");
        deleteButton.onclick = function () { deleteEmployee(uniqueID); };
        cell = document.createElement("td");
        cell.appendChild(deleteButton);
        row.appendChild(cell);

        document.getElementById("employeeList").appendChild(row);
        updateEmployeeListVisibility();
    }

    function createCellWithText(text) {
        var cell = document.createElement("td");
        cell.appendChild(document.createTextNode(text));
        return cell;
    }
```

```
function handleDeleteStateChange() {
    if(xmlHttp.readyState == 4) {
        if(xmlHttp.status == 200) {
            deleteEmployeeFromList();
        }
        else {
            alert("Error while deleting employee.");
        }
    }

}

function deleteEmployeeFromList() {
    var status =
                    xmlHttp.responseXML.getElementsByTagName("status")
                    .item(0).firstChild.nodeValue;
    status = parseInt(status);
    if(status != 1) {
        return;
    }

    var rowToDelete = document.getElementById(EMP_PREFIX + deleteID);
    var employeeList = document.getElementById("employeeList");
    employeeList.removeChild(rowToDelete);

    updateEmployeeListVisibility();
}

function updateEmployeeListVisibility() {
    var employeeList = document.getElementById("employeeList");
    if(employeeList.childNodes.length > 0) {
        document.getElementById("employeeListSpan").style.display = "";
    }
    else {
        document.getElementById("employeeListSpan").style.display = "none";
    }
}
</script>
</head>

<body>
    <h1>Employee List</h1>
```

```
<form action="#">
  <table width="80%" border="0">
      <tr>
          <td>Name: <input type="text" id="name"/></td>
          <td>Title: <input type="text" id="title"/></td>
          <td>Department: <input type="text" id="dept"/></td>
      </tr>
      <tr>
          <td colspan="3" align="center">
              <input type="button" value="Add" onclick="addEmployee();"/>
          </td>
      </tr>
  </table>
</form>

<span id="employeeListSpan" style="display:none;">
<h2>Employees:</h2>

<table border="1" width="80%">
  <tbody id="employeeList"></tbody>
</table>
</span>
</body>
</html>
```

Clicking the Add button initiates the database insert operation. The addEmployee function is called by the Add button's onclick event. The addEmployee function employs createAddQueryString to build a query string containing the employee name, title, and department information entered by the user. After creating the XMLHttpRequest object and setting the onreadystatechange event handler, the request is submitted to the server.

Listing 4-14 details the Java servlet that handles this request. Upon receipt of the request, the servlet's doGet method is called. This method retrieves the value of the query string's action parameter and directs the request to the appropriate method. In the case of an addition, the request is directed to the addEmployee method.

Listing 4-14. EmployeeListServlet.java

```
package ajaxbook.chap4;

import java.io.*;
import java.net.*;
import java.util.Random;

import javax.servlet.*;
import javax.servlet.http.*;

public class EmployeeListServlet extends HttpServlet {
```

```java
protected void addEmployee(HttpServletRequest request
                                   , HttpServletResponse response)
throws ServletException, IOException {

    //Store the object in the database
    String uniqueID = storeEmployee();

    //Create the response XML
    StringBuffer xml = new StringBuffer("<result><uniqueID>");
    xml.append(uniqueID);
    xml.append("</uniqueID>");
    xml.append("</result>");

    //Send the response back to the browser
    sendResponse(response, xml.toString());
}

protected void deleteEmployee(HttpServletRequest request
                                   , HttpServletResponse response)
throws ServletException, IOException {

    String id = request.getParameter("id");
    /* Assume that a call is made to delete the employee from the database */

    //Create the response XML
    StringBuffer xml = new StringBuffer("<result>");
    xml.append("<status>1</status>");
    xml.append("</result>");

    //Send the response back to the browser
    sendResponse(response, xml.toString());
}

protected void doGet(HttpServletRequest request, HttpServletResponse response)
throws ServletException, IOException {
    String action = request.getParameter("action");
    if(action.equals("add")) {
        addEmployee(request, response);
    }
    else if(action.equals("delete")) {
        deleteEmployee(request, response);
    }
}
```

```java
    private String storeEmployee() {
        /* Assume that the employee is saved to a database and the
         * database creates a unique ID. Return the unique ID to the
         * calling method. In this case, make up a unique ID.
         */
        String uniqueID = "";
        Random randomizer = new Random(System.currentTimeMillis());
        for(int i = 0; i < 8; i++) {
            uniqueID += randomizer.nextInt(9);
        }

        return uniqueID;
    }

    private void sendResponse(HttpServletResponse response, String responseText)
    throws IOException {
        response.setContentType("text/xml");
        response.getWriter().write(responseText);
    }
}
```

The addEmployee function is responsible for coordinating the database insertion and the server response. The addEmployee method delegates to the storeEmployee method to perform the actual database insert. In a real-world implementation, the storeEmployee method would likely call a database service that would handle the details of performing the database insert. In this simplified example, the storeEmployee fakes the database insert by generating a random unique ID that mimics the ID that a real database insert might return. The generated unique ID is then returned to the addEmployee method.

Assuming a successful database insertion, the addEmployee method then continues by preparing the response. The response is a simple XML string that returns a status code to the browser. The XML is created via string concatenation and then written to the response's output stream.

The browser handles the server's response by calling the handleAddStateChange method. This method is called whenever the XMLHttpRequest object signals a change in its internal ready state. Once the readystate property indicates that the server response has completed successfully, the updateEmployeeList function is called, followed by the clearInputBoxes function. The updateEmployeeList function is responsible for adding the successfully inserted employee information to the list of employees that appears on the page. The clearInputBoxes function is a simple utility method that clears out the input boxes so they're ready for the next employee.

The updateEmployeeList function adds a row to the table that lists the employee information. It starts by using the document.createElement method to create an instance of a table row. The row's id attribute is set to a value that includes the unique ID generated by the database insert. The id attribute value uniquely identifies the table row so that it can be easily removed from the table if the Delete button is ever used.

The updateEmployeeList function uses a utility function named createCellWithText to create table cell elements that contain the specified text. The createCellWithText function creates table cells for the employee name, title, and department information entered by the user. Each cell is then added to the previously created table row.

The last item to create is the Delete button and the table cell that contains it. You can create the Delete button by using the `document.createElement` method to create a generic input element whose `type` and `value` attributes are set to `button` and `Delete`, respectively. You then create a table cell to house the Delete button and add the Delete button as a child element to the table cell. You then add the cell to the table row and add the row, which now contains cells for the employee name, title, department, and Delete button to the employee list table.

Deleting an employee works much the same way as adding an employee. The Delete button's `onclick` event handler calls the `deleteEmployee` function, passing the employee's unique ID to the function. A simple query string is created indicating the desired action (delete) and the unique ID of the employee record to delete. The request is submitted after the XMLHttpRequest object's `onreadystatechange` property is set to the desired event handler.

The `EmployeeListServlet` servlet uses the `deleteEmployee` method to handle the employee delete use case. This simplified example assumes that another method handles the details of actually performing the database delete. Assuming a successful database delete, the `deleteEmployee` method prepares the XML string that is returned to the browser. Like the employee add use case, this use case returns a status code to the browser. Once created, the XML string is written back to the browser through the response object's output stream.

The browser handles the server response through the `handleDeleteStateChange` function, which forwards to the `deleteEmployeeFromList` method if the response is successful. The `deleteEmployeeFromList` function retrieves the status code from the XML response; the function immediately exits if the status code indicates an unsuccessful delete. Assuming a successful delete operation, the function continues by retrieving the table row representing the deleted information by using the `document.getElementById` method. The row is then deleted from the table body using the table body's `removeChild` method.

WHY ISN'T THE SETATTRIBUTE METHOD USED TO SET THE DELETE BUTTON'S EVENT HANDLER?

You may have noticed the method by which the Delete button's event handler is set. You probably expected that the code to set the Delete button's `onclick` event handler would look something like this:

```
deleteButton.setAttribute("onclick", "deleteEmployee('" + unique_id + "');");
```

Indeed, this code is technically correct, follows W3C standards, and works in most modern browsers with the notable exception of Internet Explorer. Fortunately, a workaround is available for Internet Explorer and also works in Firefox, Opera, Safari, and Konqueror.

The workaround consists of referencing the Delete button's `onclick` event handler using dot notation and then setting the event handler using an anonymous function that calls the `deleteEmployee` function.

Figure 4-14 shows the dynamic update example in action.

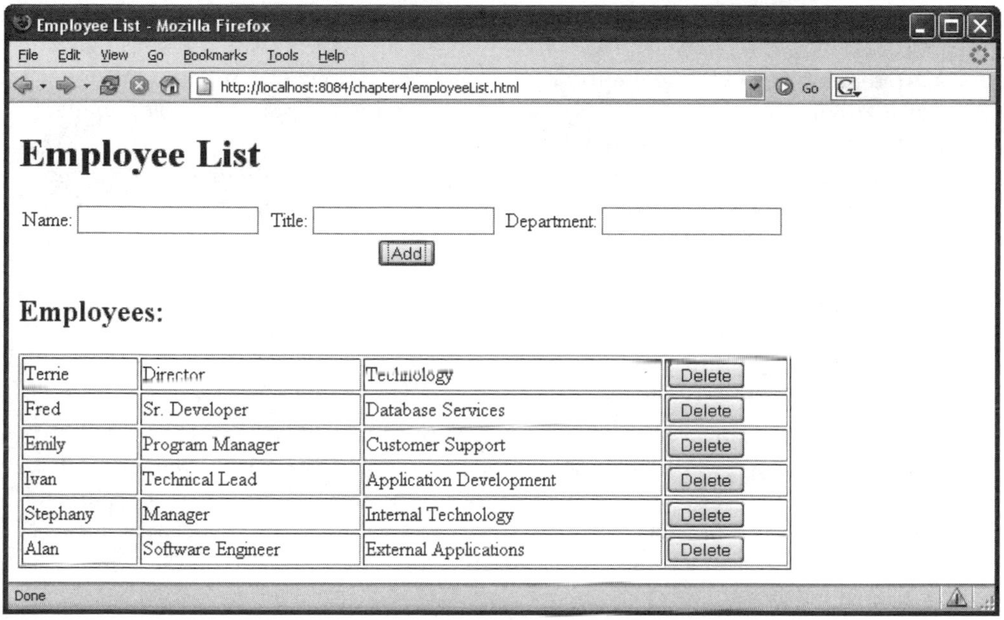

Figure 4-14. *Each name is dynamically added to the list each time the Add button is clicked, without refreshing the page each time.*

Accessing Web Services

Web Services are the latest attempt to solve an age-old software engineering problem: calling services or methods on one machine from another machine, even when the machines use completely different hardware or software. A few years ago a lot of hype surrounded Web Services, as some considered them the Holy Grail of distributed software development. Since then much of the sheen has worn off, and Web Services have settled into a comfortable niche as a useful tool for enabling disparate computer systems to interoperate with one another.

Web Services are typically used as the communication pipeline between computer systems, much like Common Object Request Broker Architecture (CORBA), Remote Method Invocation (RMI), or Distributed Component Object Model (DCOM). The difference is that Web Services are vendor neutral and can be implemented by a wide variety of programming tools and platforms. To enable a high level of interoperability, Web Services are a text-based protocol often implemented over HTTP. Since they are a text-based protocol, Web Services almost always use XML in some variety.

The most well-known Web Services implementation is Simple Object Access Protocol (SOAP). SOAP is a specification managed by the W3C. It is an XML protocol that provides a definition of how to call remote procedures.

A Web Services Description Language (WSDL) document is an XML document that describes how to create a client to a Web Service. By providing a WSDL document, a Web Service provider simplifies the task of creating client-side code for potential clients. WSDL and SOAP are often used together, but this is not necessary, as the two specifications are maintained separately.

Despite the efforts made to simplify SOAP implementations, SOAP remains a difficult technology to employ, and thus its use has often been relegated to situations where cross-platform interoperability is truly an important requirement. A simpler approach to Web Services called REpresentational State Transfer (REST) is gaining popularity with developers who want 80 percent of SOAP's benefits at only 20 percent of the cost.

Yahoo! has chosen REST as the protocol for its public Web Services. Yahoo! believes that REST-based services are easy to understand and likes REST's accessibility from most modern programming languages. In fact, Yahoo! believes REST has a lower barrier of entry and is easier to use than SOAP.

Using REST, you can form a request by starting with a service entry URL and then appending search parameters to the query string. The results are returned by the service as an XML document. Does this pattern sound familiar? That's right—it's identical to the Ajax examples you've been working with throughout the book.

The XMLHttpRequest object is the perfect client for REST-based Web Services. Using the XMLHttpRequest object, you can asynchronously send a request to a Web Service and parse the resulting XML response. In the case of Yahoo! Web Services, the XMLHttpRequest object can send a request to Yahoo! to search for a specified term. Once Yahoo! returns a response, JavaScript DOM methods parse the response and dynamically render the result data to the page.

Listing 4-15 demonstrates how to use Ajax techniques to access Yahoo! Web Services and render the results to the page. The text field on the page allows the user to specify the term on which to perform the search. The select box enables the user to specify how many results to display. Clicking the Submit button initiates the search.

But wait! In Chapter 3 you learned that the XMLHttpRequest object could access resources only within the same domain from which the containing document originated. Attempting to access a resource from another domain may fail because of security restrictions imposed by the browser. How do you get around that?

You have a few options. As you learned in Chapter 3, browsers implement the security sandbox differently. Internet Explorer will ask the user if it's OK to access a resource at a different domain. Firefox will automatically fail with an error, although you can avoid this with Firefox-specific JavaScript code.

Another option, and the option used in this example, is to create a gateway to Yahoo! that lives in the same domain as the XMLHttpRequest script. The gateway accepts the request from the XMLHttpRequest object and forwards it to Yahoo! Web Services. When Yahoo! responds with the results, the gateway simply routes the results to the browser. By using this approach, you avoid having to use browser-specific JavaScript. Additionally, this approach is more robust, because you could extend the gateway to include other Web Service providers.

Listing 4-15. yahooSearch.html

```
<!DOCTYPE html PUBLIC "-//W3C//DTD XHTML 1.0 Strict//EN"
  "http://www.w3.org/TR/xhtml1/DTD/xhtml1-strict.dtd">
<html xmlns="http://www.w3.org/1999/xhtml">
<head>
<title>Yahoo! Search Web Services</title>

<script type="text/javascript">
var xmlHttp;
```

```
function createXMLHttpRequest() {
    if (window.ActiveXObject) {
        xmlHttp = new ActiveXObject("Microsoft.XMLHTTP");
    }
    else if (window.XMLHttpRequest) {
        xmlHttp = new XMLHttpRequest();
    }
}

function doSearch() {
    var url = "YahooSearchGateway?" + createQueryString()
                                     + "&ts=" + new Date().getTime();
    createXMLHttpRequest();
    xmlHttp.onreadystatechange = handleStateChange;
    xmlHttp.open("GET", url, true);
    xmlHttp.send(null);
}

function createQueryString() {
    var searchString = document.getElementById("searchString").value;
    searchString = escape(searchString);

    var maxResultsCount = document.getElementById("maxResultCount").value;

    var queryString = "query=" + searchString + "&results=" + maxResultsCount;
    return queryString;
}

function handleStateChange() {
    if(xmlHttp.readyState == 4) {
        if(xmlHttp.status == 200) {
            parseSearchResults();
        }
        else {
            alert("Error accessing Yahoo! search");
        }
    }
}

function parseSearchResults() {
    var resultsDiv = document.getElementById("results");
    while(resultsDiv.childNodes.length > 0) {
        resultsDiv.removeChild(resultsDiv.childNodes[0]);
    }

    var allResults = xmlHttp.responseXML.getElementsByTagName("Result");
```

```
        var result = null;
        for(var i = 0; i < allResults.length; i++) {
            result = allResults[i];
            parseResult(result);
        }
    }

    function parseResult(result) {
        var resultDiv = document.createElement("div");

        var title = document.createElement("h3");
        title.appendChild(document.createTextNode(
                                        getChildElementText(result, "Title")));
        resultDiv.appendChild(title);

        var summary = document.createTextNode(getChildElementText(result, "Summary"));
        resultDiv.appendChild(summary);

        resultDiv.appendChild(document.createElement("br"));
        var clickHere = document.createElement("a");
        clickHere.setAttribute("href", getChildElementText(result, "ClickUrl"));
        clickHere.appendChild(document.createTextNode
                                        (getChildElementText(result, "Url")));
        resultDiv.appendChild(clickHere);

        document.getElementById("results").appendChild(resultDiv);
    }

    function getChildElementText(parentNode, childTagName) {
        var childTag = parentNode.getElementsByTagName(childTagName);
        return childTag[0].firstChild.nodeValue;
    }
    </script>
    </head>

    <body>
      <h1>Web Search Using Yahoo! Search Web Services</h1>

      <form action="#">
        Search String: <input type="text" id="searchString"/>

        <br/><br/>
        Max Number of Results:
        <select id="maxResultCount">
            <option value="1">1</option>
            <option value="10">10</option>
            <option value="25">25</option>
            <option value="50">50</option>
        </select>
```

```
    <br/><br/>
    <input type="button" value="Submit" onclick="doSearch();"/>
  </form>

  <h2>Results:</h2>
  <div id="results"/>

</body>
</html>
```

Clicking the Submit button on the page calls the doSearch function. This function creates the target URL by using the createQueryString function that is responsible for placing the search term and maximum desired results into the query string. Note that the names of the parameters, query and results, are defined by the Yahoo! Search API.

The query string created by createQueryString is sent to the Yahoo! Search gateway. In this example, the gateway is implemented as a Java servlet named YahooSearchGatewayServlet (see Listing 4-16). The premise of this servlet is simple: forward all requests to the Yahoo! Search URL and stream the results to the browser. Certainly this gateway could be implemented in languages other than Java. The gateway is simple but solves the problem of the XMLHttpRequest object needing to access resources in another domain.

Listing 4-16. YahooSearchGatewayServlet.java

```java
package ajaxbook.chap4;

import java.io.*;
import java.net.HttpURLConnection;
import java.net.URL;

import javax.servlet.*;
import javax.servlet.http.*;

public class YahooSearchGatewayServlet extends HttpServlet {
    private static final String YAHOO_SEARCH_URL =
        "http://api.search.yahoo.com/WebSearchService/V1/webSearch?"
                    + "appid=your_app_id" + "&type=all";

    protected void processRequest(HttpServletRequest request
                                            , HttpServletResponse response)
    throws ServletException, IOException {

        String url = YAHOO_SEARCH_URL + "&" + request.getQueryString();

        HttpURLConnection con = (HttpURLConnection)new URL(url).openConnection();
        con.setDoInput(true);
        con.setDoOutput(true);
```

```
            con.setRequestMethod("GET");

            //Send back the response to the browser
            response.setStatus(con.getResponseCode());
            response.setContentType("text/xml");

            BufferedReader reader =
                    new BufferedReader(new InputStreamReader(con.getInputStream()));
            String input = null;
            OutputStream responseOutput = response.getOutputStream();

            while((input = reader.readLine()) != null) {
                responseOutput.write(input.getBytes());
            }

        }

    protected void doGet(HttpServletRequest request, HttpServletResponse response)
    throws ServletException, IOException {
        processRequest(request, response);
    }
}
```

Once Yahoo! Search returns the results to the gateway and the gateway forwards the results to the browser, the parseSearchResults function is called. This function retrieves the resulting XML document from the XMLHttpRequest object and looks for all elements with a tag name of Result.

Each Result element is passed to the parseResult function. This function creates the content that is added to the page using the Title, Summary, ClickUrl, and Url elements that are children of the Result element.

As you can see, Ajax techniques are quite powerful when combined with REST-based Web Services. If you want to access Web Services within your own domain, then you can do all this work with JavaScript. Otherwise, you should create some sort of gateway to the external resource to avoid browser security sandbox issues when trying to access a resource in another domain.

Figure 4-15 shows the results of using Yahoo! Search Web Services with Ajax.

Figure 4-15. *The results of a search using Yahoo! Search Web Services with Ajax*

CAN AJAX ALSO BE USED WITH SOAP?

Can you use Ajax with SOAP? The short answer is "yes"—you can use Ajax techniques with SOAP-based Web Services, although this requires more work than when using REST-based Web Services.

Both REST and SOAP return the response as an XML document. The most obvious difference between the two is that while REST sends the request as a simple URL with query string parameters, a SOAP request is an actual XML document that is usually sent via POST rather than GET.

Using SOAP with Ajax requires that the SOAP request's XML somehow be created, which may not necessarily be easy. One option is to create the request XML using string concatenation. While conceptually simple, this approach is somewhat messy and error prone, as it's easy to miss a double quote here or a plus sign there.

Another option is to use one XMLHttpRequest request to load a static XML document from your site that is a template for the SOAP request. Once the template is loaded, you could use JavaScript DOM methods to modify the template to fit the particular request. Once the request is ready, a second XMLHttpRequest request could send the newly created SOAP request along with the request.

Providing Autocomplete

One of the most asked-for functions we've encountered is autocomplete. Many people have used tools such as Intuit's Quicken and have become enamored with its register's ability to fill in information from previous entries. This makes data entry faster, easier, and less error prone. Though this is easy enough to add to a thick client, Web applications have lived without this feature.[1] But Google proved autocomplete was an option when it unveiled Google Suggest to its beta labs area.

Google Suggest is an amazing piece of work (see Figure 4-16). Not only does it place the drop-down area perfectly, it automatically inserts the most likely answer in the input box and grays out the area that the user didn't type. You can even use the up and down arrows in the drop-down area. By providing the number of results for a given term, the user gets a better sense of what awaits them when they actually perform a search.

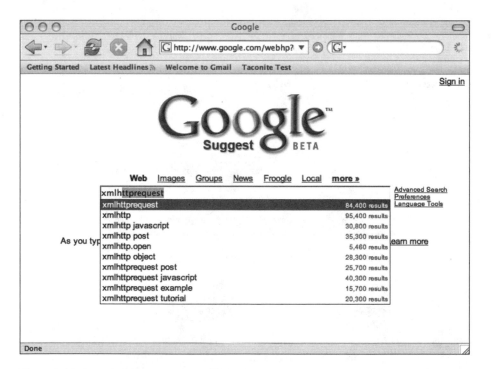

Figure 4-16. *Google Suggest—powered by Ajax*

Google Suggest has since been dissected on various Web sites (just "google" *Google Suggest!*). The example in Listing 4-17 is not quite as rich as Google's, but it gives you an idea of what you can do with Ajax. Note that in this example, the `callback()` function looks for a return code of 204 in addition to the usual suspect, 200. The 204 response code indicates there is no information from the server, and you use this indicator to clear out the name drop-down area. You'll also

---

1. One author had a client who just couldn't believe autocomplete wasn't an option for his snazzy new Web application. Like many requests, it was added to the proverbial future phase list.

notice that you are setting the mouse events for the cells via the dot notation as explained in the earlier "Why Isn't the setAttribute Method Used to Set the Delete Button's Event Handler?" sidebar. Once again, you use a calculateOffset() method to determine exactly where to position the data.

Listing 4-17. autoComplete.html

```
<!DOCTYPE HTML PUBLIC "-//W3C//DTD HTML 4.01 Transitional//EN">

<html>
  <head>
    <title>Ajax Auto Complete</title>
    <style type="text/css">

    .mouseOut {
    background: #708090;
    color: #FFFAFA;
    }

    .mouseOver {
    background: #FFFAFA;
    color: #000000;
    }
    </style>
    <script type="text/javascript">
        var xmlHttp;
        var completeDiv;
        var inputField;
        var nameTable;
        var nameTableBody;

        function createXMLHttpRequest() {
            if (window.ActiveXObject) {
                xmlHttp - new ActiveXObject("Microsoft.XMLHTTP");
            }
            else if (window.XMLHttpRequest) {
                xmlHttp = new XMLHttpRequest();
            }
        }

        function initVars() {
            inputField = document.getElementById("names");
            nameTable = document.getElementById("name_table");
            completeDiv = document.getElementById("popup");
            nameTableBody = document.getElementById("name_table_body");
        }
```

```
function findNames() {
    initVars();
    if (inputField.value.length > 0) {
        createXMLHttpRequest();
        var url = "AutoCompleteServlet?names=" + escape(inputField.value);
        xmlHttp.open("GET", url, true);
        xmlHttp.onreadystatechange = callback;
        xmlHttp.send(null);
    } else {
        clearNames();
    }
}

function callback() {
    if (xmlHttp.readyState == 4) {
        if (xmlHttp.status == 200) {
            var name =
                    xmlHttp.responseXML
                    .getElementsByTagName("name")[0].firstChild.data;
            setNames(xmlHttp.responseXML.getElementsByTagName("name"));
        } else if (xmlHttp.status == 204){
            clearNames();
        }
    }
}

function setNames(the_names) {
    clearNames();
    var size = the_names.length;
    setOffsets();

    var row, cell, txtNode;
    for (var i = 0; i < size; i++) {
        var nextNode = the_names[i].firstChild.data;
        row = document.createElement("tr");
        cell = document.createElement("td");

        cell.onmouseout = function() {this.className='mouseOver';};
        cell.onmouseover = function() {this.className='mouseOut';};
        cell.setAttribute("bgcolor", "#FFFAFA");
        cell.setAttribute("border", "0");
        cell.onclick = function() { populateName(this); } ;

        txtNode = document.createTextNode(nextNode);
        cell.appendChild(txtNode);
        row.appendChild(cell);
        nameTableBody.appendChild(row);
    }
}
```

```
        function setOffsets() {
            var end = inputField.offsetWidth;
            var left = calculateOffsetLeft(inputField);
            var top = calculateOffsetTop(inputField) + inputField.offsetHeight;

            completeDiv.style.border = "black 1px solid";
            completeDiv.style.left = left + "px";
            completeDiv.style.top = top + "px";
            nameTable.style.width = end + "px";
        }

        function calculateOffsetLeft(field) {
          return calculateOffset(field, "offsetLeft");
        }

        function calculateOffsetTop(field) {
          return calculateOffset(field, "offsetTop");
        }

        function calculateOffset(field, attr) {
          var offset = 0;
          while(field) {
            offset += field[attr];
            field = field.offsetParent;
          }
          return offset;
        }

        function populateName(cell) {
            inputField.value = cell.firstChild.nodeValue;
            clearNames();
        }

        function clearNames() {
            var ind = nameTableBody.childNodes.length;
            for (var i = ind - 1; i >= 0 ; i--) {
                nameTableBody.removeChild(nameTableBody.childNodes[i]);
            }
            completeDiv.style.border = "none";
        }

    </script>
</head>
<body>
  <h1>Ajax Auto Complete Example</h1>
  Names: <input type="text" size="20" id="names"
                                 onkeyup="findNames();" style="height:20;"/>
```

```
    <div style="position:absolute;" id="popup">
        <table id="name_table" bgcolor="#FFFAFA" border="0"
                                        cellspacing="0" cellpadding="0"/>
            <tbody id="name_table_body"></tbody>
        </table>
    </div>
  </body>
</html>
```

The server-side code mimics a dynamic search for names from a name service. A handful of names are set in the servlet, and searches are delegated to another class that has the lookup logic in it. Note that if you don't find any data, you return a response that indicates no content to the client. Listing 4-18 shows AutoCompleteServlet.java, and Listing 4-19 shows NameService.java.

Listing 4-18. AutoCompleteServlet.java

```java
package ajaxbook.chap4;

import java.io.*;
import java.util.ArrayList;
import java.util.Iterator;
import java.util.List;

import javax.servlet.*;
import javax.servlet.http.*;

public class AutoCompleteServlet extends HttpServlet {

    private List names = new ArrayList();

    public void init(ServletConfig config) throws ServletException {
        names.add("Abe");
        names.add("Abel");
        names.add("Abigail");
        names.add("Abner");
        names.add("Abraham");
        names.add("Marcus");
        names.add("Marcy");
        names.add("Marge");
        names.add("Marie");
    }

    protected void doGet(HttpServletRequest request, HttpServletResponse response)
        throws ServletException, IOException {
            String prefix = request.getParameter("names");
            NameService service = NameService.getInstance(names);
            List matching = service.findNames(prefix);
```

```
        if (matching.size() > 0) {
            PrintWriter out = response.getWriter();

            response.setContentType("text/xml");
            response.setHeader("Cache-Control", "no-cache");

            out.println("<response>");
            Iterator iter = matching.iterator();
            while(iter.hasNext()) {
                String name = (String) iter.next();
                out.println("<name>" + name + "</name>");
            }
            out.println("</response>");
            matching = null;
            service = null;
            out.close();
        } else {
            response.setStatus(HttpServletResponse.SC_NO_CONTENT);
        }
    }
}
```

Listing 4-19. NameService.java

```
package ajaxbook.chap4;

import java.util.ArrayList;
import java.util.Iterator;
import java.util.List;

public class NameService {
    private List names;

    /** Creates a new instance of NameService */
    private NameService(List list_of_names) {
        this.names = list_of_names;
    }

    public static NameService getInstance(List list_of_names) {
        return new NameService(list_of_names);
    }
```

```
public List findNames(String prefix) {
    String prefix_upper = prefix.toUpperCase();
    List matches = new ArrayList();
    Iterator iter = names.iterator();
    while(iter.hasNext()) {
        String name = (String) iter.next();
        String name_upper_case = name.toUpperCase();
        if(name_upper_case.startsWith(prefix_upper)){
            boolean result = matches.add(name);
        }
    }
    return matches;
}
}
```

Figure 4-17 shows the autocomplete example in action.

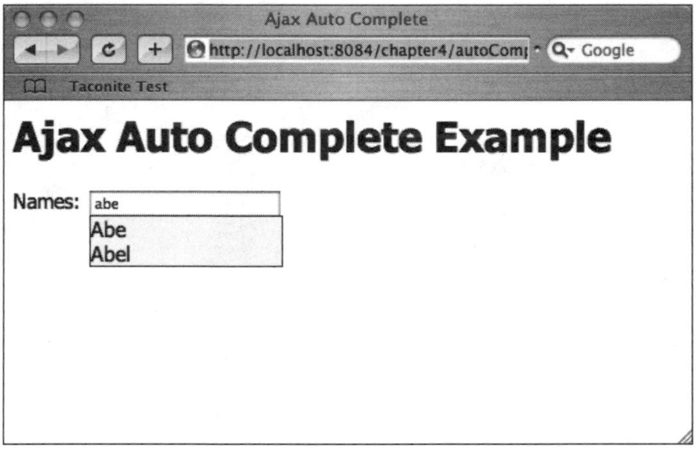

Figure 4-17. *Autocomplete example*

Summary

In this chapter, you explored several examples that showcased ways in which you can apply Ajax technology to enhance your users' experience. In many cases, you can retrofit Ajax techniques to existing applications, replacing full-page refreshes with Ajax requests that seamlessly communicate with the server and update the page content. Users may not necessarily notice that the application is performing differently, but over time they may realize that the application just works "better." You can design new Web applications with Ajax techniques right from the start. The Ajax toolset, now part of your developer toolbox, will help you build Web applications that behave more like thick client applications, much to the delight of your end users.

You've now learned the nuts and bolts of Ajax techniques. You've learned the ins and outs of the XMLHttpRequest object and how to dynamically update a Web page using JavaScript to manipulate the standard W3C DOM. You've seen several common examples where you can use Ajax techniques to replace complete page refreshes.

Now you'll shift your focus a little bit and start looking at the bigger picture. Chances are in the past you treated JavaScript as a second-class programming language and tried to avoid it as much as possible. In the next few chapters, you'll explore how to bring generally accepted software engineering techniques to your JavaScript development to help maximize productivity, minimize errors, and eliminate the amount of stress that's often associated with JavaScript development.

■ ■ ■

CHAPTER 5

Building the Ultimate Ajax Developer's Toolbox

As an experienced Web application developer, you're likely adept at applying a particular server-side technology (or, perhaps, applying several server-side technologies) to build Web applications. The past few years have seen a large push to make sever-side software development easier and more robust, while the client side has been mostly ignored. The advent of Ajax techniques has changed that, as developers now have a larger client-side toolbox with which to work. You may not be used to working with large amounts of HTML, JavaScript, and CSS, but implementing Ajax techniques will force you to do so. This chapter introduces you to some tools and techniques that will help make developing Ajax applications a little bit easier. This chapter is not an in-depth tutorial but rather provides a jump start on a number of useful tools and techniques.

Documenting JavaScript Code with JSDoc

JavaScript, like many other programming languages, suffers from a basic flaw in the average software developer's psyche: it is often easier to write (or rewrite) a certain piece of functionality than it is to read some existing code and figure out how it works. Properly adding comments to code while writing the code can greatly reduce the amount of time and effort required by other developers to understand how the code works, especially when it comes time to modify the functionality of the code.

The Java language was introduced with a tool called javadoc. This tool produces API documentation in HTML format from documentation comments in the source code. Any Web browser can easily read the resulting HTML, and since it's rendered as HTML, it can be distributed online, which provides developers with easy access to it. Providing the API documentation in an easily browsable format often eliminates the need for developers to inspect source code to figure out how a certain class or method behaves and how it should be used.

`   JSDoc is a similar tool for JavaScript (jsdoc.sourceforge.net). JSDoc is an open-source tool that is licensed under the GNU Public License (GPL). JSDoc is written in Perl, meaning that Windows users will have to install a Perl runtime environment. (Perl is a standard part of most Linux and Unix operating systems.)

Installation

To use JSDoc, Windows users must install a Perl environment such as ActivePerl (www.activeperl.com). You must also install a nonstandard Perl module named HTML::Template (www.cpan.org). The JSDoc project page provides instructions and help for those who need further assistance.

JSDoc is distributed as a gzipped tarball. To install JSDoc, simply download the tarball from the JSDoc project page and unpack it to the desired directory. You can immediately test JSDoc by going to the JSDoc directory and entering the following command:

```
perl jsdoc.pl test.js
```

JSDoc sends the resulting HTML files to a directory named js_docs_out. Open the index.html file located in this folder to browse the documentation generated from the test.js file.

Usage

Now that you've gotten this far, you can investigate how to use JSDoc to document your JavaScript code. Table 5-1 outlines the special JSDoc tags that create the HTML documentation. The tags will seem familiar to anyone used to writing javadoc comments in Java code. Each comment block to be included in the generated documentation must start with /** and end with */.

Table 5-1. *JSDoc Command Attributes*

Command Name	Description
@param @argument	Describes a function parameter by specifying the parameter name and description.
@return @returns	Describes the return value of the function.
@author	Indicates the author of the code.
@deprecated	Indicates that a function is deprecated and may be removed from future versions of the code. You should avoid using this particular piece of code.
@see	Creates an HTML link to the description of the specified class.
@version	Specifies the release version.
@requires	Creates an HTML link to the specified class that is required for this class.
@throws @exception	Describes the type of exception that a function may throw.
{@link}	Creates an HTML link to the specified class. This is similar to @see but can be embedded inside comment text.
@author	Indicates the author of the code.
@fileoverview	A special tag that when used in the first block of documentation in a file, specifies that the rest of the documentation block will be used to provide an overview of the file.
@class	Provides information about the class and is used in the constructor's documentation.
@constructor	Identifies a function as the constructor for a class.
@type	Indicates the return type of a function.

Command Name	Description
@extends	Indicates that a class subclasses another class. JSDoc can often detect this information on its own, but in some instances using this tag is required.
@private	Signifies that a class or function is private. Private classes and functions will not be available in the HTML documentation unless JSDoc is run with the `--private` command-line option.
@final	Indicates that a value is a constant value. Keep in mind that JavaScript can't actually enforce a value as being constant.
@ignore	JSDoc ignores functions that are labeled with this tag.

The JSDoc distribution includes a file named `test.js` that is a good reference example for how to use JSDoc. Recall that this is the documentation file that was created when you first tested your JSDoc installation. You can refer to this file if you have any questions regarding how to use JSDoc tags.

Listing 5-1 outlines a short example of JSDoc usage. The `jsDocExample.js` file defines two classes, Person and Employee. The Person class has one property, name, and one method, getName. The Employee class inherits from Person and adds the title and salary properties in addition to the getDescription method.

Listing 5-1. `jsDocExample.js`

```
/**
 * @fileoverview This file is an example of how JSDoc can be used to document
 * JavaScript.
 *
 * @author Ryan Asleson
 * @version 1.0
 */

/**
 * Construct a new Person class.
 * @class This class represents an instance of a Person.
 * @constructor
 * @param {String} name The name of the Person.
 * @return A new instance of a Person.
 */
function Person(name) {
    /**
     * The Person's name
     * @type String
     */
    this.name = name;
```

```
    /**
     * Return the Person's name. This function is assigned in the class
     * constructor rather than using the prototype keyword.
     * @returns The Person's name
     * @type String
     */
    this.getName = function() {
        return name;
    }
}


/**
 * Construct a new Employee class.
 * @extends Person
 * @class This class represents an instance of an Employee.
 * @constructor
 * @return A new instance of a Person.
 */
function Employee(name, title, salary) {
    this.name = name;

    /**
     * The Employee's title
     * @type String
     */
    this.title = title;

    /**
     * The Employee's salary
     * @type int
     */
    this.salary = salary;
}

/* Employee extends Person */
Employee.prototype = new Person();

/**
 * An example of function assignment using the prototype keyword.
 * This method returns a String representation of the Employee's data.
 * @returns The Employee's name, title, and salary
 * @type String
 */
Employee.prototype.getDescription = function() {
    return this.name + " - "
        + this.title + " - "
        + "$" + this.salary;
}
```

While not as complete an example as the `test.js` file included in the JSDoc distribution, this example shows the most common usages of JSDoc (see Figure 5-1). The `@fileoverview` tag gives an overview of the `jsDocExample.js` file. The `@class` tag describes the two classes, and the `@constructor` tag flags the appropriate functions as object constructors. The `@param` tag describes a function's input parameters, and the `@returns` and `@type` tags describe the function's return value. These are the tags you're likely to use most often and the ones that will prove most useful to other developers browsing the documentation.

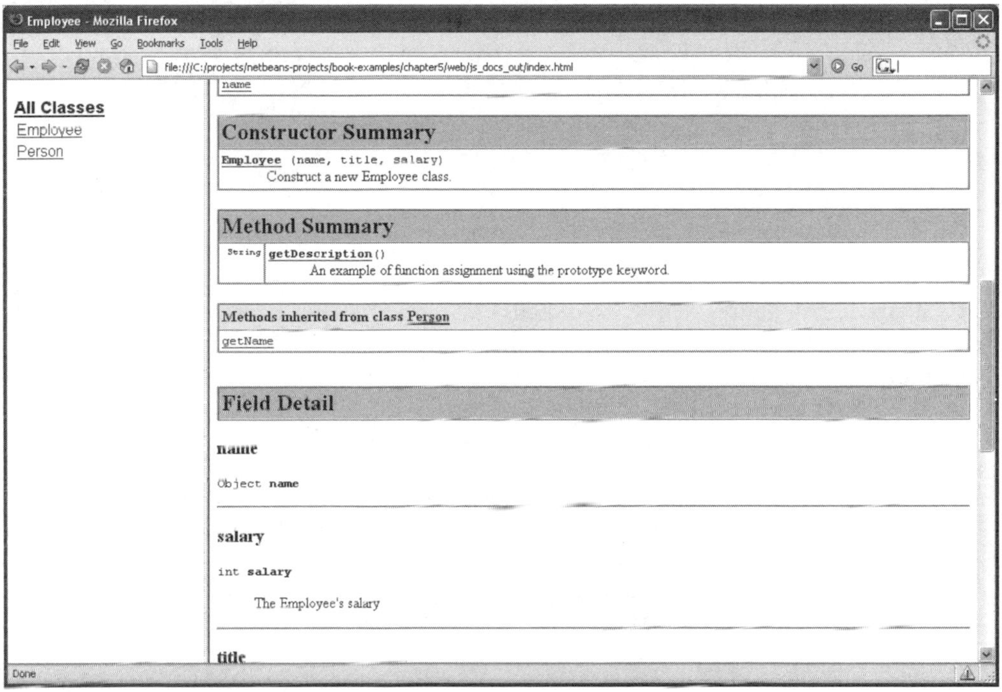

Figure 5-1. *The documentation produced from the* `jsDocExample.js` *file by JSDoc*

Validating HTML Content with Firefox Extensions

Today's modern browsers do a good job of implementing the standard W3C DOM. Authors can count on nearly universal browser support as long as they create content that follows standard HTML or XHTML.

Often that is easier said than done. Unlike compiled languages such as C++ or Java, HTML does not have a compiler that translates the human-readable code into machine-readable binary code. It's the role of the Web browser to interpret the human-readable HTML or XHTML code into an internal representation of the DOM and render the content appropriately on-screen.

The browser wars of the late 1990s saw browser makers such as Microsoft and Netscape adding proprietary HTML tags in an effort to gain market share. This, along with HTML's lack of a strict compiler, has led to massive amounts of nonstandard Web pages. Today's modern browsers, while supporting the latest in W3C standards, also attempt to be as forgiving as possible to the poorly written HTML page. Most browsers work by having two rendering modes, based on the doctype of the HTML page (if it's available): strict and quirks. Web browsers use a *strict* mode when the doctype indicates that a Web page is written to follow a certain W3C recommendation, such as HTML 4.1 or XHTML 1.0. Web browsers use a *quirks* mode when a doctype is not available or when the page has a number of conflicts with the specified doctype.

As a developer, you should strive to create pages that adhere to a certain W3C standard. Doing so not only makes your Web pages accessible to all modern Web browsers but also makes your own life easier by ensuring that the browser can create an accurate representation of the DOM from the HTML code. The browser may not be able to create an accurate representation of the DOM if the page is poorly written, forcing the browser into rendering the page using a quirks mode. An incorrect representation of the DOM may make it difficult to access and modify the DOM via JavaScript, especially in a cross-browser way.

Since HTML does not have a strict compiler, how can you ensure that the HTML code you write adheres to W3C standards? Fortunately, a couple of extensions are available for the Firefox Web browser that make it easy to validate your Web pages.

HTML Validator

HTML Validator[1] is a Firefox extension that finds and flags errors on an HTML page. HTML Validator is based on Tidy, a tool originally developed by the W3C to validate HTML code. HTML Validator embeds the Tidy tool into Firefox and allows the source code of a page to be validated locally within the browser without sending the code off to a third party.

Tidy finds HTML errors and classifies them into three categories:

- *Errors*: Problems that Tidy cannot fix or understand

- *Warnings*: Errors that Tidy can fix automatically

- *Accessibility warnings*: HTML warnings for the three priority levels defined by the W3C Web Accessibility Initiative (WAI)

HTML Validator displays the status of the page and the number of errors in the lower-right corner of the browser, providing fast feedback during the development cycle (see Figure 5-2).

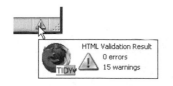

Figure 5-2. *HTML Validator summarizes the errors on a page using an icon on the status bar.*

HTML Validator provides even more help when you view the source of a Web page by accessing the View ➤ Page Source menu item. The Firefox view-source window opens as normal, but with HTML Validator enabled, the window includes two new panes (see Figure 5-3). The HTML Errors and Warnings pane lists all the errors found on the page. Clicking any of the items in the list jumps the main source window to the location of the problem in the HTML source. The Help pane fully describes the problem and offers suggestions on how you can fix the problem.

---

1. https://addons.mozilla.org/extensions/moreinfo.php?application=firefox&category=
Developer%20Tools&numpg=10&id=249

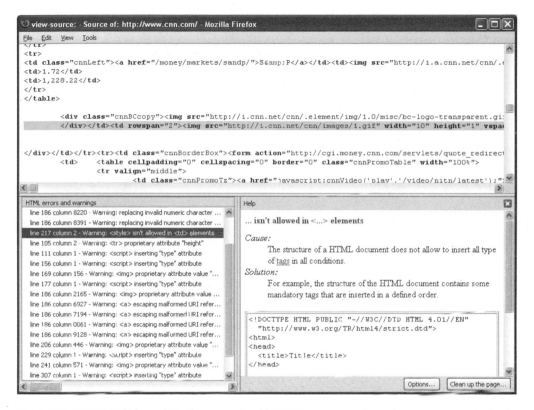

Figure 5-3. *HTML Validator lists the errors in the HTML source code and suggests ways to fix the problem when viewing a page's source.*

The bottom of the Firefox view-source window includes a Clean Up the Page button. This button launches a window that further helps you fix any errors on the page (see Figure 5-4). The Cleanup the Page window opens with four tabs along the top: Cleaned Html, Original Html, Cleaned Browser, and Original Browser.

The Cleaned Html tab is the most useful for Web developers. This tab lists the source code of the page after you put the page through HTML Validator for fixing. HTML Validator will do its best to automatically fix all the errors on the page, and the output is listed on this tab. The Original Html tab lists the source code of the page in its original form, before it was processed by HTML Validator.

Sometimes fixing the HTML errors on a page will change the way in which the browser renders the page, which may or may not be a desirable effect. The Cleaned Browser tab shows how the page will now look using the fixed source code provided by HTML Validator, while the Original Browser tab displays the page using the original source code.

In sum, HTML Validator is a powerful tool that can help you clean up your HTML and make it comply with W3C standards and recommendations. Unfortunately, HTML Validator is available only for Windows platforms. Luckily, another Firefox extension provides similar functionality to HTML Validator and is available on all platforms.

Figure 5-4. *The Cleanup the Page dialog box of HTML Validator will suggest new source code that fixes the errors found in the original source HTML.*

Checky

Checky[2] is another Firefox extension that helps developers write better HTML pages. Unlike HTML Validator, which validates the source code locally, Checky sends the page source off to various third-party sites to perform the HTML validation.

You can access Checky by right-clicking any page in Firefox and selecting the Checky menu item (see Figure 5-5). The Checky menu item contains several subitems that perform various tasks. The HTML/XHTML menu item lists several sites that offer HTML validation services. Clicking any of the sites in the list opens a new tab in Firefox that points to the validation site. Checky automatically fills in the address of the page to validate and starts the validation process.

As you can see in Figure 5-6, the code to be validated needs to be publicly available on the Internet so the validation site can access the HTML.

Checky also provides access to sites that validate more than just HTML. The Links menu lists sites that will validate all the links on a page, ensuring that all the links connect to existing URLs. The CSS menu lists sites that will validate any of the CSS files used on the page to ensure that they follow standard CSS rules.

Take the time to test some of the validation sites provided by Checky. Using these validation tools will make your code more standards compliant and will reduce the time spent manually attempting to track down problems or issues.

---

2. https://addons.mozilla.org/extensions/moreinfo.php?application=firefox&category=
Developer%20Tools&numpg=10&id=165

Figure 5-5. *You can access Checky via a context menu in Firefox.*

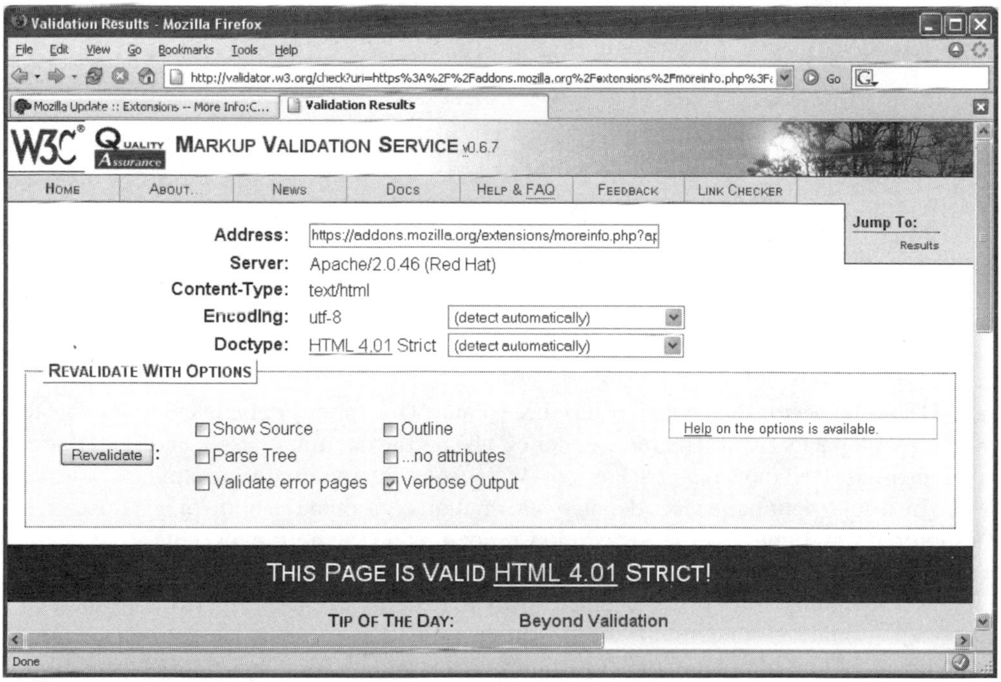

Figure 5-6. *The results of HTML validation using the W3C's online validator, accessed using Checky*

Searching for Nodes Using DOM Inspector

DOM Inspector is a tool packaged with the Mozilla Suite and Firefox browser. DOM Inspector allows you to view a structured representation of a Web page and even gives you the ability to search for specific nodes and to dynamically update nodes in the DOM. In Firefox, you can access DOM Inspector via the Tools menu item. To inspect a Web page using DOM Inspector, enter the desired URL into the textbox, and click the Inspect box; alternatively, select a window from the File ➤ Inspect a Window menu, which lists the Web pages currently open within the browser (see Figure 5-7).

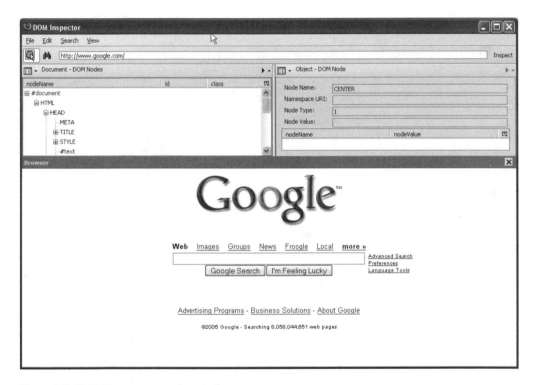

Figure 5-7. *DOM Inspector main window*

The DOM Inspector main window has three panes. The upper-left pane is a hierarchical view of the Web page's DOM. The root element is always the document itself, and from there every node in the Web page is listed. For most Web pages, the root node will almost always be HTML. The upper-right pane gives detailed information regarding the node that is selected in the structured view pane. If a browser window is not open in the bottom part of the window, you can open it by selecting the View ➤ Browser menu item.

DOM Inspector is a powerful tool that allows you to quickly traverse the structure of a given Web page and view and modify the individual nodes that make up the Web page's DOM. You can normally find nodes manually by drilling down through the items in the structured view. You can also find individual nodes using the Search ➤ Find Nodes menu item. This search functionality allows you to find nodes based on the id attribute, tag name, or attribute name and value (see Figure 5-8).

The easiest way to find nodes in DOM Inspector is by using the mouse. To find a node in the structured view, select the Search ➤ Select Element by Click menu item, and click the item in the browser window. The selected item should blink momentarily with a red border, and its node will be selected in the structured view pane.

Once you have selected a particular node in the structured view pane, you can start inspecting and modifying its properties. For example, you can right-click a node, select Cut from the context menu, select another node in the structured view, right-click, and then select Paste from the context menu. Doing so effectively moves the selected node from one spot in the DOM to another. Figure 5-9 displays how the main image on the Google search page was moved to another part of the page using this method.

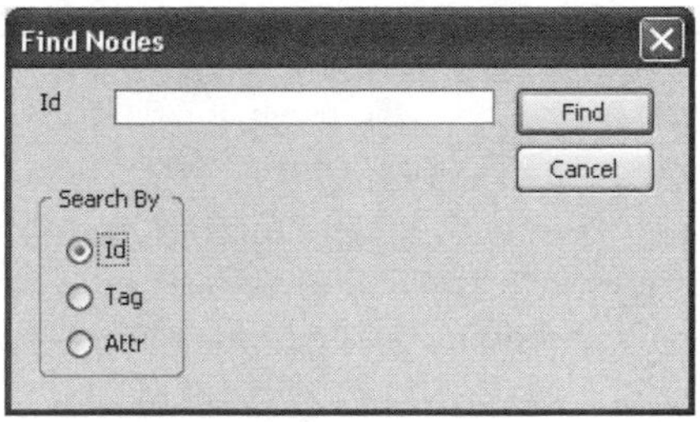

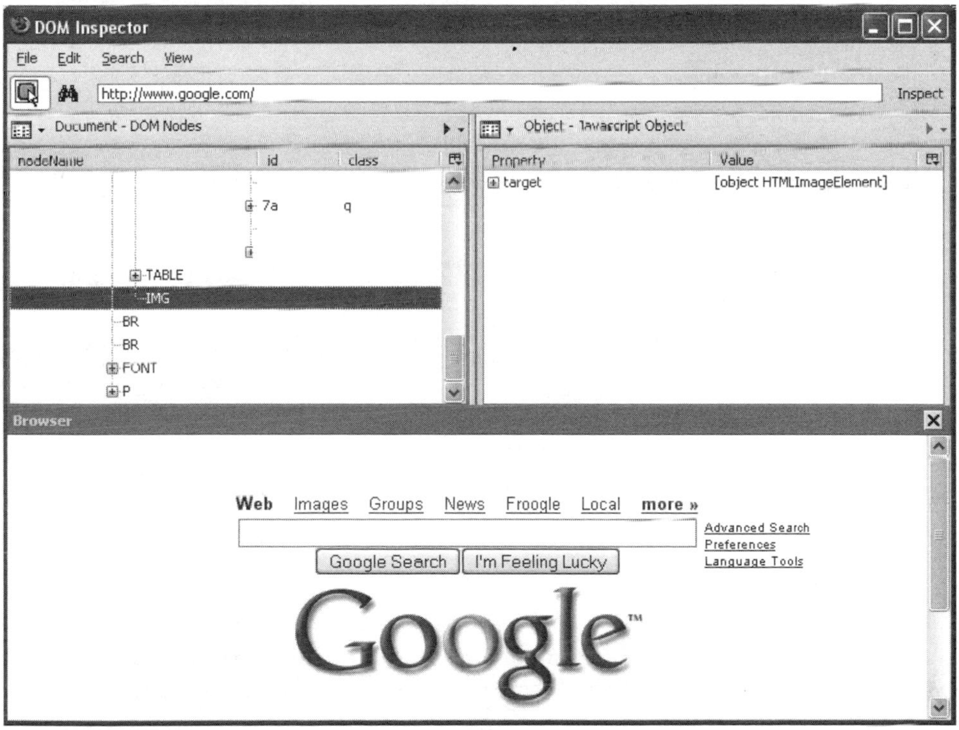

Figure 5-8. *DOM Inspector's Find Nodes dialog box*

Figure 5-9. *The results of moving the main image on the Google search page using DOM Inspector*

You can find more functionality in the upper-right information pane. This window displays various types of information about the node selected in the structured view pane. You can toggle the types of information available using the drop-down list icon in the top header area. The available types of information are DOM Node, Box Model, XBL Bindings, CSS Style Rules, Computed Style, and JavaScript Object. The Box Model and XBL Bindings information types are more useful when developing applications using Mozilla's XML User Interface Language (XUL) toolkit.

The DOM Node information type shows basic information about the node such as its tag name, its node value, and the node's attributes. Right-clicking a node displays a context menu with an Edit menu item that allows you to modify the value of a node's attribute. For instance, try it on a font node by changing the `size` attribute. Figure 5-10 shows how the size of the fonts above the input box on the Google search page were increased using this technique.

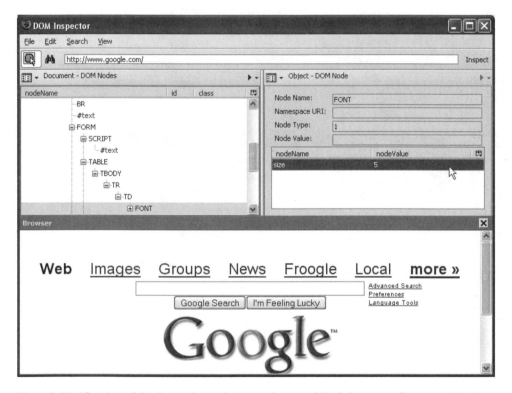

Figure 5-10. *The size of the fonts above the input box modified dynamically using DOM Inspector*

The JavaScript Object information type lists the DOM properties and methods available for the selected node. This can be a powerful feature when trying to determine what properties and methods are available for a specific DOM node. For example, in addition to a normal method such as `appendChild`, methods such as `insertRow` and `deleteRow` are listed for a table node.

Right-clicking in the information pane when it's set to the JavaScript Object information type displays a context menu with an Evaluate JavaScript menu item. Selecting this menu item launches a pop-up window that allows you to evaluate a JavaScript expression against the selected node. Figure 5-11 shows the JavaScript evaluation menu opened for the body node of the Google search page and shows that executing the JavaScript expression as shown in the evaluation window will append the specified text to the end of the page. Note that the target is used as the variable name and refers to the selected node, in this case the body element.

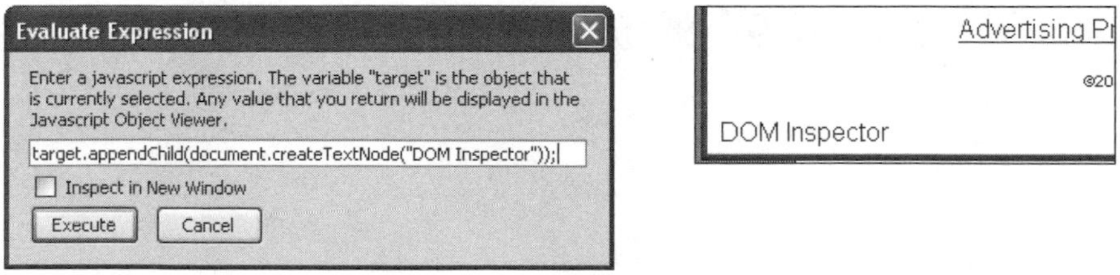

Figure 5-11. *Using the JavaScript evaluation window to dynamically add a text node to the body of the page (left) and the result in the browser pane (right)*

The CSS Style Rules and Computed Style information types display information about the selected node's style rules. The Computed Style information type lists all the style-related attributes as the browser's rendering engine sees them, including styles set explicitly using the `style` attribute, styles specified in external CSS files, or styles inherited from parent nodes.

Now that you've seen a brief overview of DOM Inspector's features, you can begin to imagine the scenarios in which it may prove to be a useful tool in your development environment. You can use DOM Inspector to inspect DOM nodes created dynamically via the `document.createElement` methods to ensure their property values are as you expect them to be. You could also use DOM Inspector to troubleshoot why a particular node doesn't have the style rules applied to it that you expect. As you become more familiar with DOM Inspector's capabilities, you'll undoubtedly find scenarios in which it will be an invaluable tool during your Web development process.

Performing JavaScript Syntax Checking with JSLint

JSLint is a JavaScript verifier (www.jslint.com) that scans JavaScript source code looking for problems. If JSLint finds a problem, the tool displays a message describing the problem and the approximate location of the error in the source code. JSLint flags structural problems in addition to coding-style conventions that often lead to unintended behavior or errors. JSLint does not guarantee that the logic is correct, but it does help find errors that may cause the browser's JavaScript engine to throw an error.

JSLint defines a set of coding conventions that is stricter than the language defined by the ECMA. These coding conventions are harvested from years of experience and follow this age-old rule of programming: just because you can do it doesn't mean you should. JSLint attempts to promote good JavaScript coding habits by flagging what it determines to be risky coding practices, in addition to flagging instances that are outright errors (see Figure 5-12).

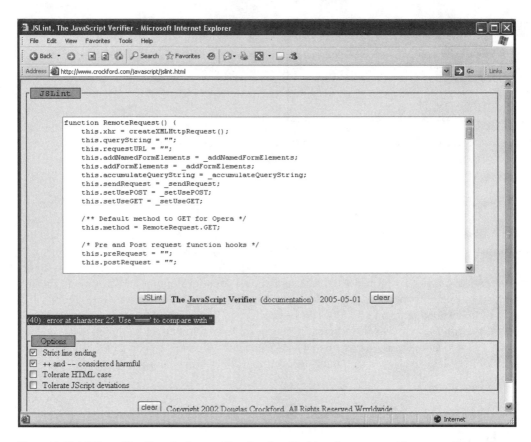

Figure 5-12. *JSLint offers JavaScript verification by checking for errors and poor coding styles.*

The following is a partial list of structural errors that JSLint will flag as being suspect coding practices. (You can find the complete list in JSLint's documentation.)

- JSLint expects that all lines end with a semicolon. While JavaScript does allow a linefeed character to act as a line termination character, this is considered ambiguous and poor coding style.

- Statements using `if` and `for` must use curly braces for the statement blocks.

- In JavaScript, unlike other programming languages, a block does not introduce variable scope. JavaScript supports only function-level scope. Thus, JSLint accepts only blocks that are part of `function`, `if`, `switch`, `while`, `for`, `do`, and `try` statements and will flag any other blocks as errors.

- A `var` may be declared only once, and it must be declared before it is used.

- JSLint flags code that comes immediately after a `return`, `break`, `continue`, or `throw` statement as unreachable code. These statements must be immediately followed by a closing curly brace.

JSLint is an especially good tool for beginning JavaScript programmers because it helps teach good JavaScript coding practices. It can reduce debugging time by flagging areas that could potentially be causing logic errors or other unintended behavior. Be sure to try JSLint if you are having trouble debugging a particular piece of JavaScript code.

Performing JavaScript Compression and Obfuscation

We all know that JavaScript is an interpreted language that executes within the client's browser. In other words, JavaScript is downloaded as plain text to the browser, which then executes the JavaScript code as needed.

The user can always read JavaScript source code by using the browser's view source functionality, which displays the complete HTML markup of the page, including any JavaScript blocks. Even if the JavaScript source is placed in an external file and referenced with the `script` tag's `src` attribute, the user can still download and read it. Because the JavaScript source is always available to anybody viewing the page, you should not place proprietary or sensitive logic algorithms in JavaScript. Such logic is best left on the server where it is more secure.

The size of JavaScript files can become an issue as JavaScript usage grows in Ajax-based applications. Because it is an interpreted language, JavaScript is never compiled to machine-level binary code, which is a more efficient storage format for executable code. A large number of JavaScript files can slow an application down because it needs to download the source from the server to the browser before it can be executed. In addition, a large set of JavaScript code will only become larger if the code is commented with a tool such as JSDoc, as described earlier.

You can probably see that JavaScript's lack of a binary executable package has two problems: poor security and large source code downloads. Is there a way around these problems?

JavaScript's increasing popularity has produced a number of tools that can help solve these problems. The simplest compression tools simply strip JavaScript source of all comments and line-feed characters, which helps reduce the size of the source code download. Removing comment lines and line-feed characters can reduce the size of a JavaScript file by 30 percent or more, depending on the situation. Note that all statements in the JavaScript source must correctly terminate with a semicolon before the source can be compressed with such tools. If this isn't the case, you'll receive errors or unintended behavior. So, before compressing your JavaScript source, be sure to use JSLint to ensure that all statements end with a semicolon!

Other tools go one step further by offering obfuscation services. *Obfuscation* is the process of scanning through source code and changing field and function names from their original names to coded, nonsensical names in an effort to prevent others from learning the intent and inner workings of the source code. Obfuscation is typically not needed for languages such as C++ that are compiled to machine-level binary instructions. Even modern languages such as Java and C#, which are compiled to intermediate bytecodes rather than binary instructions, require obfuscation tools for maximum security. JavaScript, being a completely interpreted language, is another example.

One freeware tool that offers both compression and obfuscation services is MemTronic's HTML/JavaScript Cruncher-Compressor (`hometown.aol.de/_ht_a/memtronic/`). This tool supports multiple levels of JavaScript compression. The lowest level of compression, called *crunching* in the tool's nomenclature, simply removes all comments and line-feed characters. According to the tool's documentation, this can lead to bandwidth savings of 20–50 percent. Using the "crunch" mode, we saw the size of one JavaScript file reduced by 30 percent.

The highest level of compression, named *compressing* in the tool's vernacular, actually compresses the JavaScript source with a real compression scheme, with autodecompression added to the file. The tool claims bandwidth savings of 40–90 percent when using this mode and claims that the compressed output has been successfully tested on modern versions of Internet Explorer, Netscape, Mozilla, and Opera. We used the "compress" mode on the same JavaScript file used in the "crunch" test, and this time we saw the size of the file reduced by more than 65 percent (see Figure 5-13).

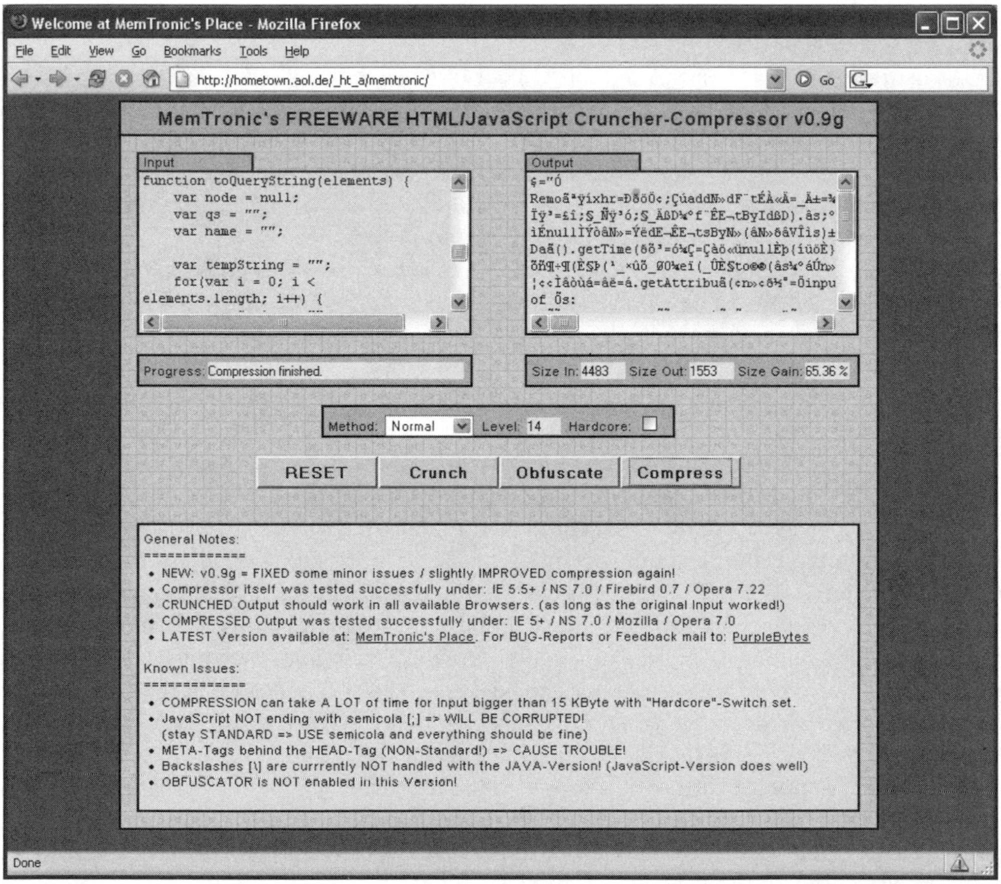

Figure 5-13. *MemTronic's HTML/JavaScript Cruncher-Compressor significantly reduces the size of JavaScript source while also making it difficult to read.*

At the time of this writing, the MemTronic tool's documentation claims that the JavaScript obfuscator is not yet complete. However, look at the output window in Figure 5-13. This is the result of a "compress" operation on a JavaScript file. The output is hardly readable and in fact contains numerous odd characters. While it may not be true obfuscation, it certainly is enough to prevent the casual user from inspecting (and possibly stealing) your JavaScript source.

Using the Web Developer Extension for Firefox

The Web Developer extension for Firefox adds a multitude of useful Web developer tools to the browser. You access the tools via a toolbar that is added to your browser once you install the extension (see Figure 5-14). The extension is available for all platforms for which Firefox is currently available, meaning it includes Windows, OS X, and Linux. The Web Developer extension for Firefox is available at `chrispederick.com/work/firefox/webdeveloper/`.

Figure 5-14. *The Web Developer extension's toolbar added to Firefox*

The Web Developer extension provides more than 80 individual tools that do everything from converting GET requests to POST requests (and vice versa) to allowing live editing of a page's CSS rules. Too many tools exist to list them individually, but the following are the general tool categories:

- The Disable menu provides the ability to disable browser functionality such as JavaScript, CSS, cookies, and animated images.

- The CSS menu contains tools related to CSS rules and style sheets.

- You can use the Forms menu to convert GET requests to POST requests (and vice versa), automatically populate form values, and remove maximum lengths from input elements.

- You can outline and hide images using functionality located in the Images menu.

- You can inspect various information relating to the page such as cookie information, link information, and response headers from the Information menu.

- The Miscellaneous menu provides tools for clearing the browser's cache, history, and session cookies, as well as zooming in or out on the page.

- You can outline tables, table cells, frames, block-level elements, and more using the Outline menu.

- The Resize menu displays the current window size in the title bar along with other tools for resizing the current window.

- You can find quick links to third-party sites for validating CSS, HTML, and download speed under the Tools menu.

- The View Source button provides easy access to viewing the page's source.

- The Options menu provides custom editing of the Web Developer extension's colors, shortcut keys, and behavior.

Some Web developers have described the tools and functionality provided by the Web Developer extension as "indispensable," "the best," and "essential." Install it to experiment with its various tools and determine whether it aids your development and debugging process.

Implementing Advanced JavaScript Techniques

We're assuming the audience of this book has at least a basic working knowledge of JavaScript. A complete tutorial on JavaScript fills a complete book itself, so we'll avoid trying to teach the language here. Instead, this section discusses some of the advanced and possibly little-known features of JavaScript and how you can incorporate them into your Ajax development.

We'll first cover a little history about JavaScript so you know where it has been and how it got here. Brendan Eich of Netscape developed JavaScript in 1995. His task was to develop a way to make Java applets more accessible to the nontechnical Web designers who created and maintained Web sites. Eich decided that a loosely typed language devoid of compilers was the appropriate choice.

Various names were attached originally to Eich's creation, but it was finally renamed to JavaScript in an effort to capitalize on Java's newfound marketing success. JavaScript swiftly became the most popular scripting language on the Web, thanks to a low barrier of entry and an ability to be copied and pasted from one page into another. Early revisions of JavaScript and the Navigator DOM gave rise to the DOM Level 0 standard, which defined form elements and images as children of their elements.

Not to be outdone, Microsoft created its own scripting language called VBScript. VBScript was functionally similar to JavaScript but had a Visual Basic–like syntax and worked only in Internet Explorer. Microsoft also supported an implementation of JavaScript (which by now had been and standardized and named ECMAScript by ECMA) as JScript. While the syntax of the various flavors of JavaScript were nearly identical, the vast differences in the implementations of the DOM among browsers made cross-browser scripts almost impossible to create. Using a lowest common denominator approach usually led to scripts that could do no more than the most trivial of tasks.

By 1998 Netscape had opened the source code for its browser and decided to rewrite the browser from scratch with a focus on closely following W3C standards. At that same time, version 5 of Internet Explorer had by far the best implementation of the W3C DOM and ECMAScript. The first complete release of the open-source Netscape code under the *Mozilla* banner came in 2002. This started a trend in the browser space: more and more browsers worked to comply with Web standards maintained by the W3C and ECMA. Today, modern browsers such as Firefox, Mozilla, Opera, Konqueror, and Safari all adhere closely to Web standards, greatly simplifying the task of writing cross-browser HTML and JavaScript. Internet Explorer 6, not much changed from the version 5 browser of 1998, exhibits the most nonstandard behavior.

Object-Oriented JavaScript via the prototype Property

JavaScript supports a form of inheritance through a linking mechanism rather than through the classical inheritance model supported by fully object-oriented languages such as Java. Each JavaScript object has a built-in property named prototype. The prototype property holds a reference to another JavaScript object that acts as the current object's parent.

An object's prototype property is used only whenever a function or property of the object is referenced via the dot notation method but is not found on the object. When this situation occurs, the object's prototype object is inspected for the requested property or function. If it doesn't exist on the object's prototype property, then the prototype's prototype is examined and so forth up the chain until the requested function or property is found or the end of the chain is reached, in which case the value undefined is returned. In this sense, the inheritance structure is more of a "has a" relationship than an "is a" relationship.

The prototype mechanism takes some getting used to for those who are accustomed to a more classically based inheritance scheme. The prototype mechanism is dynamic and can be configured at runtime at will, without the need for a recompile. You can add properties and functions to an object only when necessary, and you can join disparate functions together dynamically to create dynamic, highly versatile objects. The highly dynamic nature of the prototype mechanism can be both a curse and a blessing, as it can be difficult to learn and apply but powerful and robust when applied correctly.

The dynamic nature is akin to the concept of polymorphism found in classical inheritance schemes. Two objects may share the same properties and functions, but the function methods may be completely different, and the properties may hold different data types. This polymorphism allows JavaScript objects to be generically handled by other scripts and functions.

Figure 5-15 shows the prototype inheritance scheme at work. The script defines three classes of objects: Vehicle, SportsCar, and CementTruck. Vehicle is considered the base class from which the other two classes inherit. Vehicle defines two properties, wheelCount and curbWeightInPounds, that represent the Vehicle's number of wheels and total weight, respectively. JavaScript does not support the concept of an abstract class (a class that cannot be instantiated and must be extended by other classes), so for the base Vehicle class the wheelCount defaults to 4 and curbWeightInPounds defaults to 3,000.

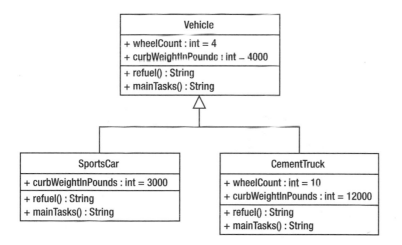

Figure 5-15. *The relationships between the* Vehicle, SportsCar, *and* CementTruck *objects*

Note how the UML diagram depicts that the SportsCar and CementTruck objects override the refuel and mainTasks functions of vehicle, because a normal Vehicle, a SportsCar, and a CementTruck all perform these tasks differently. A SportsCar has the same number of wheels as a Vehicle, so there is no need for SportsCar to override the Vehicle's wheelCount property. A CementTruck has more wheels and weighs more than a Vehicle, so it overrides both the wheelCount and curbWeightInPounds properties.

Listing 5-2 contains the JavaScript code that defines the three classes. Pay special attention to how the prototype keyword attaches properties and functions to the object definition.

Also note that each object is defined by a constructor function that has the same name as the object type.

Listing 5-2. inheritanceViaPrototype.js

```javascript
/* Constructor function for the Vehicle object */
function Vehicle() { }

/* Standard properties of a Vehicle */
Vehicle.prototype.wheelCount = 4;
Vehicle.prototype.curbWeightInPounds = 4000;

/* Function for refueling a Vehicle */
Vehicle.prototype.refuel = function() {
    return "Refueling Vehicle with regular 87 octane gasoline";
}

/* Function for performing the main tasks of a Vehicle */
Vehicle.prototype.mainTasks = function() {
    return "Driving to work, school, and the grocery store";
}


/* Constructor function for the SportsCar object */
function SportsCar() { }

/* SportsCar extends Vehicle */
SportsCar.prototype = new Vehicle();

/* SportsCar is lighter than Vehicle */
SportsCar.prototype.curbWeightInPounds = 3000;

/* SportsCar requires premium fuel */
SportsCar.prototype.refuel = function() {
    return "Refueling SportsCar with premium 94 octane gasoline";
}

/* Function for performing the main tasks of a SportsCar */
SportsCar.prototype.mainTasks = function() {
    return "Spirited driving, looking good, driving to the beach";
}


/* Constructor function for the CementTruck object */
function CementTruck() { }

/* CementTruck extends Vehicle */
CementTruck.prototype = new Vehicle();
```

```
/* CementTruck has 10 wheels and weighs 12,000 pounds*/
CementTruck.prototype.wheelCount = 10;
CementTruck.prototype.curbWeightInPounds = 12000;

/* CementTruck refuels with diesel fuel */
CementTruck.prototype.refuel = function() {
    return "Refueling CementTruck with diesel fuel";
}

/* Function for performing the main tasks of a SportsCar */
CementTruck.prototype.mainTasks = function() {
    return "Arrive at construction site, extend boom, deliver cement";
}
```

Listing 5-3 details a small Web page that demonstrates the inheritance mechanism of the three objects. The page simply contains three buttons, with each button creating one type of object (Vehicle, SportsCar, or CementTruck) and passing the object to the describe function. The describe function is responsible for displaying the values of each object's properties and the return values of the object's functions. Notice how the describe method doesn't know whether the object it's describing is a Vehicle, SportsCar, or CementTruck—it just assumes that the object has the appropriate properties and functions and lets the object return its own values.

Listing 5-3. inheritanceViaPrototype.html

```
<!DOCTYPE html PUBLIC "-//W3C//DTD XHTML 1.0 Strict//EN"
  "http://www.w3.org/TR/xhtml1/DTD/xhtml1-strict.dtd">
<html xmlns="http://www.w3.org/1999/xhtml">
<head>
<title>JavaScript Inheritance via Prototype</title>

<script type="text/javascript" src="inheritanceViaPrototype.js"></script>

<script type="text/javaScript">

function describe(vehicle) {
    var description = "";
    description = description + "Number of wheels: " + vehicle.wheelCount;
    description = description + "\n\nCurb Weight: " + vehicle.curbWeightInPounds;
    description = description + "\n\nRefueling Method: " + vehicle.refuel();
    description = description + "\n\nMain Tasks: " + vehicle.mainTasks();
    alert(description);
}

function createVehicle() {
    var vehicle = new Vehicle();
    describe(vehicle);
}
```

```
function createSportsCar() {
    var sportsCar = new SportsCar();
    describe(sportsCar);
}

function createCementTruck() {
    var cementTruck = new CementTruck();
    describe(cementTruck);
}
</script>
</head>

<body>
  <h1>Examples of JavaScript Inheritance via the Prototype Method</h1>

  <br/><br/>
  <button onclick="createVehicle();">Create an instance of Vehicle</button>

  <br/><br/>
  <button onclick="createSportsCar();">Create an instance of SportsCar</button>

  <br/><br/>
  <button onclick="createCementTruck();">Create an instance of CementTruck</button>

</body>
</html>
```

Figure 5-16 depicts the results when each of the three objects is created and described using the describe function.

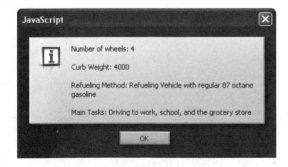

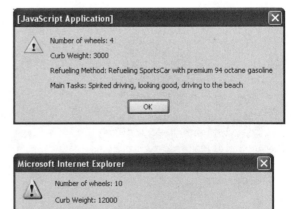

Figure 5-16. *The results of creating the* Vehicle, SportsCar, *and* CementTruck *objects and describing them using the* describe *function*

Private Properties and Information Hiding with JavaScript

The true die-hard fans of object-oriented design will notice that when using the prototype method for adding properties and functions to a JavaScript object, the added properties and functions are public and accessible to all other objects. For functions this typically isn't a problem, as most functions should be exposed to external clients anyway. But in the case of properties, the fans of object-oriented design will point out that public properties break the concept of information hiding. Object-oriented design dictates that an object's properties should be private and therefore not accessible to external clients. External clients should be able to access an object's private properties only through publicly available functions.

A little known fact about JavaScript is that it is possible to create private properties that are not accessible to external clients and instead are accessible only via the object's methods. Douglas Crockford[3] has demonstrated a method of creating private properties in JavaScript. It's rather simple, as summarized here:

- Private properties are defined in the constructor function using the var keyword.

- Private properties can be publicly accessed only by *privileged functions*. A privileged function is a function that has been defined in the constructor using the this keyword. Privileged functions are accessible to external clients but also have access to the object's private properties.

Let's consider the Vehicle class from the earlier example. Say you want to make the wheelCount and curbWeightInPounds properties private and accessible only via publicly available methods. The new Vehicle object now looks like Listing 5-4.

Listing 5-4. *The Rewritten* Vehicle *Object*

```
function Vehicle() {
    var wheelCount = 4;
    var curbWeightInPounds = 4000;

    this.getWheelCount = function() {
        return wheelCount;
    }

    this.setWheelCount = function(count) {
        wheelCount = count;
    }

    this.getCurbWeightInPounds = function() {
        return curbWeightInPounds;
    }

    this.setCurbWeightInPounds = function(weight) {
        curbWeightInPounds = weight;
    }
```

---

3. http://www.crockford.com/

```
    this.refuel = function() {
        return "Refueling Vehicle with regular 87 octane gasoline";
    }

    this.mainTasks = function() {
        return "Driving to work, school, and the grocery store";
    }
}
```

Note how the wheelCount and curbWeightInPounds properties are defined within the constructor using the var keyword, making the properties private. The properties are no longer public, and attempting to access the value of the wheelCount property via dot notation, like so:

```
var numberOfWheels = vehicle.wheelCount;
```

will return undefined instead of the actual value of wheelCount.

Since the properties are now private, you need to provide publicly available functions that can access these properties. The getWheelCount, setWheelCount, getCurbWeightInPounds, and setCurbWeightInPounds functions do just that. The Vehicle object now satisfies the concept of information hiding by allowing access to private properties only via publicly available functions.

Classical Inheritance in JavaScript

The prototype-based inheritance scheme of JavaScript works well enough, but it's not a natural way of programming for those used to the class-based inheritance schemes in languages such as C++ and Java. For those who would rather eschew the prototype-based method of inheritance and use a more classically based approach, read on.

Bob Clary[4] of Netscape proposed a method by which an object could inherit the properties and functions from another object using a single, generic script. The script simply copies the properties and functions of the "parent" object to the "child" object. For this purpose, we'll show how to modify the script slightly so that only the properties and functions that *don't exist* on the child object are copied to the child object; doing so allows functions on the child object to override functions on the parent. The generic function for creating an inheritance relationship between two objects looks like this:

```
function createInheritance(parent, child) {
    var property;
    for(property in parent) {
        if(!child[property]) {
            child[property] = parent[property];
        }
    }
}
```

The createInheritance function takes two arguments, the parent object and the child. The function simply iterates through all the members of the parent object (a member being

---

4. http://devedge-temp.mozilla.org/toolbox/examples/2003/inheritFrom/index_en.html

either a property or a function), and if the member does not exist on the child object, it is copied to the child object.

Using the createInheritance function is rather trivial: first create an instance of the child object, and then use the createInheritance function, passing to it the child object and an instance of the parent object, like so:

```
var child = new Child();
createInheritance(new Parent(), child);
```

All the properties and methods on the parent object that don't exist on the child object will be copied to the child object.

Putting It All Together

You've now seen how private properties are possible in JavaScript and how JavaScript can support a more class-based approach to inheritance like C++ and Java. To demonstrate how it all works, we'll show how to convert the earlier example that used the Vehicle, SportsCar, and CementTruck objects to use the new pattern of information hiding and inheritance. Listing 5-5 lists the new object definitions.

Listing 5-5. classicalInheritance.js

```
function Vehicle() {
    var wheelCount = 4;
    var curbWeightInPounds = 4000;

    this.getWheelCount = function() {
        return wheelCount;
    }

    this.setWheelCount = function(count) {
        wheelCount = count;
    }

    this.getCurbWeightInPounds = function() {
        return curbWeightInPounds;
    }

    this.setCurbWeightInPounds = function(weight) {
        curbWeightInPounds = weight;
    }

    this.refuel = function() {
        return "Refueling Vehicle with regular 87 octane gasoline";
    }

    this.mainTasks = function() {
        return "Driving to work, school, and the grocery store";
    }
}
```

```
function SportsCar() {
    this.refuel = function() {
        return "Refueling SportsCar with premium 94 octane gasoline";
    }

    this.mainTasks = function() {
        return "Spirited driving, looking good, driving to the beach";
    }
}

function CementTruck() {
    this.refuel = function() {
        return "Refueling CementTruck with diesel fuel";
    }

    this.mainTasks = function() {
        return "Arrive at construction site, extend boom, deliver cement";
    }
}
```

Note how the SportsCar and CementTruck objects do not define their own wheelCount and curbWeightInPounds properties and the associated accessor functions, as these will be inherited from the Vehicle object.

As before, you need a simple HTML page to test the new objects. Listing 5-6 lists the HTML page that will test these new objects. Pay special attention to the createInheritance function and how it's used to create the inheritance relationships between the Vehicle and SportsCar objects and the Vehicle and CementTruck objects. Also note that the describe function has been modified to attempt to access the wheelCount and curbWeightInPounds properties directly. Doing so should result in a value of undefined being returned.

Listing 5-6. classicalInheritance.html

```
<!DOCTYPE html PUBLIC "-//W3C//DTD XHTML 1.0 Strict//EN"
    "http://www.w3.org/TR/xhtml1/DTD/xhtml1-strict.dtd">
<html xmlns="http://www.w3.org/1999/xhtml">
<head>
<title>Classical Inheritance in JavaScript</title>

<script type="text/javascript" src="classicalInheritance.js"></script>

<script type="text/javaScript">
function createInheritance(parent, child) {
    var property;
    for(property in parent) {
        if(!child[property]) {
            child[property] = parent[property];
        }
    }
}
```

```javascript
function describe(vehicle) {
    var description = "";
    description = description + "Number of wheels (via property): "
                                                + vehicle.wheelCount;
    description = description + "\n\nNumber of wheels (via accessor): "
                              + vehicle.getWheelCount();
    description = description + "\n\nCurb Weight (via property): "
                              + vehicle.curbWeightInPounds;
    description = description + "\n\nCurb Weight (via accessor): "
                             + vehicle.getCurbWeightInPounds();
    description = description + "\n\nRefueling Method: " + vehicle.refuel();
    description = description + "\n\nMain Tasks: " + vehicle.mainTasks();
    alert(description);
}

function createVehicle() {
    var vehicle = new Vehicle();
    describe(vehicle);
}

function createSportsCar() {
    var sportsCar = new SportsCar();
    createInheritance(new Vehicle(), sportsCar);
    sportsCar.setCurbWeightInPounds(3000);
    describe(sportsCar);
}

function createCementTruck() {
    var cementTruck = new CementTruck();
    createInheritance(new Vehicle(), cementTruck);
    cementTruck.setWheelCount(10);
    cementTruck.setCurbWeightInPounds(10000);
    describe(cementTruck);
}
</script>
</head>

<body>
  <h1>Examples of Classical Inheritance in JavaScript</h1>

  <br/><br/>
  <button onclick="createVehicle();">Create an instance of Vehicle</button>

  <br/><br/>
  <button onclick="createSportsCar();">Create an instance of SportsCar</button>

  <br/><br/>
  <button onclick="createCementTruck();">Create an instance of CementTruck</button>

</body>
</html>
```

Clicking each of the buttons on the page produces the results shown in Figure 5-17. Note that as expected, attempting to access the private properties directly simply returns undefined.

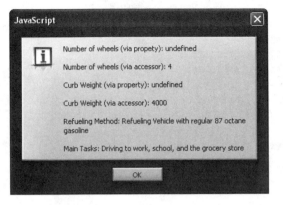

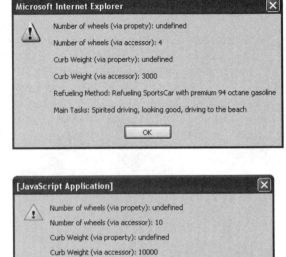

Figure 5-17. *The results of creating the* Vehicle, SportsCar, *and* CementTruck *objects and describing them using the* describe *function. The private properties cannot be accessed directly, as shown by the* undefined *values in the alert boxes.*

Summary

In this chapter, we introduced a number of tools and techniques that can make your development process a much more enjoyable experience. JSDoc helps you document your JavaScript code so it can be more easily understood and used by other developers. You'll surely write some of your own reusable JavaScript libraries if you start using Ajax techniques frequently, and you'll want to document the code with JSDoc to make it easy for others to use those libraries.

Tools such as HTML Validator and Checky help you ensure that the HTML code you write is valid HTML. Invalid HTML can cause undesirable behavior, so using valid HTML or XHTML eliminates one potential cause of errors. Valid XHTML or HTML is also more likely to be rendered identically across multiple browser platforms.

The DOM Inspector tool ships with Firefox and other Mozilla browsers and lets you inspect the nodes of an HTML document as a structured tree. DOM Inspector allows you to view each node, inspect its attribute values, and even change them on the fly. You can move nodes dynamically from one spot in the page to another, without rewriting the HTML. DOM Inspector is useful for inspecting nodes that have been dynamically created via JavaScript.

JSLint is a JavaScript verifier tool. While it can't determine that the logic of JavaScript is correct, it can help identify errors in the language syntax or areas that could be prone to error because of poor coding styles.

Removing comment lines and carriage return characters in JavaScript can greatly reduce the size of the JavaScript file and the time it takes to download to the client browser. MemTronic's HTML/JavaScript Cruncher-Compressor not only removes comment lines and carriage returns but actually compresses the JavaScript code to make it download even faster. A nice side effect of the compression is that it makes the JavaScript rather difficult to read, which helps secure the inner workings of your JavaScript code from prying eyes.

The Web Developer extension for Firefox provides a number of useful tools and utilities for the active Web developer. The tools allow you to resize images, dynamically edit CSS style rules, and change form methods from GET to POST (and vice versa), just to name a few.

Finally, you saw some advanced JavaScript techniques such as object-oriented programming. First you saw how JavaScript uses a prototype-based scheme to mimic inheritance. Then you saw how JavaScript supports the concept of information hiding using private properties that are accessible only via publicly available methods. Finally, you saw a technique by which JavaScript can mimic classically based inheritance schemes, like those used by C++ and Java. This technique will likely prove to be a more natural coding style for those accustomed to fully object-oriented languages.

These tools and techniques can make your life as an Ajax developer much easier and more enjoyable. Try them all so you can pick the ones you like; also, you may come across others on the Web that you'll find useful.

CHAPTER 6

■■■

Testing JavaScript with JsUnit

By now, it should be obvious that to really make the most of Ajax, you're going to need to write some JavaScript. Frameworks and toolkits can ease some of the burden, but in the end, you'll probably have more JavaScript than normal. Having written a fair amount of JavaScript ourselves, we know this can be daunting, but in this chapter we'll put a few more arrows in your quiver.

Specifically, we'll introduce test-driven development (TDD) and show how you can apply it to JavaScript. While this approach won't instantly solve all your coding problems, it should at least help you get home in time to eat dinner with your family. We'll start with a brief overview of TDD and the ubiquitous JUnit. Once we have established the foundation, we'll discuss JsUnit and show how you can write and run tests.

Rising to the JavaScript Challenge

If you've done any amount of work with Web applications, you've probably had to write some JavaScript; of course, if you've written anything more than the simplest of functions, your opinion of JavaScript might not be too high. Browser incompatibilities, a lack of decent development tools, no code completion, and no debuggers—it's enough to make most developers long for vi.[1]

We know your pain. In Chapter 5, we discussed a number of tools to make your life easier. In this chapter, we'll show how to make developing JavaScript as easy as possible (at least until the tool vendors catch up[2]). By writing your JavaScript in the *test-first* manner, you can greatly simplify the entire process.

Introducing the Test-First Approach

Yeah, we can hear you now—"I write tests, just before the product ships." Some of you are snickering and saying something about the quality assurance department. Still others have project managers who have said something along the lines of, "We can't waste time writing tests; we need to write real code." So, what does it mean to practice TDD?

TDD rose out of the agile development movement, specifically extreme programming (XP), where it is a central principle. Rather than write your tests when you are done, often as an afterthought, TDD practitioners write the tests before they write any code. In essence, the

---

1. OK, so for some of you, vi is obvious, but c'mon, even you've got to have issues with JavaScript!
2. We fully expect the major tool vendors will solve this problem in the near future.

tests serve as the design document—rather than spending considerable time fighting a complex diagramming tool, you "sketch" the class directly in the code. You begin by writing a test for some small piece of functionality. Depending on the language, your test may not even compile yet because you reference a class that doesn't yet exist. Once you have established your test, you run it (and, yes, it will fail). You then write the smallest amount of code that will allow your test to pass. At this point, you refactor your code and add more tests.

Typically, you use a testing framework to help you write automated tests. The most famous of these frameworks is JUnit, though now a number of *x*Unit projects simplify creating tests in a number of languages. In general, these frameworks work on an *assert* basis. Developers write test methods that compare the actual result from invoking a method against an expected result. Of course, you could perform these comparisons by manually inspecting a log file or the user interface, but unlike humans, computers are fast and accurate at performing data comparison. Further, computers don't get bored when they've run the same test 1,500 times.

JUnit and its peers make writing and running tests relatively simple. This encourages developers to create a large number of tests (most likely leading to good test coverage) and run those tests often (helping developers find bugs must faster). In many cases, projects that incorporate TDD will have as much test code as production code!

Practicing TDD provides a number of important benefits:

Offers a clear end: You know when you're done—when the tests pass, your work is complete (assuming you wrote good tests). Tests create a natural boundary around your code that helps you focus on the task at hand. Once your tests pass, you have tangible proof that your code works. Running automated tests in an *x*Unit framework is orders of magnitude faster than manually testing the user interface or comparing results in a log file. Most *x*Unit tests run in a matter of milliseconds, and most practitioners run their tests several times a day. In many shops, a successful pass through the test suite is required to check code into the source tree.

Provides documentation: How often have you encountered code that you just couldn't understand? The code probably doesn't have any documentation, and the developer who wrote the code is long since gone (or on vacation). Of course, you're often exposed to this code at 3 a.m. or when some vice president is screaming for a fix yesterday, making it that much harder to take the time to figure out what the author meant. Good unit tests serve as system documentation, and they also show you exactly what the system does—most documentation we've encountered says what the system is supposed to do. Tests are like breadcrumbs left by the initial developer that show you how their classes actually work.

Improves design: Writing tests improves your designs. Tests help you think in terms of your interface—the test framework is just another client of the code. The tests help you think simply. If you really do follow the principle of "do the simplest thing that works," you won't find yourself with pages of complex algorithms. Code written to be tested often has fewer dependencies and is more decoupled since this makes it easier to test. Of course, it also has the added side effect of being easier to change!

Encourages refactoring: With a robust test suite, you are free to refactor at will. How often have you encountered code that you were hesitant to change? Fear makes you move slowly and conservatively since you can't be sure your changes won't break the system. With a good unit test suite, you can refactor mercilessly while keeping your code clean.

Increases speed: Doesn't writing all these tests slow development down? Speed (or development cost) is one of the most frequent arguments against practicing TDD and using *x*Unit frameworks. All new tools have learning curves, but once your developers are comfortable with their frameworks of choice (often this takes a little time), development velocity will actually increase. A full unit test suite gives you a way to regression test your system, meaning you can sleep a little easier after adding that new whiz-bang feature.

Gives feedback: One often-overlooked benefit of unit testing relates to rhythm. It may seem trivial, but you gain a real sense of accomplishment when your tests pass! Rather than spending days and days hacking code without any feedback, the test-code-test approach encourages you to work in small chunks, often coding little more than a few minutes at a time. Instead of facing a daunting list of features, you inch your code base forward one tiny piece at a time.

In our experience, testing is infectious, and you can find yourself addicted to the green bar. Initially, many developers are skeptical, but inevitably the light bulb turns on for nearly every developer. Usually it's when the tests catch a bug for the first time or when adding that new feature takes minutes instead of hours; regardless of when it occurs, usually developers realize that tests matter.

Introducing JUnit

Since JUnit serves as the inspiration for JsUnit, we'll start with a brief overview of JUnit before diving into the details of JsUnit. For a truly detailed look at JUnit, take a look at any of the excellent books on the topic. While JUnit isn't the only answer for testing (TestNG and Fit/FitNesse are worth investigating), JsUnit is essentially a "port" of JUnit for use in testing JavaScript, which is why we're discussing JUnit here.

JUnit is one of the most widely used *x*Unit test frameworks. Written by Erich Gamma and Kent Beck, JUnit is commonly used on Java-based open-source software, and most common IDEs support it out of the box. Writing tests in JUnit is fairly trivial —you simply create a class that implements TestCase, write some methods that start with test and have some asserts in them, and then run your tests with your favorite test runner. By default, JUnit will automatically run any method that is prefixed with test, though you can override this behavior to suit your needs.

By the time you write your second or third test, you will find you have some common code that can be refactored. Since you've probably read *The Pragmatic Programmer*, by Andrew Hunt and David Thomas (Addison-Wesley, 1999), you know you shouldn't repeat yourself, so you pull out the common code into a fixture by overriding the setUp() and tearDown() methods, which are called before and after (respectively) every test you run.

At first you may have only a few tests, but eventually their numbers will grow, and you'll need some ways to organize them. In JUnit, you create TestSuites that consist of a collection of test methods or even entire test classes. (TestSuites can hold anything that implements the Test interface.) If you prefer greater control over your tests, you can manually add them to the TestSuite, or you can simply tell JUnit to do the work for you by passing your TestCase to the TestSuite constructor.

JUnit supports a number of test runners. Some IDEs have their own proprietary runners, and you are free to make your own if you want. JUnit comes with both a textual runner and a graphical runner that reports on the outcome of running your tests. (The graphical runner has a handy "red bar fail"/"green bar pass" approach.) JUnit tests are also commonly triggered by your commit or build process.

Exploring JsUnit

At the start of 2001, Edward Hieatt began work on a "port" of JUnit for use in testing JavaScript in the browser. Since then, JsUnit has had nearly 10,000 downloads and counts almost 300 people as members of its newsgroup. JsUnit supports the common *x*Unit functions and is written entirely in JavaScript. If you're comfortable with JUnit (or similar *x*Unit frameworks), you'll find JsUnit pretty intuitive.

The usual suspects are present: setUp() and tearDown() are there, though as functions instead of methods; test functions (instead of test methods) are grouped into test pages (instead of test cases); and JsUnit comes with its own HTML-based test runners. Table 6-1 compares the two frameworks.

Table 6-1. *JUnit vs. JsUnit*

JUnit	JsUnit
Test class extends TestCase	Test page includes jsUnitCore.js
Test methods	Test functions
Test classes	HTML-based test pages
TestSuites	HTML-based test suites
Various test runners	HTML/JavaScript-based test runner
setUp() and tearDown() methods	setUp() and tearDown() functions
Runs in the virtual machine	Runs in a browser
Written in Java	Written in JavaScript

Getting Started

Getting started with JsUnit is trivial—simply download the JsUnit zip file from the JsUnit Web page (www.edwardh.com/jsunit/). Expanding the archive results in a jsunit folder that you can actually put on your Web server to make JsUnit easier to use on a team or across an organization. Most of the "meat" of JsUnit is in the jsunit/app directory—here you'll find jsUnitCore.js, jsUnitTracer.js, and jsUnitTestManager.js, amongst others. If you want to run the actual JsUnit tests, you can do so using the testRunner.html file to run any of the test pages found in the jsunit/tests directory. If you are using IntelliJ and want to actually work on JsUnit, the jsunit/intellij directory contains all the appropriate files to get you started.

Writing Tests

Writing tests in JsUnit is similar to writing tests in JUnit. Test functions can't take any parameters and must begin with the prefix test, for example, testDateValidation(). Your test functions are contained on a *test page*, which is analogous to a Test class in JUnit. The test page must include the jsUnitCore.js file found in the jsunit/app directory when you expand the JsUnit zip file. Including this JavaScript file is no different from adding an external JavaScript file to your page; you simply reference the file with the script element `<script language="JavaScript" src="jsUnitCore.js"></script>`, keeping in mind that, unless you are working in the `jsunit/app` directory, you will need to provide relative path information to the `jsUnitCore.js` file. Of course, you are free to include any number of other functions or JavaScript files in your test page; in fact, putting many of your JavaScript functions in separate files is a good practice. Test functions can also reside in separate JavaScript files; however, if you do this, you need to use the `exposeTest➥ FunctionNames()` method so JsUnit can find them. In fact, if you need to set up your tests against different page content, putting the test functions in a separate file avoids the pain of copy-and-paste issues.

In general, JsUnit will automatically discover the test functions just as JUnit finds all your test methods. However, some operating system/browser combinations don't work. If you find that your test functions aren't being discovered as you would expect, using the `exposeTestFunctionNames()` method should do the trick.

Assert Methods

Now that you know a bit about test functions and test pages, you need to write some actual tests! Just like in JUnit, you do that by using *assert methods*. Assert methods are the basic building block of any unit test; they are simple Boolean expressions that indicate whether a given statement is true or false. When an assertion fails, an error is raised, and you get the proverbial red bar. JsUnit doesn't have quite as rich a set of assert methods as JUnit, but it has what you need to test your JavaScript. Note that all the comments are optional (just like JUnit—even "incorrectly" putting the optional parameter first instead of last) except with the `fail()` method.

```
assert([comment], booleanValue)
assertTrue([comment], booleanValue)
assertFalse([comment], booleanValue)
assertEquals([comment], value1, value2)
assertNotEquals([comment], value1, value2)
assertNull([comment], value)
assertNotNull([comment], value)
assertUndefined([comment], value)
assertNotUndefined([comment], value)
assertNaN([comment], value)
assertNotNaN([comment], value)
fail(comment)
```

To see these methods put to the test (literally and figuratively), look no further than the test pages included with the JsUnit download. JsUnit also provides a variable, `JSUNIT_UNDEFINED_VALUE`, that maps to the JavaScript `undefined` variable.

Enough talk—let's take a look at a simple test! This example has a simple function that adds two numbers together, and it has two tests: one for positive integers, another for negative integers. To test your function, create the simple Web page shown in Listing 6-1, which includes the `jsUnitCore.js` file and contains both the functions to test and the test methods. Of course, with production code, you probably wouldn't mix your test code with the functions it's testing, but it'll do for a first taste.

Listing 6-1. *Simple Test Page*

```html
<!DOCTYPE HTML PUBLIC "-//W3C//DTD HTML 4.01 Transitional//EN">

<html>
  <head>
    <title>A Simple Test Page</title>
    <script language="JavaScript" src="../jsunit/app/jsUnitCore.js"></script>
    <script language="JavaScript">
        function addTwoNumbers(value1, value2) {
            return value1 + value2;
        }

        function testValidArgs() {
            assertEquals("2 + 2 is 4", 4, addTwoNumbers(2, 2));
        }

        function testWithNegativeNumbers() {
            assertEquals("negative numbers: -2 + -2 is -4", -4, ➥
addTwoNumbers(-2, -2));
        }
    </script>
  </head>
  <body>
    This is a simple test page for addTwoNumbers(value1, value2).
  </body>
</html>
```

Running these tests gives you the results shown in Figure 6-1. (We'll describe the test runner in greater detail in the following pages.)

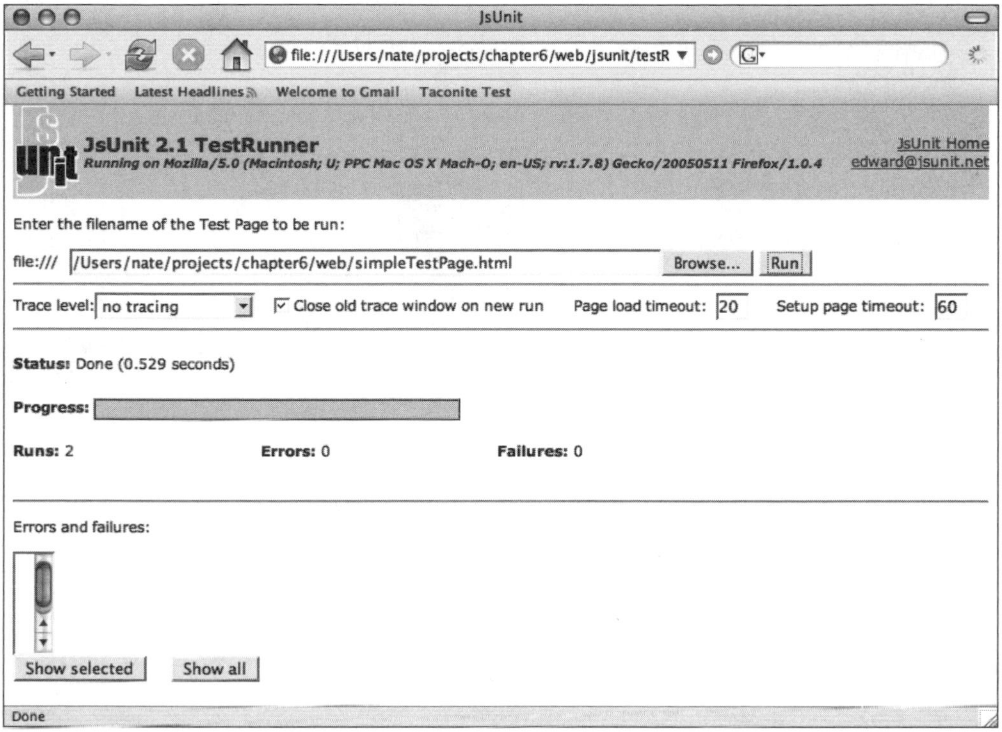

Figure 6-1. *Simple test results*

Obviously, it's unlikely that you will mix your production functions with the test functions in a test page. Instead, you'd probably put your production code in a separate JavaScript file that you would then include in your test page. This approach would look like Listing 6-2.

Listing 6-2. *A More Typical Approach*

```html
<!DOCTYPE HTML PUBLIC "-//W3C//DTD HTML 4.01 Transitional//EN">

<html>
  <head>
    <title>Another Test Page</title>
    <script language="JavaScript" src="../jsunit/app/jsUnitCore.js"></script>
    <script language="JavaScript" src="simpleJS.js"></script>
    <script language="JavaScript">

        function testValidArgs() {
            assertEquals("2 + 2 is 4", 4, addTwoNumbers(2, 2));
        }
```

```
        function testWithNegativeNumbers() {
            assertEquals("negative numbers: -2 + -2 is -4", -4, ➥
addTwoNumbers(-2, -2));
        }
    </script>
  </head>
  <body>
    This is a simple test page for the simpleJS file.
  </body>
</html>
```

The JavaScript file truly is simple, as shown in Listing 6-3.

Listing 6-3. simple.js

```
function addTwoNumbers(value1, value2) {
        return parseInt(value1) + parseInt(value2);
}
```

As you would expect, the results are the same (see Figure 6-2).

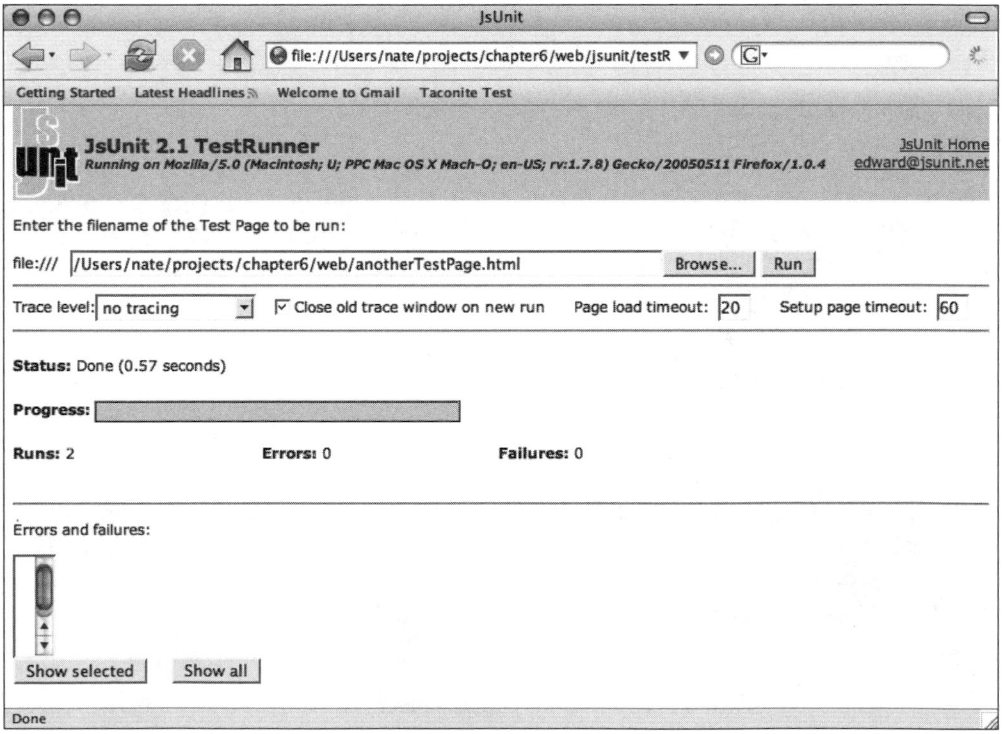

Figure 6-2. *Results from a typical approach*

As you can see, your two test functions were automatically discovered, and typically that's what will happen. However, if you launch your test page and nothing happens when you click Run, you may need to use exposeTestFunctionNames() to make sure JsUnit can find your tests, as shown in Listing 6-4.

Listing 6-4. *Using* exposeTestFunctionNames()

```
<!DOCTYPE HTML PUBLIC "-//W3C//DTD HTML 4.01 Transitional//EN">

<html>
  <head>
    <title>A Test Page With exposeTestFunctions</title>
    <script language="JavaScript" src="../jsunit/app/jsUnitCore.js"></script>
    <script language="JavaScript" src="simpleJS.js"></script>
    <script language="JavaScript">

        function testValidArgs() {
            assertEquals("2 + 2 is 4", 4, addTwoNumbers(2, 2));
        }

        function testWithNegativeNumbers() {
            assertEquals("negative numbers: -2 + -2 is -4", -4, ➥
addTwoNumbers(-2, -2));
        }

        function exposeTestFunctionNames() {
            var tests = new Array(2);
            tests[0] = "testValidArgs";
            tests[1] = "testWithNegativeNumbers";
            return tests;
        }
    </script>
  </head>
  <body>
    This is a simple test page that uses exposeTestFunctionNames.
  </body>
</html>
```

As you would expect, this works (see Figure 6-3).

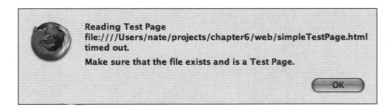

Figure 6-3. *Running a test that uses* `exposeTestFunctionNames()`

If you see an error message like the one in Figure 6-4, chances are either you forgot to include `jsUnitCore.js` in your test page or the path to the file is incorrect. Check your test page, and run it again.

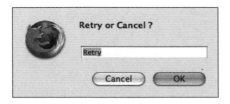

Figure 6-4. *JsUnit error message*

When you click OK, you will be prompted to retry or cancel the test, as shown in Figure 6-5.

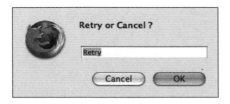

Figure 6-5. *Retry or cancel*

setUp() and tearDown()

Like its cousin JUnit, JsUnit supports setUp() and tearDown(). The JsUnit flavor is similar to JUnit in that setUp() and tearDown() are optional, with setUp() being called before every test and tearDown() being called after every test. Before you run off and start using setUp() and tearDown() extensively, you need to know about the two key differences between the JUnit and JsUnit implementations of the setUp() and tearDown() methods. In JUnit, each test run results in the creation of a new instance of the Test class, meaning any instance variables that are declared are "reset" between test runs. JsUnit, however, does not reload the test page for each test run, so the variable state will be preserved across tests. The other key difference concerns test order. With JUnit, the order your tests are executed in is not guaranteed. In JsUnit, tests will be executed in the order they are declared in your test page, starting at the top.[3]

Listing 6-5 shows a rather contrived example of using the setUp() and tearDown() methods. This builds on the simple add method you created before, but this time you'll add a form to the equation. You'll use the setUp() and tearDown() methods to populate the form and then clean up after yourself.

Listing 6-5. *Using* setUp() *and* tearDown()

```
<!DOCTYPE HTML PUBLIC "-//W3C//DTD HTML 4.01 Transitional//EN">

<html>
  <head>
    <title>Using setUp and tearDown</title>
    <script language="JavaScript" src="jsunit/app/jsUnitCore.js"></script>
    <script language="JavaScript" src="simpleJS.js"></script>
    <script language="JavaScript">

        function setUp() {
            document.getElementById("value1").value = "2";
            document.getElementById("value2").value = "2";
        }

        function testValidArgs() {
            assertEquals("2 + 2 should equal 4", 4, addNumbers());
        }

        function addNumbers() {
            var val1 = document.getElementById("value1").value;
            var val2 = document.getElementById("value2").value;
            return addTwoNumbers(val1, val2);
        }
```

---

3. The normal caveats about tests depending on each other still apply, though. Just because your tests will be executed in a defined order doesn't imply you should write tests that depend on execution order!

```
        function tearDown() {
            document.getElementById("value1").value = "";
            document.getElementById("value2").value = "";
        }

    </script>
  </head>
  <body>
    <form id="test">
        <input type="text" size="3" id="value1"/>
        <input type="text" size="3" id="value2"/>
        <input type="button" value="Add" onclick="addNumbers()"/>
    </form>
  </body>
</html>
```

As you might expect, the results are pretty typical (see Figure 6-6).

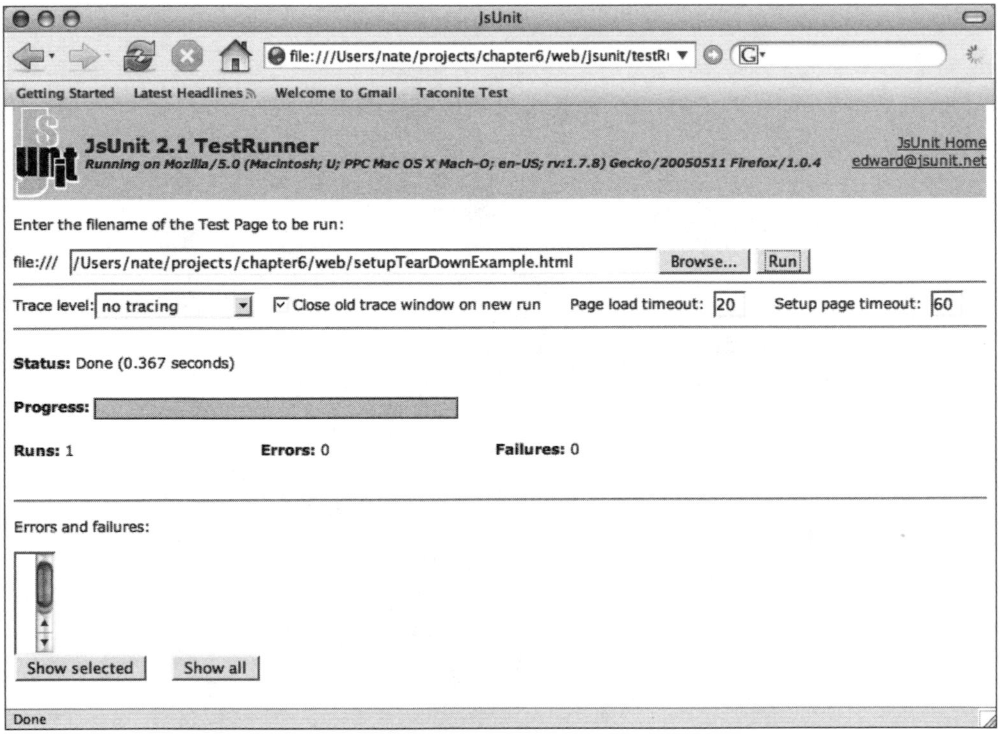

Figure 6-6. *Running the* setUp()/tearDown() *example*

JsUnit contains another feature that you won't find in JUnit: the setUpPage() function. Some in the JUnit community think its lack of "one-time setup" and "one-time teardown" is a flaw in its design. Some have gone so far as to extend JUnit or create new test frameworks that have this feature baked in; in addition, the JUnit frequently asked questions (FAQ) site even describes one way to approximate this behavior.[4] Most books about JUnit also discuss approaches to this issue.

JsUnit, however, does contain one-time setup; the setUpPage() function is called exactly once per test page and before any of your test functions are called. By now, you've probably figured out that this is a great place to stash preprocessing, especially if you need to load any data to your page before running the tests. Unlike the setUp() and tearDown() functions, there is a little more to using setUpPage() than just putting your processing in the function. If you do choose to use this feature, make sure you set the setUpPageStatus variable to complete when your function is done—this tells JsUnit it can move on and fire the tests on your test page.

How about an example? Let's return to the simpleJS.js file and add three functions to round out the math features. Include subtract, multiply, and divide functions, as shown in Listing 6-6.

Listing 6-6. simpleJS2.js

```
function addTwoNumbers(value1, value2) {
    return parseInt(value1) + parseInt(value2);
}

function subtractTwoNumbers(value1, value2) {
    return parseInt(value1) - parseInt(value2);
}

function multiplyTwoNumbers(value1, value2) {
    return parseInt(value1) * parseInt(value2);
}

function divideTwoNumbers(value1, value2) {
    return parseInt(value1) / parseInt(value2);
}
```

Now use the setUpPage() function to set up some simple test data, as shown in Listing 6-7. Please note the last line of the function—you have to tell JsUnit that you're done setting up your page.

---

4. junit.sourceforge.net/doc/faq/faq.htm#organize_3

Listing 6-7. *Using the* setUpPage() *Function*

```html
<!DOCTYPE HTML PUBLIC "-//W3C//DTD HTML 4.01 Transitional//EN">

<html>
  <head>
    <title>Using setUp and tearDown</title>
    <script language="JavaScript" src="jsunit/app/jsUnitCore.js"></script>
    <script language="JavaScript" src="simpleJS2.js"></script>
    <script language="JavaScript">
        var arg1;
        var arg2;

        function setUpPage() {
            arg1 = 2;
            arg2 = 2;
            setUpPageStatus = "complete";
        }

        function testAddValidArgs() {
            assertEquals("2 + 2 should equal 4", 4, addTwoNumbers(arg1, arg2));
        }

        function testSubtractValidArgs() {
            assertEquals("2 - 2 should equal 0", 0, subtractTwoNumbers(arg1, arg2));
        }

        function testMultiplyValidArgs() {
            assertEquals("2 * 2 should equal 4", 4, multiplyTwoNumbers(arg1, arg2));
        }

        function testDivideValidArgs() {
            assertEquals("2 / 2 should equal 1", 1, divideTwoNumbers(arg1, arg2));
        }

    </script>
  </head>
  <body>
    This is an example of using setUpPage.
  </body>
</html>
```

This is starting to get a tad boring—yet another green bar (see Figure 6-7).

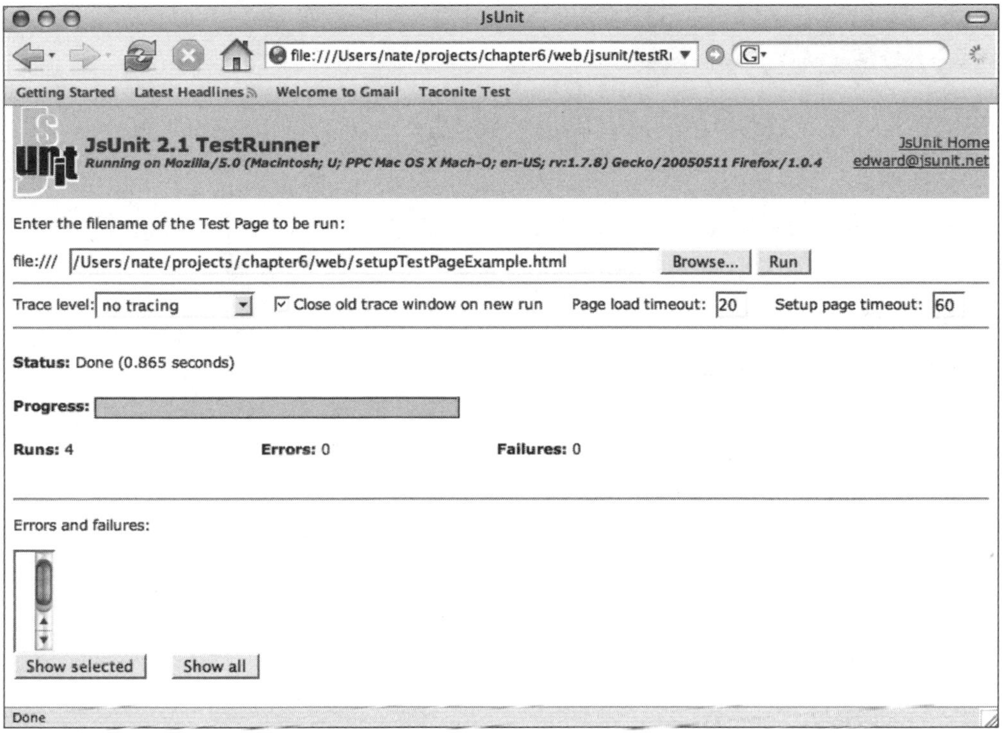

Figure 6-7. *Running the* setUpPage() *test*

Test Suites

Once you have a few test pages, you'll want to organize them into *test suites*, which are just like the similarly named TestSuites from JUnit. Test suites group various test pages, allowing you to run similar tests together by running a single suite. Test suites are nothing more than special test pages that include a list of test pages or other test suites (thereby allowing you to have a master suite) that run in sequence.

You can define test suites in a similar fashion to test pages with two exceptions. First, they cannot contain any test functions. Second, your test suite must contain a suite() function that returns a JsUnitTestSuite object. You can use two methods to add items to a test suite: addTestPage(testPage), which adds an individual test page to your suite, and addTestSuite(testSuite), which adds a suite to your, well, suite. Keep in mind that when you add a test page to a test suite, you need to provide a fully qualified or relative pathname to your file *in relation to the test runner*. In other words, if your jsunit folder is in the same directory as your test pages, then the test runner is one folder deeper than your tests. If you see an error like the one shown in Figure 6-8, make sure you've provided the path relative to the test runner. When you want to add other test suites to your test suite, keep in mind that the argument to addTestSuite must be of type JsUnitTestSuite, which is declared in the same page as the suite function. Helpfully, you will find a test suite example in the jsunit/tests directory. Listing 6-8 also shows an example.

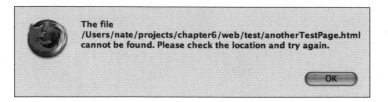

The file /Users/nate/projects/chapter6/web/test/anotherTestPage.html cannot be found. Please check the location and try again.

OK

Figure 6-8. *Running a test suite with a path error*

Listing 6-8. *A Simple Test Suite*

```html
<!DOCTYPE HTML PUBLIC "-//W3C//DTD HTML 4.01 Transitional//EN">

<html>
  <head>
    <title>Sample Test Suite</title>
    <script language="JavaScript" src="jsunit/app/jsUnitCore.js"></script>
    <script language="JavaScript">

        function sampleSuite() {
            var sampleSuite = new top.jsUnitTestSuite();
            sampleSuite.addTestPage("../anotherTestPage.html");
            sampleSuite.addTestPage("../simpleTestPage.html");
            return sampleSuite;
        }

        function suite() {
            var testSuite = new top.jsUnitTestSuite();
            testSuite.addTestSuite(sampelSuite());
            testSuite.addTestPage("../setupTearDownExample.html");
            return testSuite;
        }

    </script>
  </head>
  <body>
    This is a simple test suite.
  </body>
</html>
```

As you might expect, this results in a green bar (see Figure 6-9).

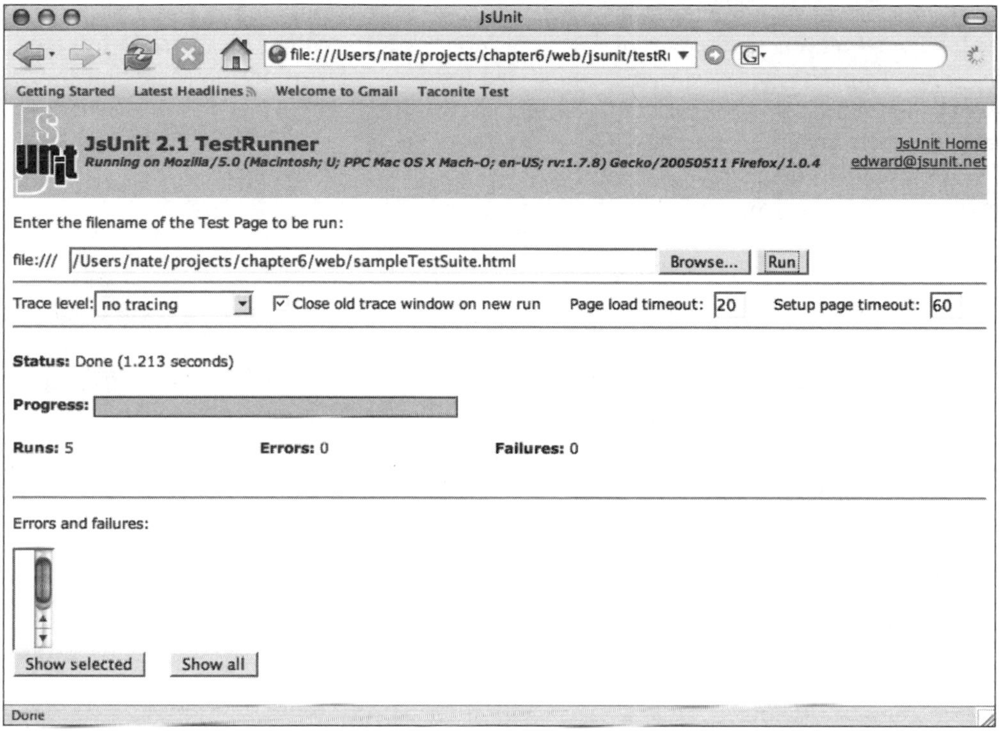

Figure 6-9. *Running the test suite*

Tracing and Logging

One of the most painful parts of writing JavaScript is tracing your way through the code. Unlike many other languages, you don't have a nifty logging library that lets you print statements in a coherent manner—instead, you are forced to use alert(). Of course, alert() works, but it isn't an optimal solution. It can be painful to click your way through a host of alert() functions as you work your way through a problem, and once you've fixed the bug, you have to go in and remove all your alert() code. Of course, around the time you finish deleting all the extraneous alert() functions, another bug crops up that is in nearly the same place the last one was, forcing you to put in all new alert() functions. Are you still wondering why many people aren't huge fans of JavaScript?

To improve the lives of JavaScript developers, JsUnit supports tracing! JsUnit contains the following three functions that can be called from any test (note in each instance that the value argument is optional):

```
warn(message, [value])
inform(message, [value])
debug(message, [value])
```

JsUnit supports three tracing levels: warn, info, and debug. When you run your tests, you specify which level you want to output. The three levels cascade in this order: warn, info, debug. This means if you choose debug when running your tests, you will see any messages that are sent from the warn(), inform(), or debug() functions. Selecting warn will display messages only from the warn() function, while selecting info will result in messages from warn() and inform() to be displayed. The default is no tracing. Now let's add some trace methods to the simple example and see what happens (see Listing 6-9).

Listing 6-9. *Adding Trace Functions to a Test*

```
<!DOCTYPE HTML PUBLIC "-//W3C//DTD HTML 4.01 Transitional//EN">

<html>
  <head>
    <title>A Simple Test Page with Tracing</title>
    <script language="JavaScript" src="jsunit/app/jsUnitCore.js"></script>
    <script language="JavaScript">
        function addTwoNumbers(value1, value2) {
            warn("this is a warning message");
            warn("this is a warning message with a value", value1);
            return value1 + value2;
        }

        function testValidArgs() {
            inform("this is an inform message");
            assertEquals("2 + 2 is 4", 4, addTwoNumbers(2, 2));
        }

        function testWithNegativeNumbers() {
            debug("this is a debug message");
            assertEquals("negative numbers: -2 + -2 is -4", -4, ➥
addTwoNumbers(-2, -2));
        }
    </script>
  </head>
  <body>
    This is a simple test page for addTwoNumbers(value1, value2) with tracing.
  </body>
</html>
```

To see the output from your trace functions, you need to enable tracing in the test runner by selecting the appropriate trace level. By selecting debug, you will see messages from all three functions, and the Close Old Trace Window on New Run checkbox allows you to keep the trace results from previous runs if you want (see Figure 6-10).

We won't bore you with yet another green bar in the test runner; instead, Figure 6-11 shows the output of the trace functions.

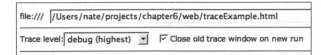

Figure 6-10. *Setting the trace level*

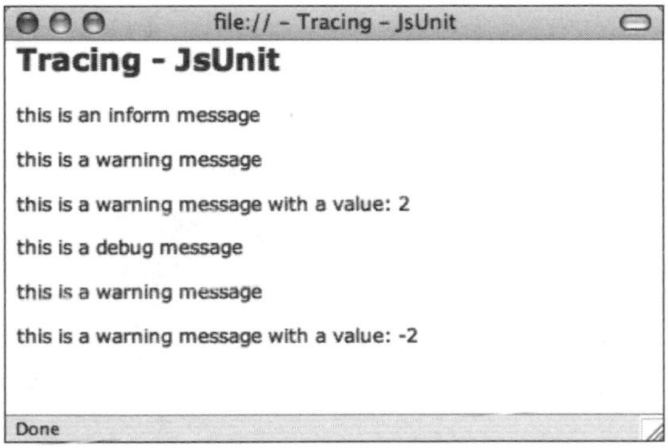

Tracing - JsUnit

file:// – Tracing – JsUnit

this is an inform message

this is a warning message

this is a warning message with a value: 2

this is a debug message

this is a warning message

this is a warning message with a value: -2

Done

Figure 6-11. *The trace output*

Running Tests

Now that you've written some tests, you need to run them, and to do this you can use the JsUnit test runner. You've already seen lots of examples of firing the test runner, but how do you do this? To access the runner, point your target browser to the testRunner.html file found in the jsunit folder. The test runner looks like Figure 6-12.

The test runner is fairly similar to the graphical runners that are often used in the JUnit space. (However, interestingly, the hotly awaited JUnit 4 does not include a graphical test runner, and one is not expected to be added.) To run a test, you select the file to run by clicking Choose File. As you would expect, the progress bar remains green, as shown in Figure 6-13, until the test runner encounters a failure. The Runs field indicates the total number of test functions; any errors or failures will also be reported.

An *error* comes from the browser and indicates that something was wrong with the test page, and a *failure* indicates one of your asserts actually failed. The specific error or failure will be displayed in the Errors and Failures text box; to see more details about the error or failure, double-click the test function in question. Alternatively, highlight it, and select Show Selected. In the event of a failure, an alert will display the expected and actual values plus any message you added to your assert. If you're seeing an error, the message will (probably) help you narrow down what is wrong.

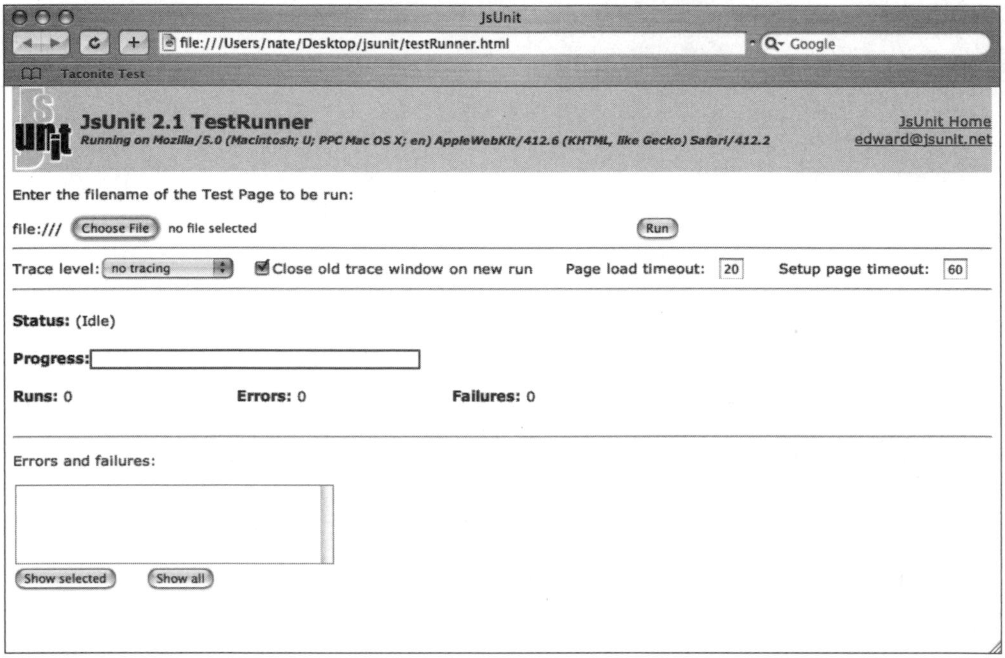

Figure 6-12. *The JsUnit test runner*

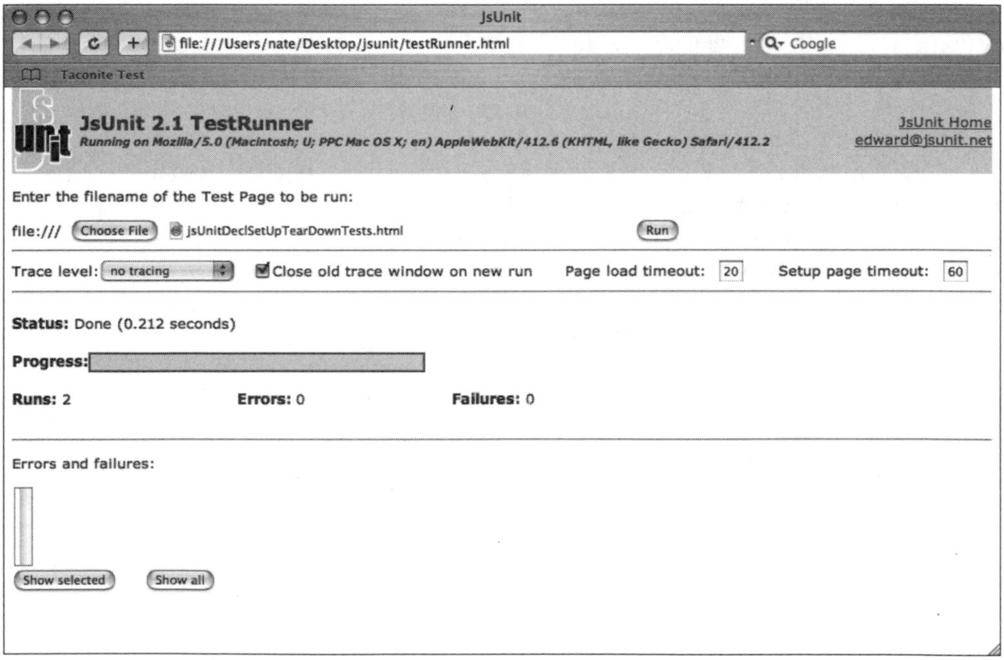

Figure 6-13. *The JsUnit test runner on success*

Let's return to the example that demonstrated the setUp() and tearDown() functions so you can make one small adjustment to this example. In the addNumbers() function, add a deliberate mistake by attempting to retrieve an element that doesn't exist, as shown in Listing 6-10.

Listing 6-10. *A Deliberate Mistake*

```
function addNumbers() {
  //arg1 doesn't exist!
  var val1 = document.getElementById("arg1").value;
  var val2 = document.getElementById("value2").value;
  return addTwoNumbers(val1, val2);
}
```

Running this test results in, as you would expect, a red bar! Notice that the Errors and Failures text box shows an error (see Figure 6-14).

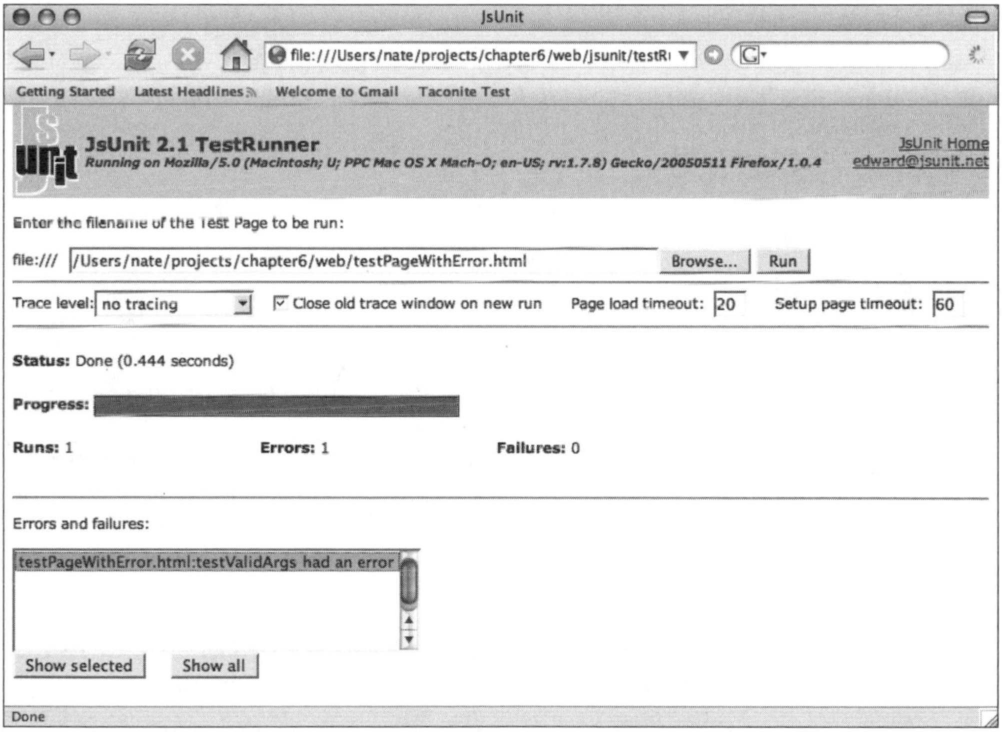

Figure 6-14. *The JsUnit test runner error*

Upon further investigation, you will see the detail information shown in Figure 6-15. This tells you that arg1 doesn't have any properties and that you should investigate the addNumbers() method to see what's happening.

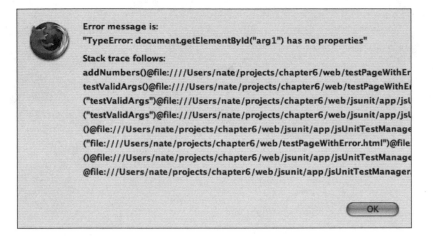

Figure 6-15. *Error details*

Failures look the same in the runner (they result in a red bar), but the details are different. For those familiar with JUnit, the failure information will look downright familiar. Let's return to your test with the simpleJS.js file. Pretend that you expect 2 + 2 to equal 5, as shown in Listing 6-11, and see what happens.

Listing 6-11. *Another Deliberate Mistake*

```
function testValidArgs() {
  assertEquals("we really do know that 2 + 2 is 4", 5, addTwoNumbers(2, 2));
}
```

As you would expect, the test runner will show a red bar, but the detail alert is a bit different, as shown in Figure 6-16.

The details of the failure are quite helpful, as shown in Figure 6-17. You see any message that you entered in the assert function, and you get the expected and actual values along with a stack trace that shows you where the failure occurred.

At this point, we've talked about every field in the test runner except two: Page Load Timeout and Setup Page Timeout. The Page Load Timeout field deals with how patient the test runner will be with your test page—if your page takes longer than the number in this box (expressed in seconds), the test runner will throw an error that looks like Figure 6-18. If you see this error, make sure your test page is actually a test page. (In other words, make sure you've included the jsUnitCore.js file, make sure the path statement is correct, and if you're accessing the page across the network, make sure it's available.) Of course, if you are doing distributed testing, you may need to increase the time in the Page Load Timeout field!

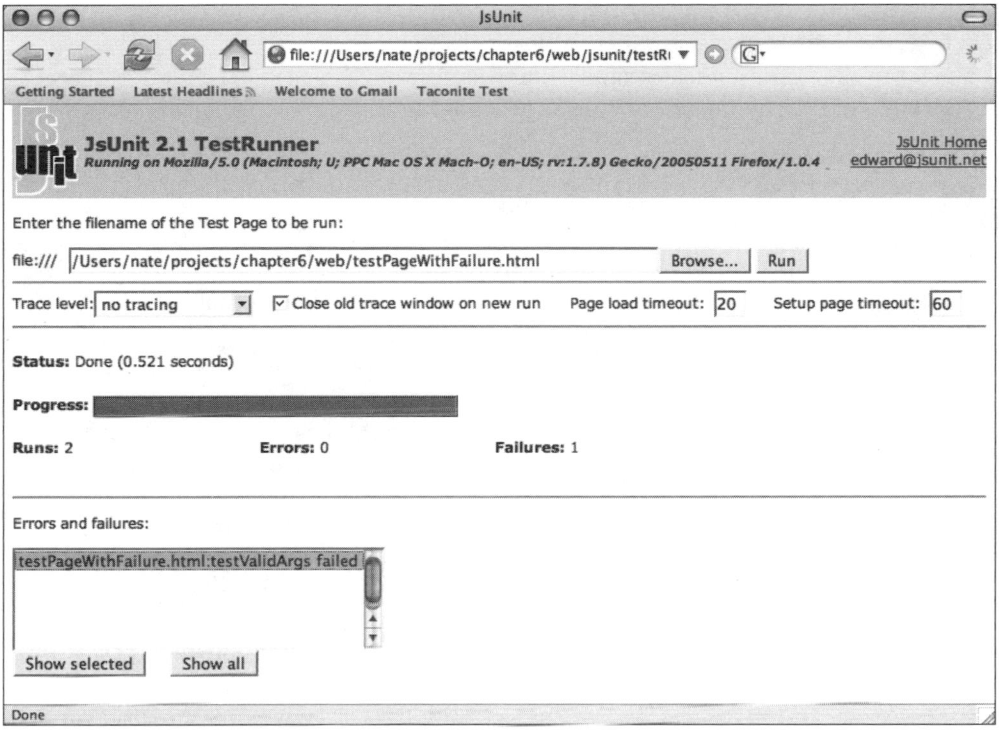

![JsUnit TestRunner window showing a test run with a failure. URL bar contains file:///Users/nate/projects/chapter6/web/jsunit/testR. Test page field contains /Users/nate/projects/chapter6/web/testPageWithFailure.html with Browse... and Run buttons. Trace level: no tracing. Close old trace window on new run checked. Page load timeout: 20. Setup page timeout: 60. Status: Done (0.521 seconds). Runs: 2, Errors: 0, Failures: 1. Errors and failures: testPageWithFailure.html:testValidArgs failed. Show selected and Show all buttons.]

Figure 6-16. *The JsUnit test runner failure*

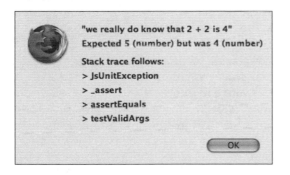

Figure 6-17. *Failure details*

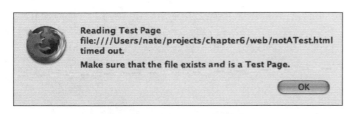

Figure 6-18. *Page timeout alert*

When you click OK, you will be given a chance to retry or cancel the test, as shown in Figure 6-19.

The Setup Page Timeout field is similar, but it applies only if you've used the `setUpPage()` function. It represents the amount of time (in seconds again) that the JsUnit test runner will wait for your `setUpPage()` function to finish. Don't forget that if your test page has a `setUpPage()` function, the test runner will wait until you set the `setUpPageStatus` variable to `complete`. As you would expect, the test runner will let you know that something unexpected happened, as shown in Figure 6-20.

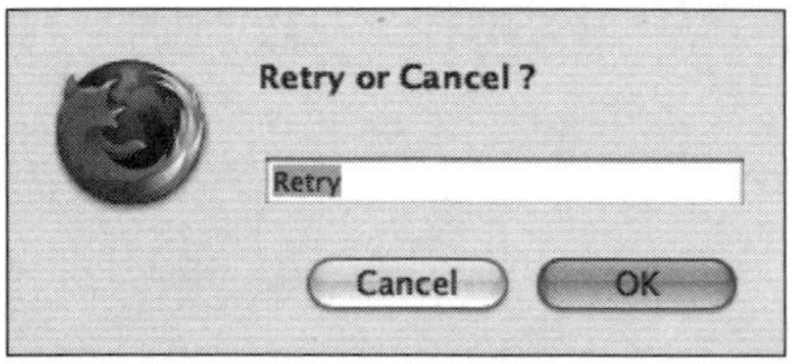

Figure 6-19. *Retry or cancel*

As with a page load timeout, you will have an opportunity to retry or cancel. Most likely, this means you forgot to tell JsUnit that your `setUpPage()` function was done. If you remembered to set the `setUpPageStatus` variable to `complete`, then you may want to look at what you are doing in your `setUpPage()` function. You may need to increase the Setup Page Timeout setting or find a way to speed up your setup work.

Figure 6-20. *Setup page timeout error*

Using Standard and Custom Query Strings

So, the test runner is pretty great, but it can get really annoying to open it and browse to your test pages or test suites day after day. Luckily, you can use certain query strings to prepopulate the file to run, have the test runner automatically run the tests, and even pass parameters to your tests!

Let's start with the basics. Say you have a test suite that you run every morning, just after you've had your morning mocha. Of course, you could always just open the test runner file, browse to your test suite, and click Run; however, if you've recently read *Pragmatic Project Automation*, by Mike Clark (Pragmatic Programmers, 2004), you'll want a way to automate this repetitive task. Luckily, the test runner supports the `testPage`[5] query string. Putting the following in your browser's address bar (adjusted for your environment, of course) will launch the test runner in your browser with the given test populated for you:

```
file:///Users/nate/projects/chapter6/web/jsunit/testRunner.html➥
?testPage=/Users/nate/projects/chapter6/web/sampleTestSuite.html
```

As if it's magic, you'll be greeted with the test runner, and the argument you passed to the `testPage` parameter will now be in the file box, as shown in Figure 6-21. Notice that you no longer have a Browse button—since you've already told the test runner what you want to run, it just gets in the way.

---

5. Interestingly, `testpage` will also work.

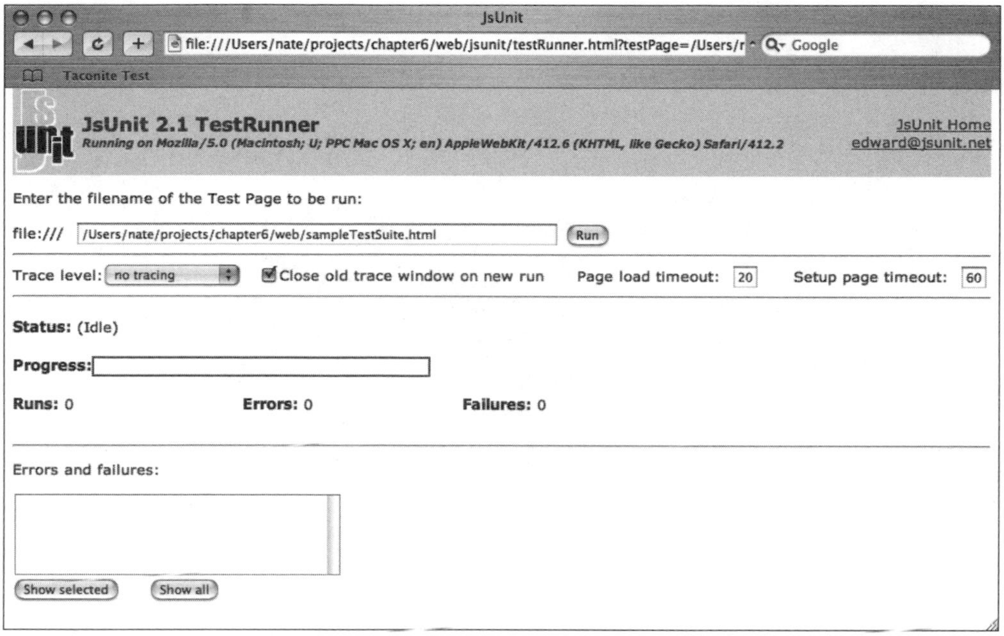

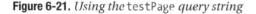

Figure 6-21. *Using the* testPage *query string*

Of course, smart developers would create bookmarks to the suites they run often. Now, if you think testPage is pretty slick, you may want to give autoRun a spin! As you might guess from the clever name, you can use autoRun[6] in conjunction with testPage to load your favorite test page or test suite and then run it automatically. A sample query string might look like this:

```
file:///Users/nate/projects/chapter6/web/jsunit/testRunner.html?testPage=➥
/Users/nate/projects/chapter6/web/testPageWithExposeTests.html&autoRun=true
```

You should now see a pretty green bar (see Figure 6-22). Note that the Run button is present. (You still can't browse to a different test suite or test page, but why would you want to do that?) Therefore, you can always rerun your tests easily. Again, efficient programmers would likely add bookmarks for this query in their target browsers.

You might think that testPage and autoRun are all any developer could ask for, but there's more! Behind the scenes, the test runner is loading each test page into a hidden frame. Most of the time this will be fine, but if you have code that just has to be run in a visible frame and you're using Internet Explorer, you can tell the test runner to show your page in a visible frame. If you incorporate showTestFrame into your query string, JsUnit will display your page in a visible frame. If you enter showTestFrame=true, the test page will display in a frame with a default height. If this default doesn't work, you can always pass an integer value and set the frame to the height of the parameter in pixels.

---

6. Guess what? autorun also works.

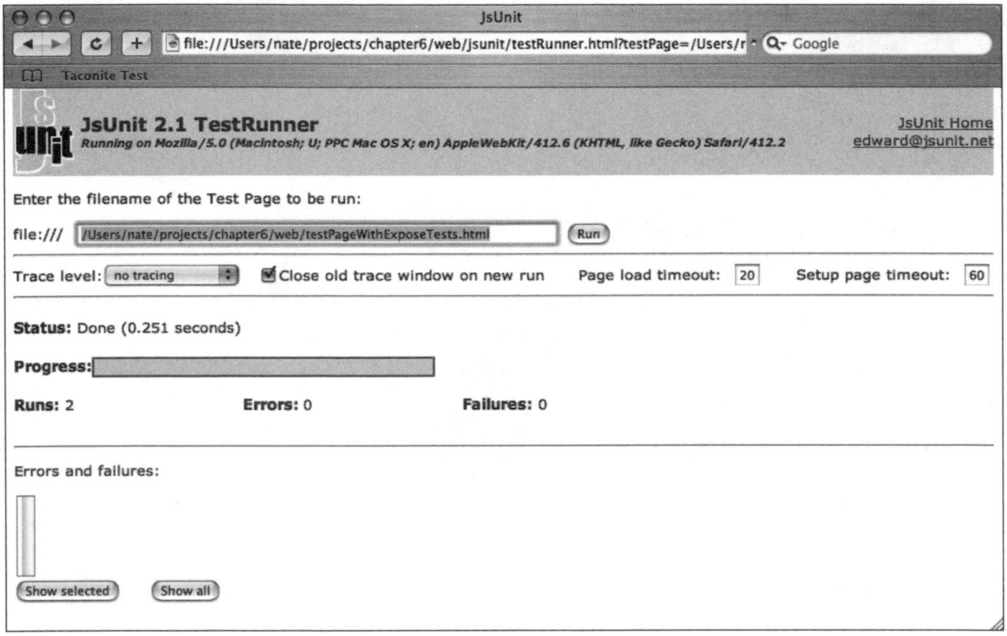

Figure 6-22. *Results of using* testPage *with* autoRun

Sometimes you may want to pass specific values to your test pages or test suites. You can add any parameter/argument pair to your query string and retrieve these values in your test page or test suite using top.jsUnitParmHash.parameterName or top.jsUnitParmHash['parameter➡ Name']. Say you open your test runner with this path: file:///Users/nate/projects/chapter6/ web/jsunit/testRunner.html?key=1. You can then access the parameter key using either top.jsUnitParmHash.key or top.jsUnitParmHash['key']. This might be useful if you want to run only certain tests—Listing 6-12 shows a contrived example.

Listing 6-12. *An Example of a Test Suite Using a Custom Query*

```
<!DOCTYPE HTML PUBLIC "-//W3C//DTD HTML 4.01 Transitional//EN">

<html>
  <head>
    <title>Sample Test Suite</title>
    <script language="JavaScript" src="jsunit/app/jsUnitCore.js"></script>
    <script language="JavaScript">

        function sampelSuite() {
            var suiteToRun = top.jsUnitParmHash.suite;
            var sampleSuite = new top.jsUnitTestSuite();
            if(suiteToRun == "other") {
                sampleSuite.addTestPage("../anotherTestPage.html");
            } else {
```

```
                sampleSuite.addTestPage("../simpleTestPage.html");
            }
            return sampleSuite;
        }

        function suite() {
            var testSuite = new top.jsUnitTestSuite();
            testSuite.addTestSuite(sampelSuite());
            testSuite.addTestPage("../setupTearDownExample.html");
            return testSuite;
        }

    </script>
  </head>
  <body>
    This is a simple test suite that uses custom queries.
  </body>
</html>
```

As you'd expect, appending ?suite=other to the path in your test runner results in
anotherTestPage.html being run and simpleTestPage.html being skipped (see Figure 6-23).
Of course, with the current flow control logic, leaving this parameter off results in just the
opposite: simpleTestPage.html will be run, and anotherTestPage.html will be skipped.

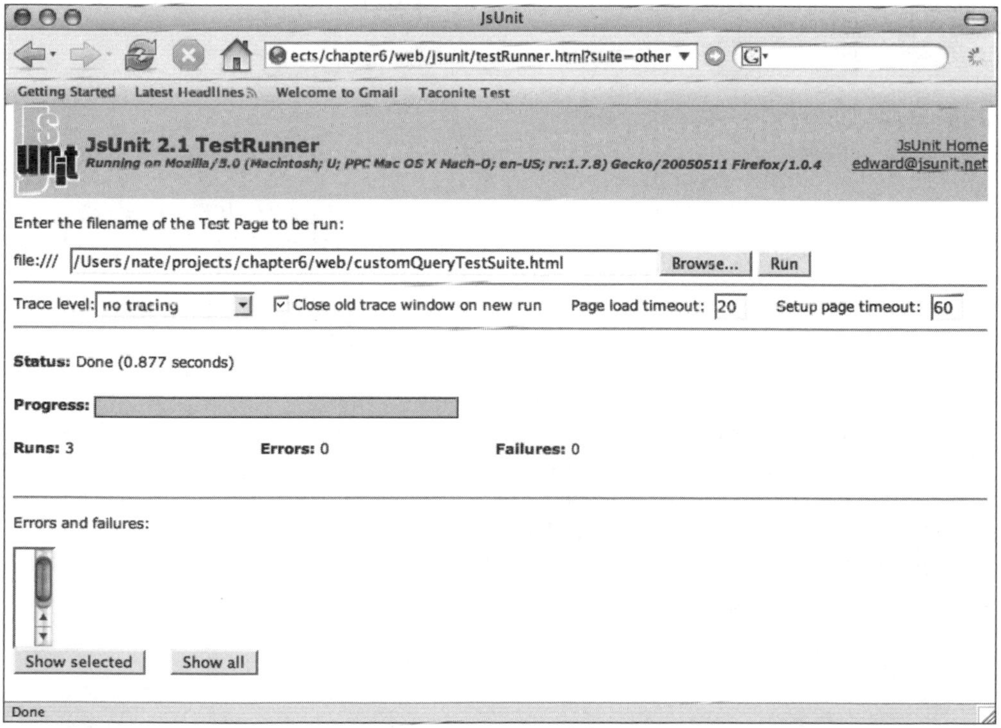

Figure 6-23. *Running a test suite with a custom query parameter*

While this is obviously a simple example, you can probably see how using custom parameters can be useful in running test suites or test pages under various circumstances. Of course, you'll probably want to add those special query strings to your browser's bookmark folder for ease of use later.

Another interesting standard parameter is debug. Don't confuse this parameter with the debug trace level—they aren't the same. The debug parameter is for those doing development work on JsUnit. You probably won't do much with this query string, but it's there should your curiosity be piqued (see Figure 6-24).

```
⊖ ⊖ ⊖                    about:blank
enter window.jsUnitTestManager._nextPage()
enter window.jsUnitTestManager._currentSuite()
exit window.jsUnitTestManager._currentSuite()==[jsUnitTestSuite]
enter window.jsUnitTestSuite.hasMorePages()
exit window.jsUnitTestSuite.hasMorePages()==true
enter window.jsUnitTestManager._currentSuite()
exit window.jsUnitTestManager._currentSuite()==[jsUnitTestSuite]
enter window.jsUnitTestSuite.nextPage()
exit
window.jsUnitTestSuite.nextPage()=="file:////Users/nate/projects/chapter6/web/a
enter
window.jsUnitTestManager.loadPage("file:////Users/nate/projects/chapter6/web/ar
enter window.jsUnitTestManager.setStatus("Opening Test Page
"file:////Users/nate/projects/chapter6/web/anotherTestPage.html"")
enter window.jsUnitTestManager._setTextOnLayer("mainStatus", "Status:
Opening Test Page
"file:////Users/nate/projects/chapter6/web/anotherTestPage.html"")
exit window.jsUnitTestManager._setTextOnLayer("mainStatus", "Status:
Opening Test Page
"file:////Users/nate/projects/chapter6/web/anotherTestPage.html"")==null
```

Figure 6-24. *Output from the* debug *query*

Two other standard parameters make sense only in relation to the JsUnit Server: submitResults and resultId. They'll make more sense when we cover the JsUnit Server in just a minute, but adding submitResults=true to your test runner's browser path will tell JsUnit to send the results of the test to JsUnit's "acceptor" servlet. What does that buy you? Well, we're spoiling the surprise, but using this parameter causes the results of the test run to create an XML representation (with the same structure as JUnit's XML output) of the results that can be retrieved later.

The resultId query makes sense only when used with submitResults=true. Based on what little we've told you about how the JsUnit Server works, you might have guessed that each test run that is submitted to the JsUnit Server has some kind of unique identifier. You can let JsUnit come up with its own ID, but if you absolutely must use your favorite number, you can do so by passing it via the resultId parameter.

Working with JsUnit Server

Although passing various parameters to the test runner can make it easier to automate tests, you may soon tire of manually running your tests on a regular basis, especially when you factor in multiple browsers on multiple operating systems. You may also want to keep track of the results of previous runs for auditing or quality assurance purposes. The JsUnit Server seeks to address these issues by providing XML logging of test results, running tests from JUnit or Ant scripts, and running tests from JUnit or Ant on remote machines.

JsUnit Server lets you run your entire test suite on your operating system/browser combinations at the press of a button. In addition, in an important step, you can make testing your JavaScript part of your build process by adding it to your Ant script. The JsUnit Server consists of a set of Java servlets that run inside the embeddable Jetty open-source Web server, saving you the hassle of installing and configuring a Web server/servlet container on every machine on which you want to test. Once you've configured it, the process really is as simple as pushing a button!

Configuring the Server

Before you can take advantage of the JsUnit Server, you need to configure it. You can accomplish this by modifying the `build.xml` file found in the `jsunit` folder. At the head of this file, you'll find a set of properties that you can modify to fit your needs. Most of these variables are self-explanatory—see Table 6-2 for the details.

Table 6-2. *Server Configurations*

Environment Variable	Contents
browserFileNames	A comma-separated list of the full paths to the executables of the browsers you want to test.
url	The URL to the test runner, including the appropriate query string to auto-run the appropriate test suite.
port	The port the JsUnit Server is running on; omitting this variable results in port 8080 being used.
resourceBase	Defines the document root of the JsUnit Server. A blank value (the typical setting) results in the `jsunit` installation directory.
logsdirectory	The directory where the results of running tests will be written. A blank value defaults to `jsunit/logs`.
remoteMachineURLs	A comma-separated list of the URLs of any remote machines on which you want to run tests. These remote machines require a configured installation of the JsUnit Server.

Once you're configured for the test suite (or test page, for that matter) and browser combinations, you simply run the `standalone_test` target. In the NetBeans development environment, this will look like Figure 6-25.

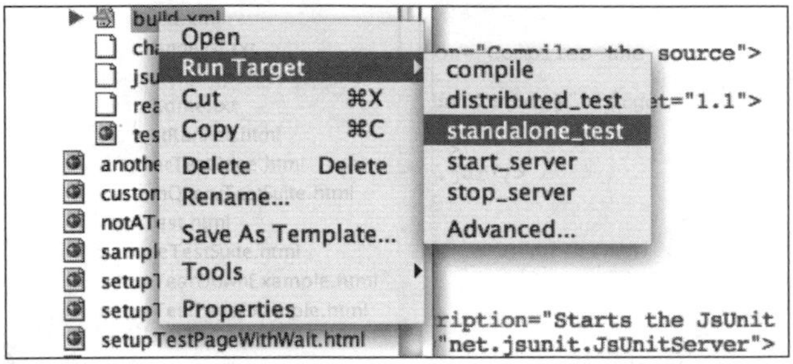

Figure 6-25. *Running the* standalone_test *target from NetBeans*

Running this target results in the Jetty server being started on the port you specified. Once the server is running, the browsers you specified will launch, and the tests you configured will run. Of course, you don't have to pay attention to the outcome—if a failure or error occurs, it will be displayed in the output from your Ant task, and it will say the task failed.

```
--------------------
testPageWithError.html:testValidArgs had an error:
Error message is: "TypeError: document.getElementById("arg1") has no properties"
Stack trace follows:
addNumbers()@file:////Users/nate/projects/chapter6/web/testPageWithError.html:21
 testValidArgs()@file:////Users/nate/projects/chapter6/web/testPageWithError.html:16
 ("testValidArgs")@file:///Users/nate/projects/chapter6/web/jsunit/
 app/jsUnitTestManager.js:359
 ("testValidArgs")@file:///Users/nate/projects/chapter6/web/jsunit/
 app/jsUnitTestManager.js:359 ()@file:///Users/nate/projects/chapter6/web/jsunit/
 app/jsUnitTestManager.js:166 ("file:////Users/nate/projects/chapter6/web/
 testPageWithError.html")
@file:///Users/nate/projects/chapter6/web/jsunit/app/jsUnitTestManager.js:104
()@file:///Users/nate/projects/chapter6/web/jsunit/app/jsUnitTestManager.js:338
@file:///Users/nate/projects/chapter6/web/jsunit/app/jsUnitTestManager.js:335
--------------------
```

Assuming you added submitResults=true to your query string, you can also check the log file to verify the results. The logs are in the same XML format as JUnit results, so you can easily manipulate them with the same transformations you're already using with your automated JUnit suites. You can always inspect the XML files directly or use JsUnit's built-in "displayer" servlet.

To use the "displayer" servlet, first make sure the JsUnit Server is running. If it's not, simply fire the start_server target. Once it's running, open your favorite browser, and point it to localhost:8080/jsunit/displayer?id=XXX where XXX is the ID of the results log you want to see. You'll see the results of the test run, as shown in Figure 6-26.

Figure 6-26. *Viewing the results of a test run*

Running Tests on Remote Machines

If you want to run your test suite on distributed machines, you need to use the `distributed_test` Ant task. Of course, you'll have to configure a JsUnit Server on each remote machine you want to use and also configure the appropriate tests and browsers. Firing the `distributed_test` Ant task invokes a JUnit test (`net.jsunit.DistributedTest`) that will in turn call a servlet on each remote machine supplied in the configuration. This servlet runs the same JUnit-based test that is triggered when you are simply running locally (`net.jsunit.StandaloneTest`). The tests are then run on the browsers that were configured on the remote machines with the results sent to the originator.

Getting Help

We've really only scratched the surface of JsUnit in this chapter, so we won't be hurt if you feel the need to look elsewhere for additional information. Of course, the first place to stop (indeed, where much of the information for this chapter came from) is the JsUnit Web site at www.edwardh.com/jsunit/. If you have specific questions, you can always e-mail the creator of JsUnit, Edward Hieatt, or you can join the group at groups.yahoo.com/group/jsunit/. You won't get flooded with e-mails—the list averaged fewer than ten e-mails a month in 2005. Still, this can be an excellent resource for common questions. If you find any bugs, you can submit them to the SourceForge bug tracker at https://sourceforge.net/tracker/?group_id=28041&atid=391976. Beyond that, give Google a spin to see what you can find.

What Else Can You Use?

Don't get us wrong—we love JsUnit, but you may want to consider some other options. The sharp folks at ThoughtWorks have released a test tool for Web applications called Selenium.[7] Selenium was developed to test an internal ThoughtWorks browser-based application, but they were kind enough to donate the code to the open-source world so the rest of us could take advantage of it. Selenium runs in all the major browsers and can be used on the common operating systems. Like JsUnit, Selenium tests run right in the browser, which makes them excellent for testing system functionality and browser compatibility. For more information, see `selenium.thoughtworks.com/index.html`.

If you are using Java on your server side, you have a handful of other options. HttpUnit is written in Java and allows you to emulate the browser. With HttpUnit, you can simulate submitting a form, test the pages returned by requests, and check rudimentary JavaScript. Typically, you would combine HttpUnit with JUnit. HtmlUnit is similar to HttpUnit except it chooses to model the pages instead of the requests and responses of HttpUnit. HtmlUnit simulates the browser and works in conjunction with JUnit. One interesting feature of HttpUnit is its ability to emulate specific browsers, thereby allowing you to test any browser-specific logic you may have.

Building upon HttpUnit is the Java-based jWebUnit. Essentially, jWebUnit greatly simplifies navigation rules and provides some ready-made assertions. Once again, you would use this tool with JUnit. Moving beyond JUnit is the acceptance-testing framework FitNesse, written by some folks at Object Mentor. What makes FitNesse unique is that your customers can use it to define what your application should do. You (or your customer!) create tables of inputs and expected outcomes that are then run against your application. Like you would expect, successful tests are green, and failures are red. FitNesse is meant to be a complement to *x*Unit-based tests—using Object Mentor's pithy language, *x*Unit makes sure you built the code right, while FitNesse makes sure you built the right code!

The moral of this short section is that you have a number of options in the testing arena. While we've highlighted free tools, proprietary options also exist, of course. At the end of the day, we recommend a blended approach that takes advantage of the various strengths of all these tools. Experiment with what we've touched on here, and search the Web for options that we didn't cover—you'll soon settle on the right approach for your team.

Summary

If you're going to do Ajax, you're going to use JavaScript. While tools and frameworks will certainly ease the pain of development, testing is still an important piece of the puzzle. Many of you have become "test infected" when it comes to your server-side code—now you have no excuse not to extend that approach to your JavaScript. We hope this brief introduction to JsUnit gives you the background you need to start using it on your team. Not only will it make your job as a developer easier, the quality of your code is bound to improve.

---

7. What's in a name? An old wives' tale says the element Selenium cures mercury poisoning.

CHAPTER 7

Exploring JavaScript Debugging Tools and Techniques

"There's no compiler to catch errors! There's no good IDE with productivity tools such as code completion! There's no good debugging environment!"

These are just a sampling of the myriad of excuses people have for avoiding JavaScript development. Ever since the browser wars of the late 1990s, JavaScript has had a reputation as being an error-prone, difficult development language. This reputation is based largely on the early, bugged-riddled versions of JavaScript that ran in the early, bugged-riddled editions of Netscape Navigator and Internet Explorer. To make matters worse, JavaScript was often written by nonprogrammers who got JavaScript to work by trying everything until something seemed to work. Freely available scripts were also available on the Web, and many of these scripts were rather poor quality, further perpetuating JavaScript's reputation as a substandard programming environment.

Today's JavaScript implementations are vastly superior to those found just a few years ago. Thanks to JavaScript syntax and behavior being standardized by the ECMA, a stable JavaScript version, and better implementation by Web browsers, programming in JavaScript is a much more enjoyable endeavor. In addition, tools such as full-fledged debugging environments, Ajax-specific debugging tools, and JavaScript error consoles provide developers with many more development tool options.

Some of the issues still remain; for example, at the time of this writing, no useful JavaScript IDE, which offers productivity tools such as code completion, exists. In addition, JavaScript is still often written by those who have no background in programming. However, more tools are available today that greatly reduce the amount of pain associated with JavaScript development and, by extension, Ajax development.

In this chapter, you'll explore some of the tools you can use when things go wrong and don't work as expected, also known as *debugging*. Having tools available to help you diagnose problems is half the battle. Once you've mastered these tools, debugging is actually kind of fun!

Debugging Ajax Requests with Greasemonkey

Ajax requests greatly enhance the user experience because they occur in the background without freezing the browser or otherwise indicating that a request to the server is taking place. The bad side effect of this behavior is that the page is more difficult to debug. Assuming that a problem with the Ajax request or response exists, it's difficult for the developer to know where the request failed. Did the server fail to read the request properly? Did the browser fail to handle the server's response correctly? Was a request to the server actually made in the first place?

Thanks to the Firefox extension Greasemonkey and an associated user script, debugging Ajax requests has become a whole lot easier.

Introducing Greasemonkey

Greasemonkey is a Firefox extension that allows you to add bits of JavaScript, known as *user scripts*, to any Web page to change its behavior. Greasemonkey is similar to other Firefox extensions that, for example, allow you to change a page's CSS style rules. Greasemonkey is really just a proxy for the user scripts that are responsible for doing the real work; you can easily download and install it from its home page at `greasemonkey.mozdev.org`.

Using an XMLHttpRequest Debugging User Script for Greasemonkey

XMLHttpRequest Debugging is a Greasemonkey user script written by Julien Couvreur. This script is an Ajax debugging console that conveniently displays every Ajax request and its associated response.

To install the XMLHttpRequest Debugging user script, first ensure that you have already successfully installed Greasemonkey for Firefox. Next, point Firefox to `blog.monstuff.com/ archives/images/XMLHttpRequestDebugging.v1.0.user.js`. This is the JavaScript file that makes up the user script. Select Tools ➤ Install User Script from Firefox's menu bar. When you install the script, be sure to enter the domain at which you want to perform the Ajax debugging in the Included Pages box. If you don't set the domain correctly, then the user script won't start properly when you want to perform Ajax debugging. You can also open this window later using Firefox's Tools ➤ Manage User Scripts menu item.

Inspecting Ajax Requests and Responses with the XMLHttpRequest Debugging User Script

Now that the user script is installed, point your browser to the page with Ajax requests you want to debug. Immediately, the XMLHttpRequest Debugging window should open. Click the "help" link at the top of the window to display the script's help module (see Figure 7-1). You can move the XMLHttpRequest Debugging window around the page by clicking its header and dragging it to the desired place. Toggle the help contents off by clicking the "help" link again.

With the XMLHttpRequest Debugging window now open, you can proceed by initiating an Ajax request. Upon initiating the request, the window will refresh itself with information pertaining to the Ajax request and the subsequent response.

XMLHttpRequest Debugging relays information about both the request and the response. The first line in the information window indicates the method of the request, such as GET or POST. The next line details the URL along with the query string that made up the request. Inspect this line carefully if you're sending request parameters as part of the query string, as you'll easily notice any errors here.

XMLHttpRequest Debugging allows you to view the body of the request by clicking the "body" link. The body of the request is usually NULL unless a string or XML document was passed as a parameter to the XMLHttpRequest object's send() method.

The bottom half of the request information window details the server response. Clicking the "headers" link shows all the response headers sent by the server. The entire contents of the server response are displayed when the "response" link is clicked. Finally, the text of the callback method called by XMLHttpRequest when the response completes is displayed by clicking the "callback" link. If that window is too small, the entire contents of both the request and response information sections can be exported to a larger browser window at any time by clicking the "export" link. Figure 7-2 shows the XMLHttpRequest Debugging window displaying the request and response values and the XMLHttpRequest object's callback function.

Figure 7-1. *The XMLHttpRequest Debugging window's help contents*

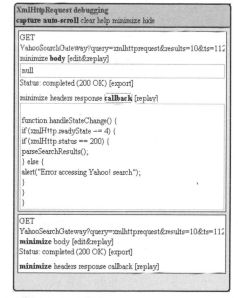

Figure 7-2. *Displaying the request and response (left) and the XMLHttpRequest object's callback function (right)*

A powerful aspect of XMLHttpRequest Debugging is that it allows you to create a new Ajax request based on a previous request. Click the "edit&replay" link to open the window, as shown in Figure 7-3. Here you'll see the data listed from the request from which you started, but now all the fields are editable. You can change the request method, update the URL, add some request headers, and even add a string of data or XML that is sent along as part of the request body. Click the "send" link to send the newly created request. This particular tool is powerful when you want to experiment with different request types and data without having to manually update the script, deploy it to the Web server, and repeat the test.

The Greasemonkey extension for the Firefox browser, combined with the XMLHttpRequest Debugging user script, is a powerful tool for Ajax debugging and development. It can help trace exactly what is happening in the browser, and if something goes wrong, you'll have the information you need to quickly debug the problem. It can help isolate whether a problem exists in the browser-side client script or in the server-side code that services the request.

Figure 7-3. *A request from the previous example was changed to use the* POST *method, and the query string was moved from the URL to the request body.*

Debugging JavaScript

Sooner or later during your Ajax development you're going to have some bugs in JavaScript code. Some of the bugs will be easy to find because they're syntactic in nature. Others will be more difficult to find because they're subtle errors in business logic. That's when a debugger tool comes in handy so you can step through the code, line by line, and verify that the scripts are flowing as expected and that the variables have the correct values.

You can use three tools to help you debug JavaScript:

Firefox JavaScript Console: Firefox JavaScript Console records all errors and warnings that occur within JavaScript. It's easy to use, and you can quickly diagnose most errors using the JavaScript Console, without resorting to a full-fledged debugging environment.

Microsoft Script Debugger: This tool integrates with Internet Explorer and provides basic debugging facilities such as the ability to set breakpoints and the ability to inspect and modify the values of variables during runtime. It's a relatively primitive tool, although it may fit nicely in situations where many Internet Explorer–specific behaviors are used or where the debugging errors occur only in Internet Explorer.

Venkman: This is a powerful JavaScript debugger available as an extension to Mozilla-based browsers such as Firefox. Venkman is a fully featured environment with excellent support for breakpoints and object inspection. Thanks to Firefox's excellent commitment to adhering to Web standards, you can be sure that if a script works in Firefox, it will work in any other standards-compliant browser.

Because debugging can be a potentially large part of the development process, we'll cover all these tools and show what they are (and aren't) capable of doing.

Using Firefox JavaScript Console

As an interpreted language, JavaScript lacks a compiler that can catch minor mistakes such as missing quotation marks or out-of-place curly braces. Tools such as JSLint can help, but they will miss plenty of errors.

Often these errors don't manifest themselves until the script is executed within the browser. A common complaint regarding JavaScript development is that browsers don't give descriptive error messages when JavaScript errors occur.

Firefox has a great tool called JavaScript Console, which is available under the Tools menu. Any JavaScript error is logged to the JavaScript Console, which describes the error and the location of the source file in which the error occurred.

Figure 7-4 displays the JavaScript Console showing a variety of errors. The first error is a string literal that is lacking a matching quotation mark at the end of the string literal. Note how JavaScript Console describes the error, indicates the location of the error (line 11), and even points to the unmatched quotation mark. The second error arises from an instance where a nonexistent property of an object was referenced.

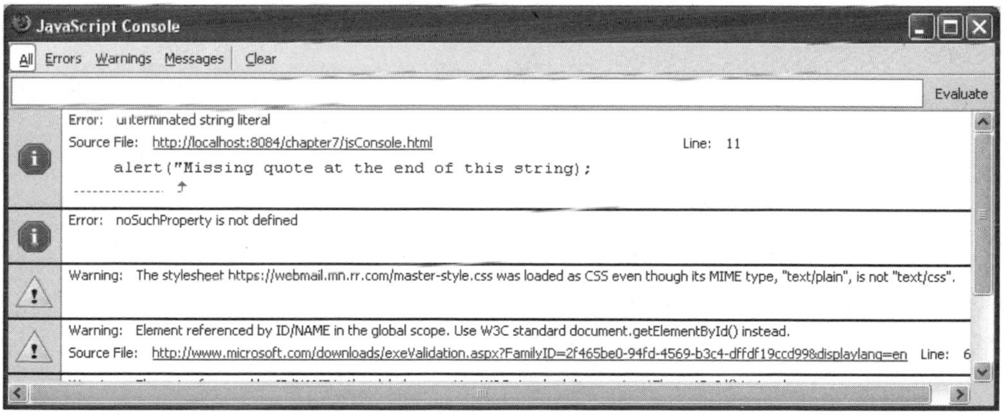

Figure 7-4. *Firefox's JavaScript Console describes the error and its location in the source file.*

The last two items in Figure 7-4 are informational warnings. These are instances in which something is technically not correct but from which Firefox can still recover. The first informational message describes a style sheet whose MIME type was sent as text/plain instead of text/css as it should be. You can correct this error by ensuring that the server supplying the page correctly sets the MIME type for CSS files to text/plain. The message shown in Figure 7-4 hints to the developer that the W3C standard of referencing an object should be used instead of a proprietary method.

Using Microsoft Script Debugger

The Microsoft Script Debugger[1] is an extension to Internet Explorer 4 (or greater) that can be used to debug both client-side scripts and server-side scripts running on Microsoft IIS. In this section, we'll focus on its client-side debugging abilities.

Installing Script Debugger is as easy as downloading and running the installation program. Once that is complete, you need to ensure that Internet Explorer has debugging enabled. To do so, open the Internet Options window available via the Tools ➤ Internet Options menu. On the Advanced tab, under the Browsing submenu, ensure that the Disable Script Debugging item is unchecked, as shown in Figure 7-5.

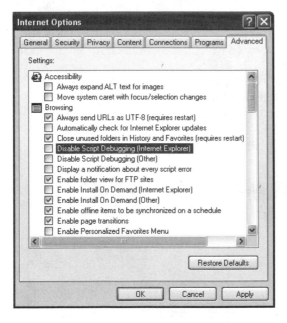

Figure 7-5. *Enabling debugging in Script Debugger*

Restart Internet Explorer, and under the View menu there should now be a Script Debugger menu item.

Script Debugger is now ready for use. Navigate to a Web page that has some JavaScript you'd like to debug. To open Script Debugger, choose the View ➤ Script Debugger ➤ Open menu item. Script Debugger should open showing the code for the HTML page you're currently viewing, as shown in Figure 7-6.

---

1. Available at http://www.microsoft.com/downloads/details.aspx?familyid=2f465be0-94fd-4569-➡ b3c4-dffdf19ccd99&displaylang=en

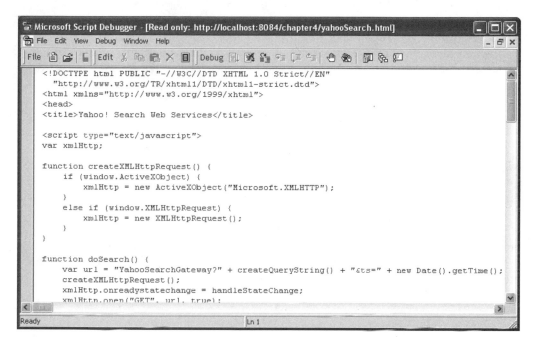

Figure 7-6. *Microsoft Script Debugger displaying the current HTML page*

The active HTML page opens in read-only mode. In other words, you can search through the document, but you are unable to make changes to the document. The page shows the entire contents of the HTML file including any embedded scripts. You can open scripts that are not embedded directly in the HTML but are included as a separate .js file by using the Running Documents window (available via the View ➤ Running Documents menu), as shown in Figure 7-7.

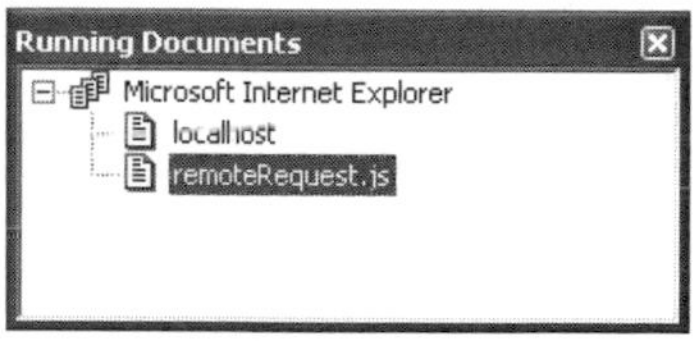

With the current document open, you can now start debugging. Select a line on which you'd like to set a breakpoint. Place the cursor on the desired line, and then press F9 or click the Toggle Breakpoint button on the menu bar. The line should become highlighted, with a dot appearing in the left gutter of the window.

Start the debugging sequence by performing the action on the page that causes the script to be run. The script should pause during execution when the selected breakpoint is encountered.

The script is now stopped, but what can you do

Figure 7-7. *Finding the current Web page and any included script files in the Running Documents window*

with it? The first simple task is to view the call stack. Click the Call Stack window on the menu bar to view the course of execution of the nested function calls. Double-clicking each item in the Call Stack list will bring you to that function call. If multiple threads are running, then each will have its own call stack.

The most useful feature of Script Debugger is the ability to view and modify variable values at runtime. The Command Window is the portal for inspecting and modifying variable values with Script Debugger. Open the Command Window by clicking the menu bar button or by selecting the View ➤ Command Window menu item.

The Command Window interface is entirely text based. It has no list of available objects to inspect or collapsible list of the object's properties under each object. You must know the name of the variable you want to inspect; it could be a JavaScript object, an object property, or the property of some item that appears on the page. To view the variable value, simply type the variable name in the Command Window, and hit the Enter key. The variable's value should display on the following line.

The process for updating the variable's value is similar to viewing its value. To update the variable's value, type the variable name followed by an equals sign, followed by the desired new value. If the value is a string, then you must enclose it within quotation marks. You can also set values to other objects by simply following the equals sign with the object variable name.

Figure 7-8 shows an instance of inspecting a variable value and then changing it. First we entered the variable name, queryString, into the Command Window, and pressed the Enter button, which displays the value of queryString on the following line. Next, we entered a line assigning a new value for queryString, with the new value being echoed after we pressed the Enter button. Finally, we inspected the value of queryString again to ensure that the new value was correctly set.

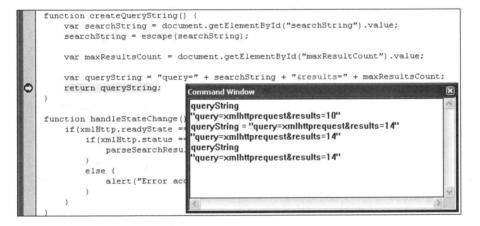

Figure 7-8. *Inspecting and modifying variable values using the Command Window*

After inspecting and possibly modifying variable values, you can continue stepping through the script, line by line. The F8 key or Step Into toolbar button will step into the next line of code, stepping into any functions that are called; the Shift+F8 key or Step Over toolbar button will execute the next line of code without stepping into any called functions. The F5 key or Run button will run the rest of the script, stopping only when another breakpoint is encountered or the script completes.

Microsoft Script Debugger is a simple but useful tool for debugging client-side scripts. Because of the primitive interface of the Command Window, the Script Debugger is probably best left for those working in an all–Internet Explorer environment or even those who are using VBScript instead of JavaScript. Still, it's another tool in the developer's toolbox that can provide a significant amount of help when needed.

Using Venkman

Venkman is the code name for the JavaScript debugging environment available for Mozilla-based browsers such as Firefox. Venkman is available as an extension for these browsers; you can install it from www.hacksrus.com/~ginda/venkman/. Venkman development started in April 2001 by Robert Ginda. Venkman is based on the Mozilla JavaScript debugging API known as js/jsd. The js/jsd API formed the basis of the Netscape JavaScript Debugger 1.1 that was available for the 4.*x* series of Netscape browsers.

Once you've installed it, you can start Venkman from the Tools ➤ JavaScript Debugger menu item on Firefox's main menu bar. Figure 7-9 shows the default layout for Venkman.

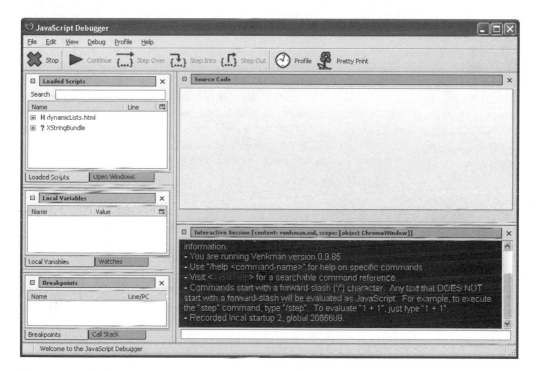

Figure 7-9. *Default window layout of Venkman*

Venkman offers a plethora of information that is divided into eight windows. The default layout consists of a large pane showing the selected source code. Smaller windows are arranged vertically on the left side of the window. Venkman's command-line interface resides on the bottom of the window under the Source Code pane.

You can drag each pane with the mouse and dock them at other locations within the main window. You can also add each pane as a separate tab to an existing pane. For example, to make the Loaded Scripts tab be a tab within the Local Variables pane, simply drag and drop the Loaded Scripts tab to the Local Variables tab. You can also undock the small window panes from the main window by clicking the docking button located on the left side of the pane's title bar, as shown in Figure 7-10. Docking the pane back to the main window is as easy as clicking the docking button again.

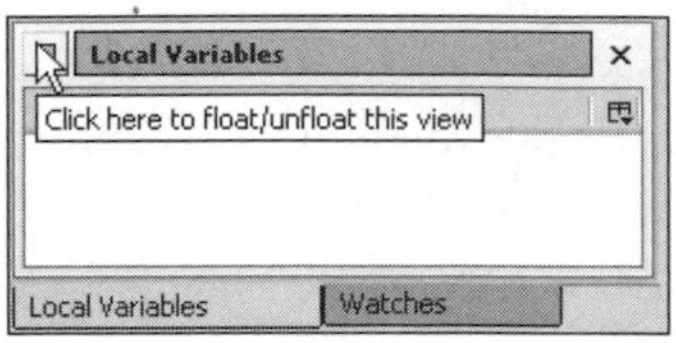

Figure 7-10. *Docking the various panes using the docking button*

As you work with Venkman, you'll get a feel for the windows that you use most often. Close the windows you don't often use by clicking the *X* button on the right side of the window's title bar. You can reopen windows by selecting the View ➤ Show/Hide menu item. If at any time you want to return the window layout to the default setting, simply use `/restore-layout factory` at the command-line interface.

Viewing Loaded Scripts

When Venkman is open, it recognizes all the JavaScript that is available to the page currently open in the browser window. Venkman recognizes JavaScript that is embedded within the HTML page using `<script>` tags and also recognizes external JavaScript files that are included in the HTML page using `<script src="js_file.js">` tags.

Venkman displays the currently available JavaScript in the Loaded Scripts window. Clicking the plus sign next to each file opens a list under the file that details all the available JavaScript functions within that file along with the line number at which the function occurs within the file and optionally the number of lines of code the function encompasses, as shown in Figure 7-11. Double-clicking a file within the Loaded Scripts window opens the file in the Source Code window and also scrolls directly to the function within the Source Code window.

Right-clicking a file in the Loaded Scripts window displays a number of options for both the file itself and the JavaScript functions contained within the file, as shown in Figure 7-12. For the file, this pop-up menu allows you to performs tasks such as disabling the debugging of eval and timeout statements, disabling the debugging of contained functions, and disabling the performance monitoring of contained functions. For individual functions, the context menu provides facilities for disabling the debugging and performance profiling.

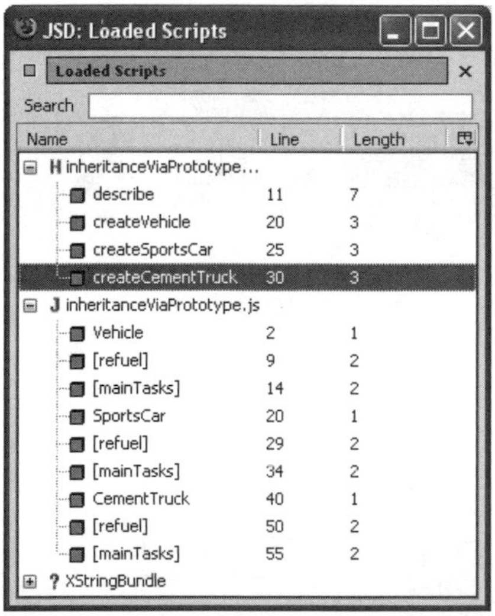

Figure 7-11. *The Loaded Scripts window displays all the scripts available within the current browser window.*

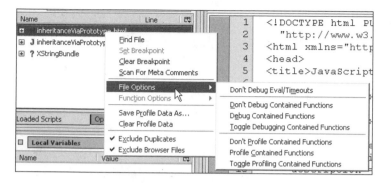

Figure 7-12. *Context menu items for a file that contains JavaScript*

Source Code

The Source Code window lists the source code for the currently open file. The file could be an HTML file, XHTML file, or JavaScript file. The Source Code window implements a tabbed theme so multiple files can be open at the same time, with each file residing in its own tab. The code has some simple colorization that improves readability. JavaScript keywords such as `function` and `var` have bold formatting, while string literals have a different colored font. On the left side of the window is the line numbering for the file. The far-left side of the Source Code window is the gutter on which debugging breakpoints can be set.

Breakpoints, Part 1

Breakpoints are the feature that really make debuggers useful. They allow you to suspend the execution of code at a point of your choosing, giving you the opportunity to inspect various variables and properties to determine the cause of bugs. Venkman supports two kinds of breakpoints: *hard* breakpoints and *future* breakpoints. This is a departure from most debugging environments, so we'll discuss the difference between the two.

A hard breakpoint is the type of breakpoint you're used to seeing in modern programming languages such as Java. It instructs Venkman to suspend processing at the breakpoint. Execution cannot continue until the user instructs it to do so. In Venkman, a hard breakpoint always exists *within the body of a function*.

A future breakpoint is similar to a hard breakpoint in that it instructs Venkman to suspend execution of the JavaScript at the breakpoint. The difference between the two is that a future breakpoint is set on lines that *do not exist within the body of a function*. These lines of code are executed as soon as they are loaded by the browser. In contrast, code that resides within the body of a function is not executed until the function is executed in response to some action or event.

Figure 7-13 shows an example page loaded with JavaScript code that has two breakpoints. The embedded JavaScript code has both a function that contains code and code that exists outside a function body. The code within the function has a hard breakpoint, and the code outside the function has a future breakpoint.

```
 8   <script type="text/javaScript">
 9
10   //The following line of code is a candidate for a Future breakpoint
11   var dateString = new Date().toString();
12
13   //Code within the body of a function can use Hard breakpoint
14   function doFoo() {
15       var x = 2 + 2;
16       var y = "hello";
17   }
18   </script>
```

Figure 7-13. *Hard and future breakpoints within the Source Code window for* breakpoints.html

To set a breakpoint on the desired lines, click in the gutter on the left side of the desired line of code. Each time you click the line, the line will cycle through one of three breakpoint settings: none, hard breakpoint, and future breakpoint. A hard breakpoint is denoted by a red *B*, and a future breakpoint is denoted by an orange *F*. Lines of code that exist outside the body of a function will cycle only through no breakpoints and future breakpoints; code within a function body will cycle through no breakpoints, hard breakpoints, and future breakpoints.

With breakpoints now set, you can try initiating an action that will cause a breakpoint to be encountered. The breakpoints.html page has a single button. Clicking the button calls the doFoo method, which does nothing more than create a couple of variables. When the doFoo button is clicked in the browser window, the doFoo method is called, and the breakpoint on line 15 is encountered. When this breakpoint is encountered, the execution of the JavaScript suspends until further notice. The Venkman window opens in front of the browser window, and the breakpoint is now highlighted, as shown in Figure 7-14.

```
 8   <script type="text/javaScript">
 9
10   //The following line of code is a candidate for a Future breakpoint
11   var dateString = new Date().toString();
12
13   //Code within the body of a function can use Hard breakpoint
14   function doFoo() {
15       var x = 2 + 2;
16       var y = "hello";
17   }
18   </script>
```

Figure 7-14. *Encountered breakpoints are highlighted within Venkman's Source Code window.*

Now that execution has been suspended, you're free to perform tasks such as inspecting variable values and viewing the call stack to determine the exact order of execution.

So far, the hard breakpoint has probably worked exactly as you expected it to work. Now, how about the future breakpoint? How can you suspend execution at the future breakpoint since there is no action or event that you control that causes its execution?

Recall that JavaScript code that exists outside the body of a function is executed as soon as the page is loaded. So, to encounter the breakpoint at line 11, you need to switch to the browser window and click the Reload button. Doing so will reload the page and suspend execution of the code at line 11. When the future breakpoint is encountered, the orange *F* icon will change to a red *B* icon, as shown in Figure 7-15.

```
 8    <script type="text/javaScript">
 9
10    //The following line of code is a candidate for a Future breakpoint
11    var dateString = new Date().toString();
12
13    //Code within the body of a function can use Hard breakpoint
14    function doFoo() {
15        var x = 2 + 2;
16        var y = "hello";
17    }
18    </script>
```

Figure 7-15. *Reloading a page with a future breakpoint set will cause the future breakpoint to be encountered and execution of the script to be suspended.*

Venkman provides a window that lists all the currently set breakpoints. This can come in handy when you're debugging a page that has multiple breakpoints set in multiple files. For example, you may be debugging an HTML page that contains embedded JavaScript written especially for that page, an included JavaScript file that represents a library of JavaScript functions maintained by your organization, and an included JavaScript file that is provided by a third-party vendor or open-source project. Each file in which a breakpoint is set is listed in the Breakpoints window, and listed under each file are all that file's breakpoints, as shown in Figure 7-16.

Name	Line/PC
F breakpoints.html	11
⊞ ● breakpoints.html	15
● doFoo	[0]
⊞ ● yahooSearch.html#	20
● doSearch	[0]
⊞ ● yahooSearch.html#	29
● createQueryString	[20]
⊞ ● yahooSearch.html#	49
● parseSearchResults	[0]

JSD: Breakpoints / **Breakpoints**

Figure 7-16. *Venkman's Breakpoints window lists all breakpoints by file.*

Stepping Through Code

With breakpoints set, you're now ready to start actually debugging code. Venkman will automatically suspend execution once a breakpoint is encountered. At that point you're in control of the script's execution. You can inspect variable values, modify variable values, and continue the script execution, either by looking at one step at a time or by restarting execution and letting it run to completion.

Venkman offers developers a few options for stepping through code once a breakpoint has been encountered. Once a breakpoint has been encountered, you can choose Continue, Step Over, Step Into, or Step Out, as shown in Figure 7-17.

Figure 7-17. *Venkman's toolbar offers several options for stepping through scripts.*

The Continue option restarts script execution. Execution will not end until either another breakpoint is encountered or the script completes. The Continue option is useful when you need to track down the location of a problem. You can set breakpoints at points along the execution chain and, each time a breakpoint is encountered, inspect variable values to see whether the problem has cropped up yet. Once the problem appears, you know the error occurred somewhere between the current breakpoint and the previous breakpoint, and you can narrow it down further from there. The Continue option is also useful when debugging an iteration. You can set a breakpoint at one point within the iteration and use the Continue option to speed through the iterated code, checking every time that execution suspends whether any problems have occurred.

The Step Over function is useful when you want to avoid stepping through a function that is called by the current function. The called function may be a function that has been extensively debugged and you *just know* the problem isn't there, or you may just want to avoid stepping through its code because you're concerned about the current function only. Keep in mind that stepping over a function does not prevent it from being executed; it merely means you're not going to step through it line by line. Instead, the function will be executed as if it were one statement.

The Step Into option is the opposite of the Step Over function. Step Into will step into a called function so you can debug the called function. Step Over and Step Into work well together when you're trying to track down the exact location of an error. Consider the situation where you're debugging the function sendAjaxRequest. This function contains several lines of logic itself, and in addition sendAjaxRequest calls createXmlHttp. The first time you step through sendAjaxRequest, carefully step over each line and watch for when the error first manifests itself. When you encounter the breakpoint for createXmlHttp, use Step Over to quickly execute createXmlHttp without stepping through it line by line. After stepping over createXmlHttp, check to see whether the error has yet shown up. If not, then you know the error does not occur within createXmlHttp. If it does show up, then you know the error occurs within createXmlHttp, and the next time debugging through sendAjaxRequest, you should step into createXmlHttp and debug from there.

You can consider the Step Out option the "antidote" to Step Into. Step Out allows you to exit debugging of the current function and return to the previous function in the call stack. If you're currently stepping through the function createXmlHttp, which was called from sendAjaxRequest, then using the Stop Out option will return to the line in sendAjaxRequest that follows the call to createXmlHttp. Step Out is particularly useful when you are in a function and don't want to step completely through it and would rather return the previous function in the call stack.

By now you may have noticed the Stop button on Venkman's toolbar and wondered what it does. Clicking the Stop button will activate Venkman's ability to suspend JavaScript immediately the next time *any* JavaScript is executed. Once you have clicked the Stop button, you can be sure that the next time any JavaScript runs, Venkman will suspend its execution. Scripts that are run automatically using setTimeout or setInterval are often difficult to debug because the script's entry point is difficult to determine. By activating the Stop function, Venkman will trap the script's entry point, and you can debug from there, as needed, as shown in Figure 7-18.

Figure 7-18. *Venkman's Stop button deactivated (left) and activated (right)*

Breakpoints, Part 2

Another powerful feature of Venkman is the ability to write custom code that executes every time a breakpoint executes. In the Breakpoints window, right-click a breakpoint, and select the Breakpoint Properties menu item, as shown in Figure 7-19.

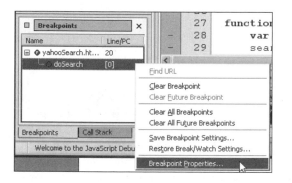

This will open the Breakpoint Properties dialog box, which is a powerful tool that allows you to modify the behavior of the breakpoint and customize it to your exact needs.

At the top of the window are two checkboxes, Enable Breakpoint and Clear Breakpoint After First Trigger. The behavior of these checkboxes is self-explanatory. The real power of the Breakpoints Properties window comes in the When Triggered, Execute checkbox, as shown in Figure 7-20.

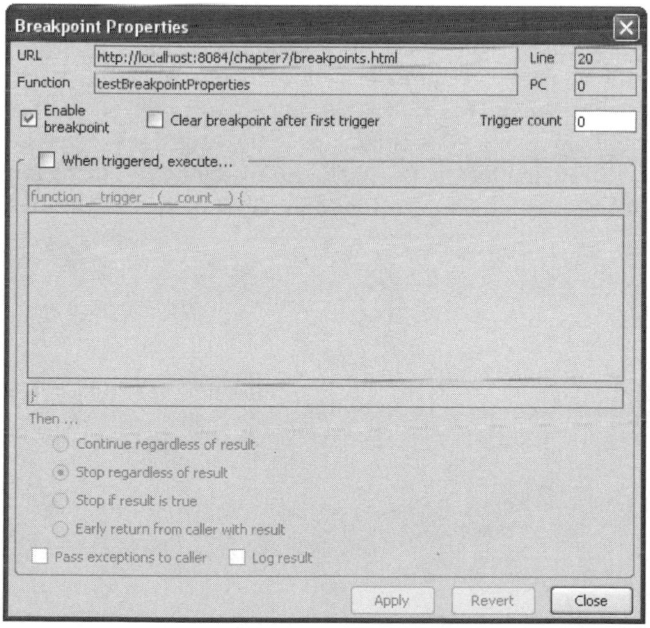

Figure 7-19. *Select the Breakpoint Properties item from the context menu of the Breakpoints window.*

Figure 7-20. *The default look of the Breakpoint Properties window*

Checking the When Triggered, Execute checkbox enables a text area. In this text area, you can write JavaScript code that will execute each time the breakpoint is encountered. Passed to this custom script is a parameter named __count__ that represents the number of times the breakpoint has been encountered.

Following the text area is a section where you can specify how the breakpoint should behave each time it is encountered. Conveniently, the behavior can depend upon the return value of the custom code entered in the text area. The behavior options are as follows:

- Continue Regardless of Result

- Stop Regardless of Result

- Stop If Result Is True

- Early Return from Caller with Result

The options are mostly self-explanatory. The option that is probably the most powerful is the Stop If Result Is True option. Choosing this option means that the breakpoint will suspend execution only if the return value from the custom code is true.

Imagine how convenient it could be to suspend execution depending on a certain condition. Consider the situation where you're iterating through a large list of objects and performing some calculations on each object. During the development process you notice that one particular object on the calculation is failing. If you're able to isolate the data source so that you're dealing with only a singular object or a small list of objects, you have no problem. However, if you can reproduce the error only when using a large list of objects, and the failing object is toward the end of the list, then you have to set a breakpoint and step through it each time, looking for the particular object on which you know the error is occurring.

This scenario is quite easy to solve if using the conditional breakpoint functionality. If you know the particular scenario that is failing, then you can write a conditional statement so that the breakpoint will suspend execution only when the condition is met.

Listing 7-1 shows a small snippet of simplistic JavaScript code. All the code does is create an array of strings and iterate over the array, and for each string in the array, another string is prepended to the string. This snippet of code shows how to conditionally stop the execution of the script based on a condition you define.

Listing 7-1. *Iterating over a String Array*

```
function testBreakpointProperties() {
    var list = ["one", "two", "three", "four", "five", "six", "seven", "eight"];

    var item = null;
    for(var i = 0; i < list.length; i++) {
        item = list[i];
        item = "Text is: "  + item;
    }
}
```

For this example, you'll want to suspend execution on only the seventh item in the list, which is the seven item. If you simply set a breakpoint within the iteration, execution will be suspended each time that line of code is encountered, and you'll have to manually restart the execution each time until you get to the item within the list in which you're interested. In this example, the list isn't very long, but if the list were several hundred items long, it would be convenient to halt execution only when a certain condition is met.

To halt execution on only the seventh item in the list, first place a breakpoint on the desired line. Then right-click anywhere in that line, and select Breakpoint Properties to open the Breakpoint Properties dialog box.

Say you have this simple scenario: you want the breakpoint to actually suspend execution only when you're working with the seventh item in the list, which is the string seven. Enable the conditional breakpoint by checking the When Triggered, Execute checkbox. Within the body of the supplied method, enter a single line of code:

```
return item == "seven";
```

Thus, the method will return true only when you're working on the seventh item in the list. Finish by checking the Stop If Result Is True radio button, instructing Venkman to suspend execution of the code only when the item is the string seven. Figure 7-21 shows the completed Breakpoint Properties dialog box.

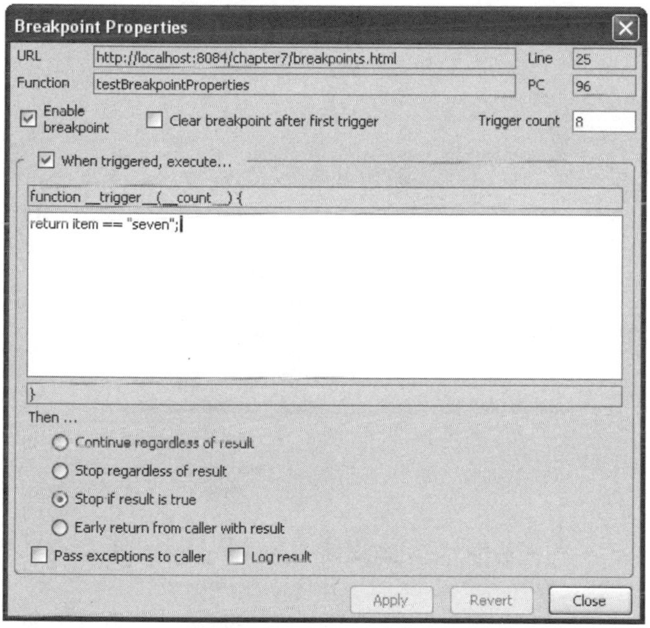

Figure 7-21. *Configuring a breakpoint to suspend execution only based on a condition*

When the function shown in Figure 7-21 is executed with the conditional breakpoint set, the breakpoint will suspend execution only on the seventh pass through the iteration, when the item variable holds the string seven.

This is a powerful technique that could come in handy in numerous scenarios. In addition to the previous example, you may want to suspend execution only every other time the breakpoint is encountered. Implementing this would entail determining whether the __count__ parameter was odd or even by using the modulo (%) operator and the Stop If Result Is True setting. Another example would be to use the Continue Regardless of Result setting and execute some sort of logging functionality each time the breakpoint is encountered. You could even use Ajax techniques to send the logging information to the server!

Local Variables List

The Local Variables window allows you to inspect and even modify variable values during script execution. The Local Variables window always displays all the variables within scope whenever a breakpoint is encountered and execution of the script is suspended.

The Local Variables window always has two top-level items, Scope and This. Scope refers to all the variables within the nearest current scope of execution. Because most JavaScript is written as a function, the nearest scope is usually *function* scope. For example, if a breakpoint within a function is encountered, then the Scope item within the Local Variables window will refer to all variables that are within that function's scope—namely, any variable defined with the keyword var within that function. Variables defined in the global scope (those defined outside any function body) are technically accessible within functions, but they are not shown within the current variable scope (see Figure 7-22).

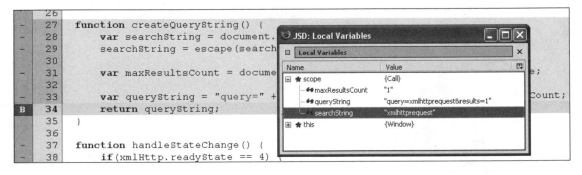

Figure 7-22. *All the variables within the current scope*

The second top-level item displayed in the Local Variables window is the this item. The this item refers to whichever object the keyword this refers. If the breakpoint occurs within a function that is part of an object, then this refers to the current object instance. The normal reference for this is the browser's window object. Note that any variables defined within the global scope will appear under the this item.

The Local Variables window uses small icons next to a variable's name to indicate the variable's data type. The data types available are boolean, double, integer, null, object, string, and void. Figure 7-23 shows the Local Variables window with each data type. Note the icon that is used for each data type.

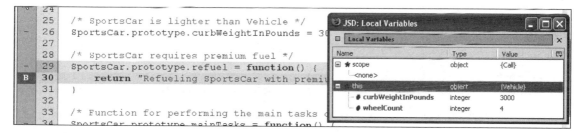

```
27   }
28
29   function allDataTypes() {
30       var booleanVar = true;
31       var doubleVar = 2.8;
32       var integerVar = 1;
33       var nullVar = null;
34       var objVar = new Object();
35       var stringVar = "String";
36       var voidVar;
37       alert("breakpoint here");
38   }
39
40
```

Figure 7-23. *The Local Variables window showing each available data type*

Other than the variable named objVar in Figure 7-23, all the data types are simple, nonobject data types, and their values are easily discernable in the Value column of the Local Variables window. Note how the objVar variable has a plus sign next to it, indicating that it can be opened to inspect the object's properties. Figure 7-24 shows the Local Variables window using an object variable type. Note that in this instance the breakpoint is set within an object's member function, meaning that within the Local Variables window the this item refers to the object instance itself while the scope item has no child items.

```
24
25   /* SportsCar is lighter than Vehicle */
26   SportsCar.prototype.curbWeightInPounds = 30
27
28   /* SportsCar requires premium fuel */
29   SportsCar.prototype.refuel = function() {
30       return "Refueling SportsCar with premiu
31   }
32
33   /* Function for performing the main tasks
34   SportsCar.prototype.mainTasks = function()
```

Figure 7-24. *Suspended within an object's member function, the Local Variable window shows the object's properties.*

In this instance, the object has two properties, curbWeightInPounds and wheelCount, and their respective values are displayed within the Local Variables window.

Up until now you've probably been using alert boxes to show the values of variables during runtime. While this technique certainly works, it takes time to pepper your script with alerts, and each alert usually shows only one variable value at a time. After the script is debugged, you'll need to remove all those alert boxes, and if you ever need to debug again, you'll end up adding alert boxes again. With Venkman, all you have to do is set a breakpoint and use the Local Variables window to inspect the values of variables, and they are all there for quick access.

Step back for a moment to think about how the Local Variables window makes Venkman an extremely powerful debugging tool. With one quick glance you are able to view the values of all the objects and variables that the JavaScript engine knows about. Using breakpoints, you can selectively suspend execution of a script and inspect the various objects and variables to ensure that the values are as you expect them to be. Since you're already using TDD techniques (you are, aren't you?), you'll know what the expected output of your script should be. If your tests are failing, you can step through the script using Venkman, and by using breakpoints in conjunction with the Local Variables window, you should be able to quickly diagnose the source of any errors.

Not only is the Local Variables window a powerful debugging tool, but it's also a great learning tool. With it you can inspect the properties of any object or variable that's available to the JavaScript interpreter. Consider the XMLHttpRequest object, which is well documented. You know it has publicly accessible properties such as `responseText`, `responseXML`, and `status`. But what if you didn't know that? Is there a way to find out? Figure 7-25 shows two views of an XMLHttpRequest object. The one on the left shows the object right after it has been created and none of its properties has been set. The one on the right shows the object's properties after a successful request has been made.

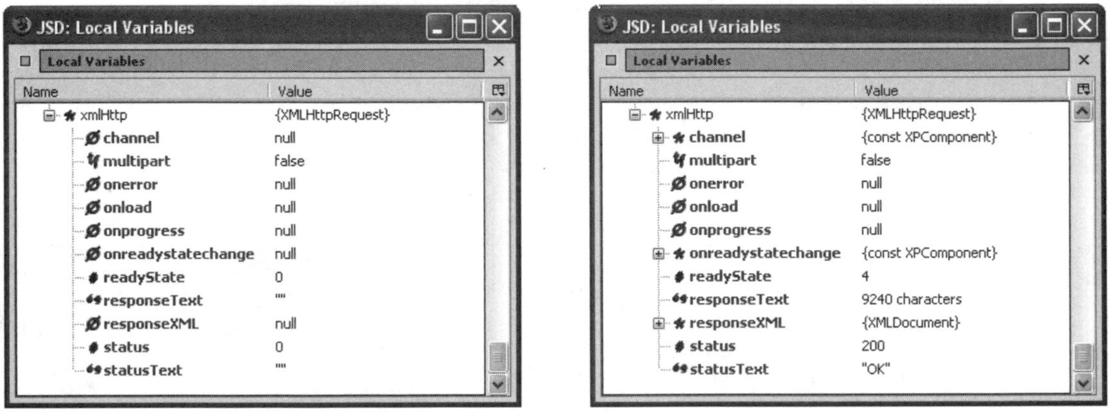

Figure 7-25. *The XMLHttpRequest object immediately following object creation (left) and immediately following a successful request (right)*

This example works well for the XMLHttpRequest object, which is well documented, but how about something that's not particularly well documented or the documentation is not easily accessible?

Consider a table row DOM object. We've mentioned that all DOM elements have properties such as `firstChild`, but what else is there? You can use Venkman and the Local Variables window to take a look. Figure 7-26 shows the Local Variables window and some of the properties available on a table row object. Did you know that it has properties named `offsetHeight`, `offsetLeft`, `parentNode`, and `previousSibling`? If so, congratulations. If not, now you know—and you may be able to put that knowledge to good use later. You may not know the meaning of all these properties, but if you know they exist and know their names, you can perform a Web search to learn more about them.

Name	Value	
⊞ ❋ childNodes	{NodeList}	
◀❹ className	""	
❄ clientHeight	26	
❄ clientWidth	674	
◀❹ dir	""	
⊞ ❋ firstChild	{HTMLTableCellElement}	
◀❹ id	"emp-66558815"	
◀❹ innerHTML	"<td>d</td><td>d</td><td>d</td><td><input value=\"Delete\" type=\"b...	
◀❹ lang	""	
⊞ ❋ lastChild	{HTMLTableCellElement}	
◀❹ localName	"TR"	
∅ namespaceURI	null	
∅ nextSibling	null	
◀❹ nodeName	"TR"	
❄ nodeType	1	
∅ nodeValue	null	
❄ offsetHeight	26	
❄ offsetLeft	3	
⊞ ❋ offsetParent	{HTMLTableElement}	
❄ offsetTop	59	
❄ offsetWidth	674	
⊞ ❋ ownerDocument	{HTMLDocument}	
⊞ ❋ parentNode	{HTMLTableSectionElement}	
∅ prefix	null	
⊞ ❋ previousSibling	{HTMLTableRowElement}	

Figure 7-26. *The Local Variables window showing some of the properties of a table row object*

If you're not already impressed with the Local Variables window, consider this: it also allows you to change the value of variables during runtime. This can be extremely powerful when you want to test the effects of different variable values on the script's output. It's also useful when you *think* you've found where a problem is occurring and want to see whether changing a variable value fixes the problem. If changing the variable value fixes the problem, then you just need to find out *why* the variable value is wrong in the first place.

Simply right-click the variable value you want to change, and select Change Value from the context menu. This opens a small prompt window in which you can modify the variable's value, as shown in Figure 7-27. You can enter any valid JavaScript expression into the prompt, including expressions such as `new Object()`. Be sure that any string literals are enclosed in either double or single quotes. Remember that in the prompt window you can also reference other variables by using the variable name.

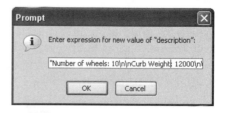

Figure 7-27. *Changing a variable value using the Change Value prompt*

Watches List

The Watches list is nearly identical to the Local Variables window in that it displays information about variables running within the current scope. The difference between the Watches list and the Local Variables window is that you, the developer, decide what variables are shown in the Watches list. In contrast, the Local Variables window shows *all* variables available to the currently executing script. Think of the Watches list as the Local Variables list on a diet.

To add a variable to the Watches list, right-click anywhere in the Watches window, and select Add Watches Expression from the context menu. A prompt window will appear, allowing you to enter a valid JavaScript expression that identifies the variable you want to watch. In most cases, you'll simply want to enter the variable name. Figure 7-28 shows the context menu and the resulting window.

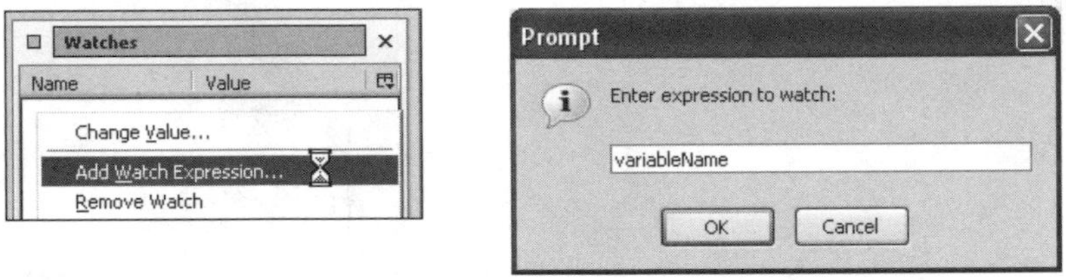

Figure 7-28. *Right-click in the Watches window (left), and then enter the name of the variable you want to watch (right).*

Remember that the Watches window will show all variables you want to watch. However, sometimes you may want to watch variables that are not within the current scope of the script. For example, if you create a watch for variable foo in function doThis, and you are stopped at a breakpoint in function doThat, then variable foo from doThis is not in scope. When this happens, Venkman will simply report a variable value of {Error}. Don't worry, this won't cause any problems—it's just Venkman's way of letting you know that the variable is not currently in scope.

In many cases, you'll want to use the Watches window more than you use the Local Variables window, simply because you get to decide what appears in the window. This leads to a much cleaner window and less time searching for the few variables you actually care about tracking.

Figure 7-29 shows three variables. The variable url is defined in another function, so its value is reported as {Error}. The variable xmlHttp is a global variable and thus shows the current value. The variable queryString is defined within the function in which script execution is currently suspended.

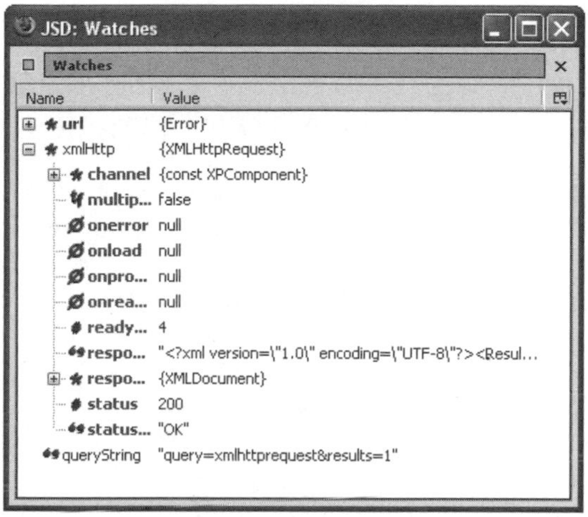

Figure 7-29. *The Watches window showing three variables*

Call Stack

Venkman keeps track of the current call stack in the Call Stack window (see Figure 7-30). This window simply shows a stack of the function call list. The function at the top of the stack is the current function; the next function in the list is the one that called the function at the top of the list, and so on. This window is useful when you have a complicated call structure and you want to see the order in which functions are called.

Double-clicking an item in the Call Stack window will bring the view in the Source Code window to the function represented by the clicked item in the call stack. The Local Variables list will update itself to show the variables in context within that function. Note that this doesn't actually change the order of execution—you've merely moved to see *where you've been,* but it doesn't change *where you're going.*

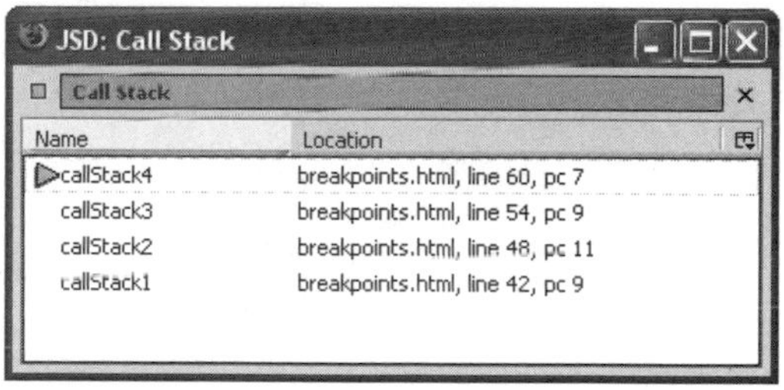

Figure 7-30. *Venkman's Call Stack window*

Performance Profiling

As you become more comfortable with Ajax techniques, you're likely to write more JavaScript than you have previously, especially if you decide to host more application logic on the browser. Doing so raises the possibility that you'll at some point encounter performance bottlenecks within the JavaScript code.

Sound software development practices teach that there is no point in optimizing code for performance unless a performance problem exists in the first place. Optimized code is almost always harder to read and maintain than code that is not optimized, so unless you truly need to optimize code for performance, avoid doing so.

Writing JavaScript is no different. In the vast majority of cases, you'll have no need to optimize any code for performance reasons. However, sometimes you'll need to do some performance tweaks. Before you can optimize code, though, you first need to determine what code needs to be optimized. Venkman has a built-in performance profiling utility that can help you do just that.

The Performance Profiling tool in Venkman automatically monitors your script and tracks the amount of time spent in each function, in addition to the number of times each function is called. The Performance Profiling tool exports its data to HTML, XML, CSV, and text formats.

To enable the Performance Profiling tool, simply click the Profile button located on the Venkman toolbar (see Figure 7-31). When activated, the Profile button will have a small green checkbox in it. From now on, the Performance Profiler will record performance metrics for all JavaScript running within the current browser window. Click the button again to stop collecting performance data.

Figure 7-31. *The Profile toolbar button when activated*

Once you've collected some performance data, it's time to view it to see where the bottlenecks occur. Select the Profile ➤ Save Profile Data As menu item, as shown in Figure 7-32. This will open the Save As window, giving you the chance to select the name of the file and the file format. The text format seems to be the most easily read format. Enter the required data, and click OK. Once you've saved the performance data, be sure to select the Profile ➤ Clear Profile Data menu item to clear out the data buffer for the next use.

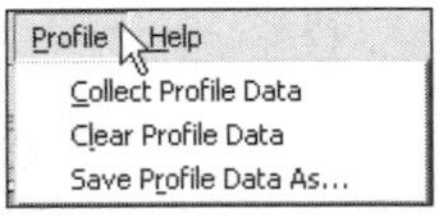

Figure 7-32. *Viewing the Profile menu*

Figure 7-33 displays an example of the profiler tool's output. For each function within the file, the profiler records the number of times the function was called; the total amount of time spent within the function; and the minimum, maximum, and average amount of time spent during each call to the function. Remember that all performance metrics are recorded in milliseconds. The output is easy to read, and you should be able to quickly determine the areas that may need further performance tuning.

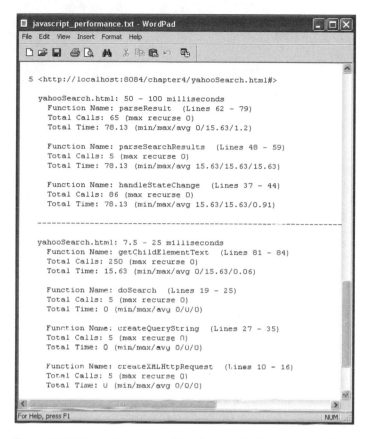

Figure 7-33. *Example output of Venkman's Performance Profiler*

Summary

Regardless of the environment in which you're developing, you're bound to make some mistakes. Some studies estimate that as much as 50 percent of a developer's time is spent figuring out other people's code and finding and fixing errors.

The tools and techniques outlined in this chapter will help you track down and terminate bugs with a minimum amount of time and effort. The Greasemonkey extension for Firefox allows a user script to run that can help you debug the actual Ajax requests and responses that are sent from the browser to the server and back again. This tool can help determine whether a bug is occurring on the browser side or the server side. The Microsoft Script Debugger is a JavaScript debugger that integrates with Microsoft Internet Explorer and provides basic debugging facilities such as breakpoints and variable inspection and editing. Venkman is a JavaScript debugger that integrates with Mozilla-based browsers such as Firefox and that provides more advanced debugging features such as intelligent breakpoints and performance profiling.

You no longer need to avoid Ajax or JavaScript development because no productivity tools are available. Using the tools and techniques described in this chapter, you can confidently begin expanding your Ajax and JavaScript development, knowing that if troubles arise, you have the tools available to find the problems and fix them.

■ ■ ■

CHAPTER 8

Putting It All Together

Well, we've covered quite a bit in this book! By now, you have a good idea of what Ajax can do for you, and you have a starter kit of examples to get you going. We've introduced you to a number of tools that will make developing Ajax applications easier, and you have no excuse to skip testing! In this chapter, we'll cover some additional topics such as patterns and frameworks and show you a more involved Ajax example.

Introducing Patterns

No technology book is complete these days without at least a casual mention of patterns. As we've said before, Ajax is quite new, so the area has a lot of churn. Also, your knowledge will certainly grow as more and more Web sites take advantage of all Ajax has to offer. Still, we'll touch on a few basic patterns in the following sections. For a more complete list of patterns, point your browser to ajaxpatterns.org. *Ajax Patterns and Best Practices* by Christian Gross (Apress, 2006) also outlines the various patterns which you'll need to quickly write appliations that work.

Implementing the Fade Anything Technique (FAT)

One of the really slick things about Ajax is that you can modify just part of a Web page. Rather than repaint the entire view, you can update just the part that changes. While this is a handy technique, it may confuse users who are expecting a full-page refresh. With this in mind, 37signals used the Yellow Fade Technique (YFT) in its flagship Basecamp product as a way of subtly indicating to the user what had changed. YFT does just what it suggests: the part of the page that changed is repainted in yellow, and it slowly fades back to the original background color.

The Fade Anything Technique (FAT) pattern is similar in nature. In essence, the only real change is the color you use to fade; after all, yellow might not be the best option for you. Implementing this technique is not terribly difficult; you can find sample code using your favorite search engine. For an example of this pattern, see Figure 8-1. The new stories are highlighted in gray, which allows users to easily identify the freshest material.

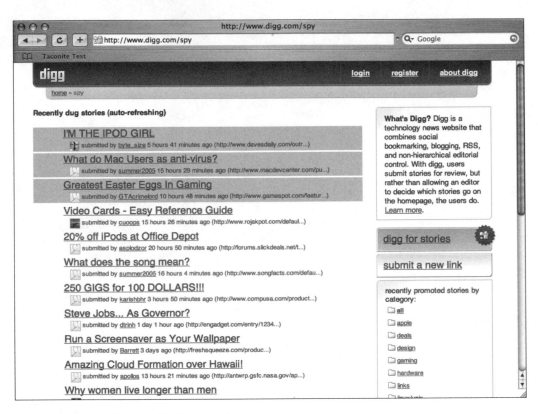

Figure 8-1. *FAT (and autorefresh) at work*

Implementing Auto Refresh

We've already shown you how to implement the Auto Refresh pattern in Chapter 4; being able to refresh parts of the page automatically is useful. Take weather, news, or other information streams that change over time—repainting just the parts that change makes a lot more sense than refreshing the entire page for a few minor changes. Of course, this might not be terribly obvious to users who are trained to hit the refresh button, which is why Auto Refresh pattern is so often paired with FAT.

Auto Refresh offers a significant benefit beyond less work for your user: it also reduces the load on your server. Rather than having thousands of users constantly hitting the refresh button, you can set a specific polling period that should spread out the requests more evenly. (Figure 8-1 showed an example of the Auto Refresh pattern.)

Implementing a Partial Page Paint

We've talked about this point quite a bit, but one of the real strengths of Ajax is that you no longer need to repaint the entire page; instead, you can just modify what has changed. Clearly, you can use this in conjunction with the FAT and Auto Refresh patterns. In fact, this can be helpful for Web applications.

Many of the existing frameworks will help you modify part of the page, and thanks to solid DOM support in modern browsers, this approach is much easier than you think. Figure 8-2 shows A9's BlockView feature, an example of the Partial Page Paint pattern. When you select a different part of the map on the left, the corresponding pictures of the street automatically change to reflect where your map is pointing (assuming pictures exist).

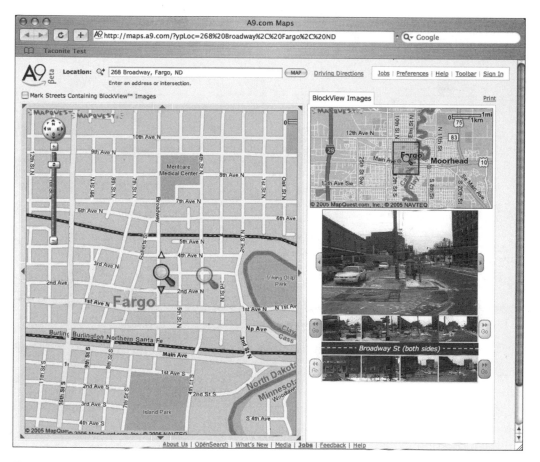

Figure 8-2. *A9's BlockView feature*

Implementing a Draggable DOM

Portals were supposed to be the solution to all our problems. Corporate intranet sites were designed to be one-stop shopping for employees to have all the information they needed at their fingertips. Your most frequently used applications, links to your key reports, industry news—a customized portal was supposed to be the answer. Unfortunately, corporate intranets never really took off, but at least part of the reason had to do with clumsy interfaces for adding new sections and moving existing ones. Typically, you had to go to a separate administration page to make your changes (a full-page refresh), save your changes, and return to your home page (another page refresh). While this approach worked, it certainly wasn't ideal.

Portals are given a new life with Ajax, especially using the Draggable DOM pattern. With this approach, the individual sections are editable right on the main page, and to customize the page, you simply grab them with your mouse and drag them to their new location. Several sites, including the personalizable Google site (www.google.com/ig), have used this pattern, as shown in Figure 8-3.

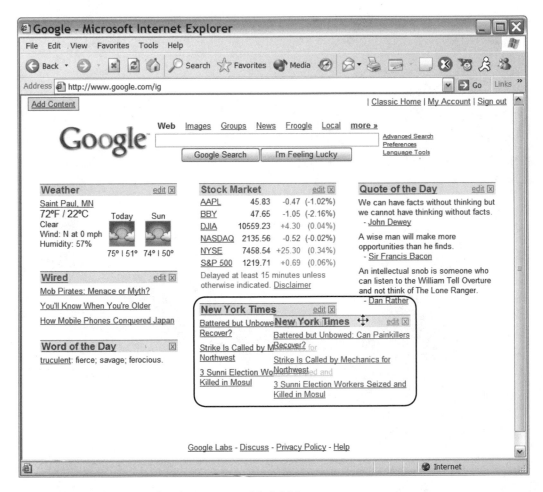

Figure 8-3. *Google Personalized uses Draggable DOM.*

Avoiding Common Gotchas

We've provided you with the tools you'll need to make Ajax development easier, but you also need to be aware of some common gotchas. You may not run into more than a couple of these issues, but before you start using Ajax everywhere, you should keep the following in mind:

Unlinkable pages: You may have noticed that in most of the figures we've shown you, the address bar doesn't change even when the page does. When you use the XMLHttpRequest object to communicate with the server, you never need to modify the URL displayed in the address bar. While this may actually be a plus in some Web applications, it also means your users cannot bookmark your page or send a URL to their friends (think about maps or driving directions). This isn't insurmountable; in fact, Google Maps now includes a Link to This Page link (see Figure 8-4). If links are key to your application or site, be aware that Ajax makes this a bit a challenge.

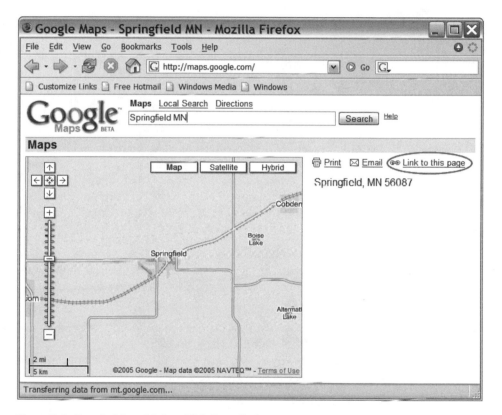

Figure 8-4. *Google Maps Link to This Page link*

Asynchronous changes: Talking to the server asynchronously is one of the real steps forward with Ajax; however, it isn't without its issues. We've talked about this a few times, but it's worth discussing again: users have been trained to expect the entire page to be repainted anytime things change, so they may not notice when you update just parts of the page. Just because you can reload parts of the page doesn't mean this is the right approach for your entire application—use this approach judiciously.

Lack of visual cues: Since the entire page doesn't repaint, users may not perceive that anything has changed. Ultimately, this is why FAT was created, but you do have other options. For instance, Gmail uses a "Loading" icon to indicate that it is doing some work (see Figure 8-5). Depending on your application, you may have to add some sort of indication so your users know what is happening.

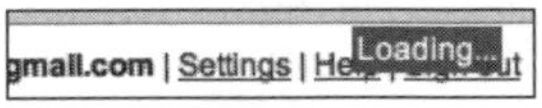

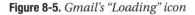

Figure 8-5. *Gmail's "Loading" icon*

The broken back button: Some Web applications deliberately disable the browser's back button, but few Web sites do. Of course, with Ajax, clicking the back button isn't going to do much of anything. If your users are expecting the back button to work, and you're using Ajax to manipulate parts of the page, you may have some problems to solve.

Code bloat: Never forget that the JavaScript that powers Ajax applications runs locally on your client. While many developers have powerful machines with reams of random access memory (RAM), some users still have older machines that just don't offer this horsepower. If you put too much JavaScript into your application, you may find sluggish response times on the client side. Even if the JavaScript runs fine, more JavaScript means larger and larger pages, which means longer download times. Until we all have broadband and dual-processor computers, keep JavaScript to a minimum.

Breaking established UI conventions: Ajax lets developers create far richer Web applications than they've created in the past. However, this doesn't obviate the need to follow normal user interface guidelines. Just because you can do something doesn't mean you should.

How will you know if you've run afoul of any of these gotchas? We can't stress this enough: test your design with representative users. Before you role out some snappy new Ajax feature, do some paper mock-ups, and run them by a few users before you spend the time and effort developing it. An hour or two of testing can save you larger issues later.

Learning Where to Go for More

This book is just a starting point—we can't cover everything having to do with Ajax (if we wanted it to be shorter than, say, a printed copy of the federal budget, that is). In addition, this space is rapidly evolving. Luckily, some excellent resources can help keep you up-to-date on Ajax.

The first place we start nearly every day is Ajaxian (www.ajaxian.com). Billed as "Ben and Dion's AJaX Mission," Ajaxian spots pretty much everything that's new in the Ajax world. (It's not unusual for Ben or Dion to post several times a day.) Industry pundits Ben Galbraith and Dion Almaer, both frequent speakers at conferences such as No Fluff Just Stuff, maintain Ajaxian.com. Lest you doubt their credentials, both were attendees of the inaugural O'Reilly/Adaptive Path Ajax Summit, and having seen both present in person, we vouch for their knowledge and true passion for the field. Without a doubt, Ajaxian.com is the first stop for news and events in the Ajax space.

Another excellent resource is Ajax Patterns (`ajaxpatterns.org`), mentioned earlier. Michael Mahemoff maintains Ajax Patterns, and although the updates may not be quite as frequent as Ajaxian, the site has impressive depth for such a new area. Don't be dissuaded by the word *Patterns* in the title, the site has plenty of information on Ajax basics, frameworks, and common gotchas.

Ajax Matters (`ajaxmatters.com/r/welcome`) has a great collection of articles and books related to Ajax. You'll find more than just references to the XMLHttpRequest object—you'll find excellent resources on JavaScript and CSS as well. Ajax Matters includes a blog, though it isn't updated frequently.

Another blog worth tracking is the appropriately named Ajax Blog (`ajaxblog.com`). This blog features a number of contributors and, as you would expect, covers a wide variety of topics in the Ajax space. Like Ajax Matters, it does a good job of discussing topics related to Ajax such as browser compatibility and tutorials.

Besides just using Google to search for information on Ajax, stopping by Google Labs (`labs.google.com`) from time to time is advisable. While not every application or feature Google Labs adds to its beta area is Ajax based, features such as Google Maps and Google Suggest certainly are primary reasons why Ajax is receiving so much attention these days. Within a few days of Google deploying something really cool, chances are good someone will have it dissected.

It's worth keeping an eye on the good people at Adaptive Path (`www.adaptivepath.com`). We owe the term *Ajax* to Jesse James Garrett, a founder of Adaptive Path; in addition, the company was a co-organizer, with O'Reilly, of the Ajax Summit. Without a doubt, Adaptive Path is a true leader in the Web design space and undoubtedly will have more to say on the topic of Ajax.

If you haven't heard of Rails or Ruby yet, head over to `www.rubyonrails.org/` and `www.ruby-lang.org/en/`. Rails is an open source Web framework that was developed by David Heinemeier Hansson of 37signals while working on the project management tool Basecamp, and it's written in the object-oriented scripting language Ruby. Proving that all good frameworks are extracted from living applications, Rails incorporates a number of fascinating features. What draws many to Rails is its convention-over-configuration approach along with its built-in ability to generate the basic scaffolding of a typical application that has a Web front end for a relational database, which seems to be all the rage these days. Several people have reported productivity gains using Ruby on Rails that are frankly staggering, and by following any of several tutorials at this site you can have an application up and running in mere minutes.[1]

What makes Rails interesting in the context of this book is its amazing support for Ajax right out of the box. Rails includes libraries to handle drag-and-drop actions along with other common Ajax approaches, and helper packages exist to ease the burden of performing tasks such as using autocomplete, calling the server, and submitting a form in the background. It's no surprise that Rails has such great support for Ajax—several of the original applications built with it are shining examples of what can be done with Ajax. Take a look at Basecamp, Backpack, and Ta-da List to get some inspiration for your next application. It's worth keeping an eye on 37signals (`www.37signals.com`), which is truly pushing the boundaries of the traditional Web applications.

---

1. The authors have indeed done this and can verify it takes longer to actually download all the components than to get an application running. One author was told about a project that took four months using the latest in the lightweight Java stack that was rewritten with Ruby on Rails in four evenings (not days, evenings).

Articles and tutorials continue to pop up weekly if not daily. While following some of the sites already listed will tip you off to most if not all of these works, it's worthwhile to peruse O'Reilly (www.oreilly.com) and the Apple Developer Connection (developer.apple.com). Both sites have been used as resources for this book and provide timely information on a range of Ajax topics.

Using a Framework

Throughout this book, we've given you a fair number of Ajax examples. And the astute observer may have noticed a fair amount of, well, duplicate code. For instance, how many times have you seen something like Listing 8-1?[2]

Listing 8-1. *The Most Repeated Chunk of Code in This Book*

```
var xmlHttp;

    function createXMLHttpRequest() {
        if (window.ActiveXObject) {
            xmlHttp = new ActiveXObject("Microsoft.XMLHTTP");
        }
        else if (window.XMLHttpRequest) {
            xmlHttp = new XMLHttpRequest();
        }
    }
```

Of course, in a production application, we'd abstract this little routine. Actually, we'd probably go further and create a special library that encapsulated the messy, repetitive aspects of Ajax. Then again, we might do a quick Google search and discover quite a few hits for *Ajax frameworks*. For a snapshot of available frameworks, check out Appendix B.

Introducing Taconite

It's shameless-plug time: the authors of this book are also the co-creators of the open-source Ajax framework Taconite. We admit this is a bit self-serving, but seriously, we think Taconite is pretty sweet. While originally built for Java Enterprise Edition–based applications, we have refactored the core of Taconite into a client-side library that can easily be used with any server-side technology. Beyond that, it wouldn't be terribly hard to port the Taconite server-side components to other technologies such as .NET.

What makes Taconite so special? Ajax is a fantastic step forward in the evolution of the Web application. However, we've struggled over the years with the inconsistencies among browsers and the difficulty inherent in developing massive quantities of JavaScript. Since we're basically lazy, we decided to just "build it once" so we could easily reuse our hard work. (Besides, we can tell our bosses it'll take three weeks, get it done in one, and spend the rest of the time following the trials and tribulations of the Minnesota Vikings.)

---

2. Seriously, how many times? Well, we counted: including this one, 19.

We know what your next question is: why should I look at Taconite? With Taconite, you don't have to deal with JavaScript and, more important, making sure it works across multiple browsers. The heart of Taconite is a parser that converts normal HTML code into a series of JavaScript commands that dynamically create the content on the browser.

The Theory of Taconite

Generating dynamic HTML has always been difficult. As we've discussed, in the early days of the Web, you had CGI and then servlets. Of course, both of these solutions worked, but at their core, they created HTML content via string concatenation. As any servlet developer will tell you, string concatenation is difficult to develop, tedious, error prone, and hard to maintain. Template models such as JSP and ASP were created to ease the burden by allowing you to use normal HTML with some special markup to develop dynamic pages. These pages are much easier to build and maintain than their "string concatenation" cousins.

As you've seen in some of our examples, using Ajax to generate dynamic content creates many of the same issues—you can use DOM methods to create content, but this approach can be irksome and often results in lots of extra code. Since you're reading this book, you're better equipped than the average developer; however, trust us when we say some DOM methods behave differently across browsers.

Many people have come to rely on `innerHTML` combined with string concatenation when they decide to put a new Ajax feature in their application. Although building the `innerHTML` content on the server (taking advantage of your favorite language) certainly helps, it still doesn't negate the issues with `innerHTML`. Though widely supported, `innerHTML` is not a W3C standard. You can do a lot with `innerHTML`, but it has its limits. For instance, you can't insert a table row between other table rows. Of course, the biggest challenge, and we're sure this will come as a shock to many of you, is that `innerHTML` behavior varies across browsers.

The Solution

Taconite solves this core issue by providing a custom parser that converts HTML into the equivalent W3C DOM methods used to create the specified content. This means you can write dynamic content using whatever HTML-generating technology with which you're most comfortable. You get the best of both worlds: you get your snazzy new Ajax feature without dealing with string concatenation or using standard W3C DOM calls. And since we're such nice guys, we've taken care of all the nasty cross-browser issues!

This parser is used by a set of custom JSP tags that allow you to write content in a way that is natural—as HTML embedded within a JSP. You no longer have to crowd your pages with a slew of `document.createElement` and `document.appendChild` commands to dynamically create new content. The JSP custom tags working with the parser take care of all this while you sit back and enjoy your refreshing iced mocha! The resulting JavaScript is returned to the browser as part of the response where the client-side JavaScript library takes over and executes these commands to produce the desired output.

Taconite doesn't try to reinvent the wheel; instead, it focuses on the Achilles heel of Ajax development: the potentially tedious task of writing large amounts of JavaScript to dynamically update your Web page. Unlike some toolkits, Taconite doesn't try to invent a new way of sending request data to the server; instead, it relies on the tried-and-true name/value pairs either embedded within the query string of a GET request or tucked safely in the body of a POST. The client-side library even automates the creation of the name/value query string—heck, we even escape the data for you. All you need to worry about is telling Taconite *what* values should be sent to the server, and it takes care of the rest.

Since all the JavaScript is created by the parser based on the HTML you specify, you don't have to worry about dealing with browser JavaScript incompatibilities. The parser takes care of them for you. Did you catch that? Taconite takes care of the incompatibilities. Seriously, you don't have to worry about it; we've done that for you. All you need to do is specify the dynamic content as HTML within a JSP, and the parser does the rest.

The beauty of Taconite's design is that it encourages you to keep all your business logic on the server side (where, frankly, it is a lot easier to write) while the browser does what it does best: it renders a user interface. Taconite trivializes the task of making Ajax requests from the browser to the server so you can reuse domain logic with ease. Of course, removing redundancy is not the only reason you should avoid business logic in the browser. Hosting domain logic on the client can open security vulnerabilities. If your logic is implemented on the browser, what's keeping a malicious user from using a tool such as Greasemonkey to update the JavaScript and insert some special processing (say a 90-percent discount on your new widget?) Taconite makes it easy to access your business routines on the server side where it's easiest to develop, debug, and secure.

Taconite's server-side library is lightweight, requiring only your favorite JSP/servlet container and nothing else. Configuration is minimal (no reams of XML here!); all you have to do is add Taconite's tag library descriptor (TLD) location to the `WEB-INF.xml` file. Thanks to its small size and zero dependencies, Taconite plays nicely with any J2EE Web framework. Whether you use Struts, Spring, MVC, WebWork, Tapestry, or something else entirely, you can use Taconite without any extra work or a steep learning curve. Just imagine integrating Taconite with Struts: the client-side JavaScript library automates the task of creating the query string that is sent to the server. Struts automatically creates and populates an ActionForm object based on the query string's values and passes the ActionForm to an Action class, where the "real" processing work begins. After domain logic has been processed, the Action class forwards the response to a JSP that uses Taconite's custom JSP tags to render the content that will dynamically update the page's contents.

We've recently ported the parser to a JavaScript library so that developers can use it outside the Java space. To use the JavaScript-based parser, the dynamic content must be valid XML embedded in a special Taconite tag. Using this approach, the content is returned as XHTML that is parsed to JavaScript and then evaluated on the browser.

Since the JavaScript is produced in a central location (the Taconite parser), we make sure it handles any known incompatibilities between browsers. We take care of these issues so you can focus on writing content in a natural way—as HTML. As new issues come up, we can update the parser without affecting any client code!

What Does Taconite Do with the Content?

So, if `innerHTML` isn't the answer, what are you actually doing on the client side? If you've looked at the W3C's Load and Save specification, you would see things such as `ACTION_APPEND_AS_CHILD` and `ACTION_REPLACE`. Taconite supports these actions and others, giving you complete flexibility with content placement. Following the ideals of the Load and Save specification should make the transition from Taconite to the W3C specification easier. Taconite currently supports the following actions, assuming that the actions are in reference to a specified context element:

- Appending as children

- Appending as first child

- Deleting

- Inserting after

- Inserting before

- Replacing children

- Replacing

Taconite isn't a toolkit—it doesn't provide widgets—but it's extremely flexible. It will render whatever you throw at it, not just what some developer thought their text box should handle. Of course, if you had to have that snappy widget, it would be pretty easy to build on top of Taconite. And, with the JavaScript-based parser, it'll work with any server-side technology you want to use.

Remember, since Taconite is open-source (licensed under the Apache license), you are free to look at the code to tweak it, learn from it, and even port it to your favorite language. Be sure to explore the Taconite home page (`sourceforge.net/projects/taconite`) for further details.

Introducing Dashboard Applications

The introduction of Mac OS X Tiger saw hundreds of new features, including a new browser with improved Really Simple Syndication (RSS) support, an automation tool to simplify common tasks, and a lightning-fast desktop search capability. One of the most talked about features of Tiger is Dashboard, essentially a collection of mini-applications (see Figure 8-6). For those of you who don't own a Mac (or don't have a friend with one), think of a Dashboard application as a replacement for all those little things you normally launch a browser for several times a day, such as checking your stocks, looking up a word in the dictionary, or checking what's on TV tonight. Rather than run off to your favorite weather site, you can simply access the Dashboard and glance at your local weather forecast!

Dashboard widgets are nothing more than bits of HTML and JavaScript, with a little bit of CSS mixed in for good measure. A good Dashboard widget has a single purpose and is small, doing one thing and doing it well. Mac OS X Tiger shipped with a handful of widgets (a calendar, a flight tracker, a stock tracker, a weather widget, and so on), but now more than a thousand are available. Dashboard widgets connect to the Internet to deliver real-time information; this means a single click keeps you up-to-date. The real beauty of Dashboard is that pretty much anyone can create their own widget—in fact, most of the widgets available for download were not written by Apple.

Unfortunately, we don't all own Macs, and at least for now, we won't be able to run Mac OS X on an Intel box. Still, that doesn't mean you can't share a bit in the features of Dashboard. In fact, in the next section, you'll use Ajax along with some freely available Web Services to mimic Dashboard in a browser.

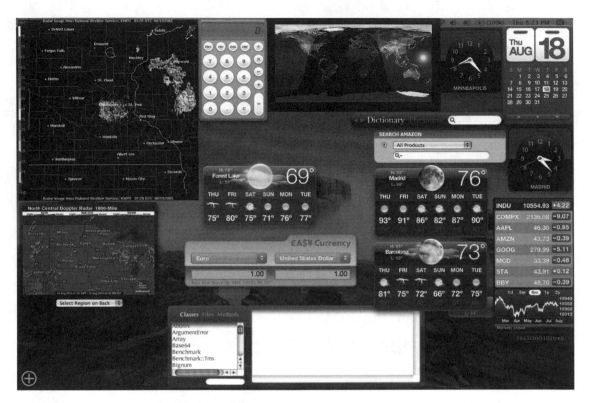

Figure 8-6. *The Dashboard in Mac OS X Tiger*

Building the Ajax Dashboard with Taconite

Up to now, all the examples in this book have been small and to the point, demonstrating one or two particular topics. The examples weren't particularly flashy, but they demonstrated an important piece of the Ajax puzzle.

This chapter's example, known as the Ajax Dashboard, is a completely cross-browser application that mimics the Mac OS X Tiger Dashboard feature. While this example isn't nearly as polished as its parent, it does serve as proof that Ajax is easy to use and can provide a huge leap in usability. The Ajax Dashboard also serves as a demonstration test bed for the Taconite framework, so you'll see how much work the Taconite framework can save you. The full source code for the Ajax Dashboard is available from the Source Code section of the Apress Web site (www.apress.com). From there you can download the source and also the prebuilt WAR file that is ready to run in any modern servlet container such as Tomcat.

Introducing the General Features

Figure 8-7 shows the Ajax Dashboard. It consists of four small windows, each containing a different mini-application. The first window provides a simple seven-day weather forecast for any valid U.S. ZIP code by showing the projected high and low temperatures along with the expected cloud cover for the day. The forecast automatically changes whenever the ZIP code changes, and Ajax automatically refreshes the forecast as long as the window is open within the browser.

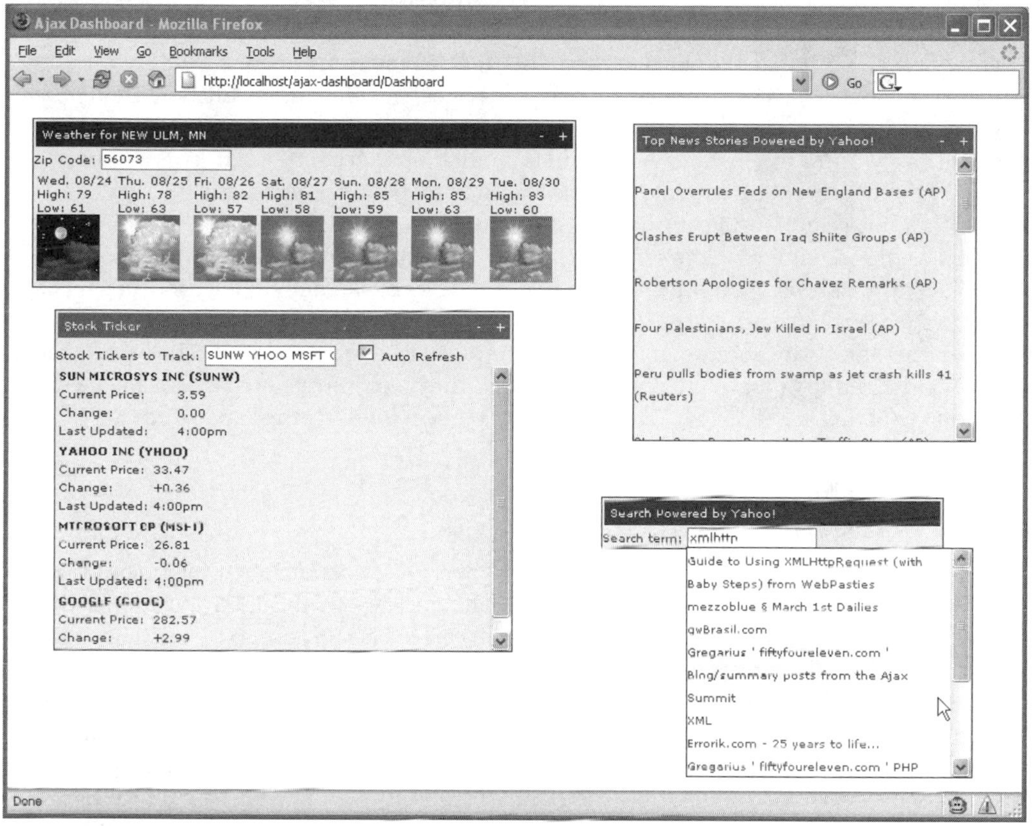

Figure 8-7. *The Ajax Dashboard example application*

The weather forecast data is supplied by a Web Service whose WSDL document is located at `www.webservicex.net/WeatherForecast.asmx?WSDL`. The National Oceanic & Atmospheric Administration (NOAA) has launched its own more complete forecast Web service at `weather.gov/forecasts/xml/`. Each time the Ajax Dashboard is opened, the Web service is contacted for the default ZIP code's weather forecast. Once open, at regular intervals or when the ZIP code is changed, the Web service is again contacted for an updated forecast. Ajax dynamically updates the forecast during these updates, so the update is seamless and does not require a complete refresh of the page.

The stock ticker window keeps track of your favorite stocks' performances on the stock market. Use it to see how fast your investments are growing and thus how soon you can retire (or, sadly, how fast they're falling and how much *longer* you'll have to work). Enter the desired stock tickers in the text box, check the box to enable the autorefresh feature, and watch how the stock prices update throughout the day, without ever having to manually refresh the page. Like the weather forecast, the stock tracker uses Ajax and automatically updates itself at set intervals to ensure that the information is up-to-date. The stock tracker retrieves its data from a Web Service whose WSDL is located at `www.swanandmokashi.com/HomePage/WebServices/StockQuotes.asmx?WSDL`.

The news window is a simple window that displays the current top news stories supplied by Yahoo!. Instead of using a Web service, Yahoo! provides the news as an RSS feed. RSS is a simple XML-based format for distributing newslike items. RSS is simpler to work with than Web services. Like the weather forecast and stock ticker windows, the news window automatically refreshes itself periodically to provide the latest headline news. Clicking an item in the news window opens the article in a separate browser window.

The last window on the Ajax Dashboard is a Yahoo! search component. This component is similar to the Yahoo! search example from Chapter 4. The big difference is that in this application, the search results display in a drop-down list box under the text box, which is updated as the user is typing the search time. This is really a combination of the Yahoo! search and autocomplete examples from Chapter 4. Clicking an item in the drop-down list opens the resource in a new browser window.

Together these four components make up the Ajax Dashboard example. The components are all good candidates for Ajax techniques because they represent data that can change rapidly, and the ability to seamlessly update the data in one window without needing to refresh the entire page is a big plus.

Introducing the Design Features

The Ajax Dashboard includes a few nice touches that set it apart from a traditional browser-based application. Each of the four components is rendered in an absolutely positioned `div` tag, and with the help of the DOM-Drag library, you can drag each component with the mouse to any position on the screen.

The DOM-Drag library, available at `www.youngpup.net/2001/domdrag`, is described by its author as a lightweight, easy-to-use, dragging API for modern DHTML browsers (see Figure 8-8). The setup requires only a couple of lines of JavaScript for each component, minimizing the hassle of using DOM-Drag. The single JavaScript file is only 121 lines long and roughly 8KB in size. The colored title bar of each Ajax Dashboard component is the "handle" for dragging the component. To move a component, simply click and hold anywhere in the colored title bar area, drag the component to the desired location, and then release the mouse button. DOM-Drag allows users to place the components wherever they choose. This enhancement, while seemingly small, gives Ajax Dashboard a feel more akin to a multiple document interface (MDI) client application than a Web page.

You may have also noticed the small plus and minus signs on the right side of the title bar for the weather forecast, stock ticker, and news stories components. These plus and minus signs, respectively, maximize and minimize the content of the component. Minimizing the component's content collapses the data so that only the title bar is visible, saving valuable screen real estate (see Figure 8-9). This may not seem like an important feature here, since Ajax Dashboard has only four components, but imagine if the application was enhanced to include several more components. A screen full of components may seem busy and hard to read, and minimizing the less frequently used components can simplify the application's appearance while still keeping the minimized components' data a single mouse click away.

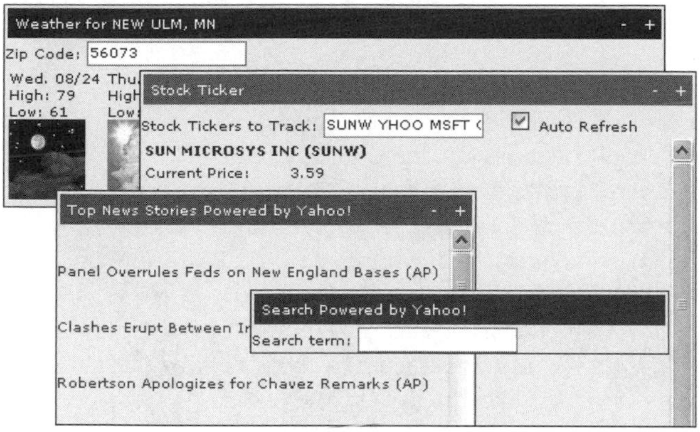

Figure 8-8. *DOM-Drag allows you to enable the individual components to be dragged to any part of the screen.*

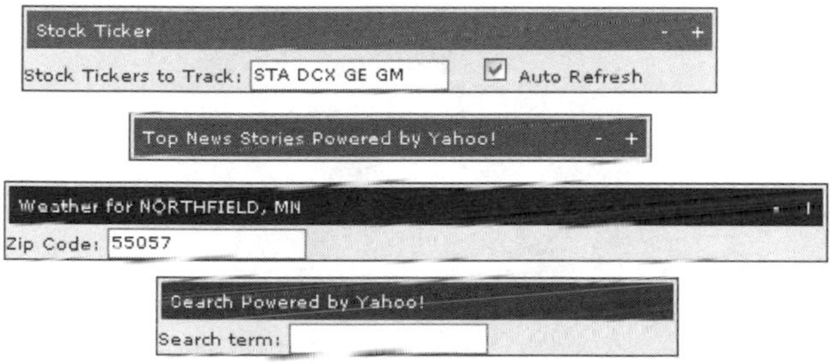

Figure 8-9. *The Ajax Dashboard components in their minimized state*

You can achieve the maximizing and minimizing effects by using a `div` element and the `display` property of its `style` attribute. You'll take a closer look at this in the next section.

Analyzing the Code

Let's begin analyzing the code that makes up the Ajax Dashboard by looking at how all the components come together on a single Web page. Listing 8-2 shows the JSP that renders the main Ajax Dashboard page.

Listing 8-2. `ajaxDashboard.jsp`

```
<%@page contentType="text/html"%>
<%@page pageEncoding="UTF-8"%>

<!DOCTYPE html PUBLIC "-//W3C//DTD XHTML 1.0 Strict//EN"
  "http://www.w3.org/TR/xhtml1/DTD/xhtml1-strict.dtd">
<html>
```

```
<head>
    <title>Ajax Dashboard</title>
    <script type="text/javascript" src="js/autocomplete.js"></script>
    <script type="text/javascript" src="js/dom-drag.js"></script>
    <script type="text/javascript" src="js/common.js"></script>
    <script type="text/javascript" src="js/weatherForecast.js"></script>
    <script type="text/javascript" src="js/stockQuote.js"></script>
    <script type="text/javascript" src="js/news.js"></script>
    <script type="text/javascript" src="js/search.js"></script>
    <script type="text/javascript" src="js/taconite/taconite-client.js"></script>
    <script type="text/javascript" src="js/taconite/taconite-parser.js"></script>
    <link type="text/css" rel="stylesheet" title="style" href="css/styles.css" >
                                                        </link>
</head>

<body>

<%@ include file="weather/weatherForecast.jsp" %>

<%@ include file="stockQuote/stockQuote.jsp" %>

<%@ include file="news/newsItems.jsp" %>

<%@ include file="search/search.jsp" %>

<script type="text/javascript" src="js/ajaxDashboard.js"></script>

<div style="position:absolute;overflow:auto;display:none;background-color:white"
                                                        id="popup">

</div>

</body>

</html>
```

This JSP is for the most part a simple placeholder for the JSPs that make up each component. At the top of the file are the references to each component's individual JavaScript file. Splitting out the JavaScript in this way makes the files more manageable and easier to change. JavaScript functions that are common to all the components are placed in the common.js file. The taconite-client.js and taconite-parser.js files are specific to the Taconite framework being used to build this example.

Each component has its own JSP, which is included in the body section of the main JSP. Breaking out the components into their own JSP files makes maintenance easier and also simplifies the process of adding or removing them to the main JSP file. Also within the body tag is a reference to a JavaScript file named ajaxDashboard.js. The absolutely positioned div tag with an id attribute value of popup is used for the search component's drop-down list, which you'll inspect in the "Building a Better Autocomplete" section.

The `ajaxDashboard.js` file consists of JavaScript that must run when the page is loaded. Located outside the body of a function, code is executed as soon as it's loaded by the browser. The majority of the code is required by the DOM-Drag library to initialize the draggable behavior of the component windows. The `initDomDrag` function located in `ajaxDashboard.js` encapsulates the code needed to initialize the draggable behavior of a component, as follows:

```
function initDomDrag(handleID, rootID) {
    var handle = document.getElementById(handleID);
    var root = document.getElementById(rootID);
    Drag.init(handle, root);
}
```

The `handle` variable refers to the `div` element that makes up the colored title bar of the component. This is the "handle" on which the mouse can be used to click and drag the rest of the component. The `root` variable refers to the parent `div` element that encloses all the component's content. The `handle` element must be a child element of the `root` element. Finally, the last line passes the `root` and `handle` variables to the DOM-Drag library to make the component draggable. For example, the following `initDomDrag` function makes the stock quote component draggable:

```
initDomDrag("stockQuoteHandle", "stockQuoteRoot");
```

Analyzing the Weather Forecast Component

Listing 8-3 details the code that renders the weather forecast window. The parent element here is the `div` element with an `id` attribute of `root`. The first child element of the outermost `div` element is another `div` element with an `id` attribute of `handle`. This `div` represents the colored title bar of the component and the area that can be clicked and dragged to move the entire component around the screen. All the components that make up the Ajax Dashboard follow this same pattern: an outmost `div` element that represents the component window, immediately followed by another `div` that defines the component's colored title bar.

In the case of the weather forecast component, the HTML that renders the title bar is followed by a `div` element that encloses the text box into which the desired ZIP code is entered. Finally, a `div` element with an `id` attribute of `weatherContent` encloses the actual weather forecast.

Listing 8-3. `weatherForecast.jsp`

```
<%@taglib uri="http://java.sun.com/jsp/jstl/core" prefix="c"%>

<div id="root" style="left:20px; top:20px;">
    <div id="handle">

        <table width="100%" border="0" class="textbox">
            <tr>
                <td align="left" class="controls">
                    <span id="forecastLocation">
                        <%@ include file="weatherLocation.jsp" %>
                    </span>
                </td>
```

```
                    <td align="right">
                        <a class="controls"
                                    href="javascript:minimize('weatherContent');">
                            -
                        </a>
                         
                        <a class="controls"
                                    href="javascript:maximize('weatherContent');">
                            +
                        </a>
                    </td>
                </tr>
            </table>

        </div>

        <div class="normalText">
            Zip Code:
            <input type="text" name="forecastZipCode" id="forecastZipCode"
                onkeyup="handleZipCodeChange();" class="normalText"
                value="<%=ajaxdashboard.Constants.DEFAULT_WEATHER_ZIP_CODE%>"/>

        </div>

        <div id="weatherContent">
            <%@ include file="weatherTable.jsp" %>
        </div>
</div>
```

You may have noticed that this JSP includes content from two other JSP files:
weatherLocation.jsp (see Listing 8-4) and weatherTable.jsp (see Listing 8-5). These two JSPs,
respectively, render the weather forecast's location and the actual forecast itself. Before you
look at why these two sections are separated into their own JSP files, take a look at their source
code. It should look pretty much the way you would expect it to look. The weatherLocation.jsp
file simply outputs the name of the current forecast location, and the weatherTable.jsp file
renders a one-row-by-seven-column table detailing the weather forecast.

Listing 8-4. weatherLocation.jsp

```
<%@taglib uri="http://java.sun.com/jsp/jstl/core" prefix="c"%>

Weather for ${forecastData.placeName}, ${forecastData.stateCode}
```

Listing 8-5. weatherTable.jsp

```
<%@taglib uri="http://java.sun.com/jsp/jstl/core" prefix="c"%>

<table>
    <tbody>
        <tr>
            <c:forEach var="forecast" items="${forecastData.details.weatherData}">
                <td>
                    ${forecast.day}

                    <br/>
                    High: ${forecast.maxTemperatureF}

                    <br/>
                    Low: ${forecast.minTemperatureF}

                    <br/>
                    <img src="${forecast.weatherImage}" alt="forecast image"/>
                </td>
            </c:forEach>
        </tr>
    </tbody>
</table>
```

The code for the weatherLocation.jsp file is rather simple. It uses the Java Standard Tag Library (JSTL) to dynamically fill in the city name and state of the weather forecast. In weatherTable.jsp, JSTL tags iterate over an array of weather data objects, where each weather data object encapsulates the forecast information for a particular day. For each weather data object, a table cell is rendered that displays the high and low temperatures along with an image describing the expected cloud cover.

By now you must be wondering: where does Ajax fit in? You'll now look at how the Ajax request is sent to the server. The following function, which appears in the weatherForecast.js file, uses the Taconite framework to send the request for a weather forecast for a particular ZIP code:

```
function updateWeatherForecast() {
    var ajaxRequest = new AjaxRequest("UpdateWeatherForecast");
    ajaxRequest.addFormElementsById("forecastZipCode");
    ajaxRequest.sendRequest();
}
```

The first thing you should notice is that the body of the updateWeatherForecast method is *only three lines long*. In comparison, the example from Chapter 4, which also sends a single parameter as part of the request, is 28 lines long, counting only the code that actually creates the XMLHttpRequest object, creates the query string, and sends the response.

The AjaxRequest object is the heart of the Taconite framework's browser-side functionality. The AjaxRequest object encapsulates its own instance of the XMLHttpRequest object, so multiple instances of AjaxRequest do not share the same instance of an XMLHttpRequest object. The AjaxRequest object defines methods that simplify building the query string that is sent as part of the Ajax request, including accumulating the specified form element values and even applying the appropriate encoding to the values. The AjaxRequest object also handles the server's response.

The first line of the updateWeatherForecast function creates an instance of the AjaxRequest object, passing to its constructor the URL that will handle the Ajax request. The second line is a call to the AjaxRequest object's addFormElementsById method, passing to it the id attribute of the ZIP code text box. This method automatically adds the ZIP code entered by the user to the query string that will be sent to the server. The addFormElementsById method can take any number of parameters. If there were two form elements whose values should be sent as part of the Ajax request, instead of calling the addFormElementsById method twice, you could simply call the method once and supply the two element IDs to the method, separating them with a comma. The last line of the updateWeatherForecast method instructs the AjaxRequest object to send the Ajax request to the specified URL.

The UpdateWeatherForecastServlet.java servlet, whose source code is shown in Listing 8-6, handles the Ajax request for updating the weather forecast. Without getting into the gory details of accessing the Web service, this servlet simply plucks the desired ZIP code of the request object and passes it the WeatherForecastService object. This object returns an instance of the WeatherForecasts object, which encapsulates all the forecast data. The WeatherForecasts object is attached as an attribute to the request object, and finally the servlet forwards the request and response to the weatherForecastAjax.jsp file.

Listing 8-6. UpdateWeatherForecastServlet.java

```java
package ajaxdashboard.servlet;

import ajaxdashboard.service.WeatherForecastService;
import java.io.*;
import java.util.Date;

import javax.servlet.*;
import javax.servlet.http.*;

public class UpdateWeatherForecastServlet extends HttpServlet {
    protected void processRequest(HttpServletRequest request
                                    , HttpServletResponse response)
                                throws ServletException, IOException {

        String zipCode = request.getParameter("forecastZipCode");
        WeatherForecastService forecastService = new WeatherForecastService();
        request.setAttribute("forecastData"
                                , forecastService.getForecastFor(zipCode));

        System.out.println("Weather updated at: " + new Date().toString());
```

```
                request.getRequestDispatcher("/jsp/weather/weatherForecastAjax.jsp")
                                              .forward(request, response);
    }
    protected void doGet(HttpServletRequest request, HttpServletResponse response)
    throws ServletException, IOException {
        processRequest(request, response);
    }
    protected void doPost(HttpServletRequest request, HttpServletResponse response)
    throws ServletException, IOException {
        processRequest(request, response);
    }
}
```

In previous examples, the response has always been returned to the browser in a format such as XML or maybe JSON, where the browser was responsible for reading the response and generating new content or updating existing content based on the results. This often requires several lines of document.createElement() or document.appendChild() calls, which can be tedious to write. For instance, the Yahoo! search example from Chapter 4 required 37 lines of code to render the results.

Compare that to Listing 8-7, which shows the contents of the weatherForecastAjax.jsp file. This file is only 19 lines long (eight of which are blank lines) and completely handles updating the weather forecast component in response to an Ajax request.

Listing 8-7. weatherForecastAjax.jsp

```
<%@ taglib uri="http://taconite.sf.net/tags" prefix="tac" %>

<tac:taconiteRoot>

    <tac:replaceChildren contextNodeID="forecastLocation" parseOnServer="true">

        <%@ include file="weatherLocation.jsp" %>

    </tac:replaceChildren>

    <tac:replaceChildren contextNodeID="weatherContent" parseOnServer="true">

        <%@ include file="weatherTable.jsp" %>

    </tac:replaceChildren>

</tac:taconiteRoot>
```

Thanks to the magic of the Taconite framework, you are no longer required to spend time writing W3C DOM methods to dynamically update the page when handling the response of an Ajax request. Instead, Taconite generates the JavaScript for you, which is returned to the browser and executed to produce the desired outcome.

Let's take a line-by-line look at weatherForecastAjax.jsp to learn what the Taconite framework is doing. The first line of the file is simply the JSP taglib declarations for the Taconite taglib.

The tac:taconiteRoot tag is the root tag for all Taconite responses. Under the covers Taconite always returns an XML document to the browser. Embedded within that XML is either JavaScript (if the parsing has been done on the server) or XHTML (if parsing is to be done on the browser). The tac:taconiteRoot emits the root tag for the return XML. All JSPs using the Taconite tag library must use the tac:taconiteRoot tag.

Every time an Ajax request is made to update the weather forecast, two items in the weather forecast component must be updated: the location (in case the ZIP code for the weather forecast location has changed) and the actual forecast. The tac:taconiteRoot tag has two tac:replaceChildren tags as its direct children. The first tac:replaceChildren tag updates the forecast location, and the second one updates the weather forecast.

The tac:replaceChildren tags are where the real work is being done to generate the newly updated content. The tac:replaceChildren tag says, "Replace all the children of the element with the specified id attribute value with the following content." The tac:replaceChildren tag has one required attribute, contextNodeID, that specifies the node whose children will be replaced with the content of the tac:replaceChildren tag.

In this case, the contextNodeID attribute of the first tac:replaceChildren tag has a value of forecastLocation. A look at Listing 8-3 will show a span element with an id attribute value of forecastLocation. The tac:replaceChildren tag is telling the Taconite framework that any child elements of the forecastLocation span element should be replaced with the content specified within the tac:replaceChildren tag. The specified content comes from the weatherLocation.jsp file, which, as you've seen previously, simply renders the location to which the weather forecast applies.

The second tac:replaceChildren tag rebuilds the actual weather forecast. The contextNodeID attribute in this case has a value of weatherContent. Looking back at Listing 8-3, you'll see a div tag with an id attribute value of weatherContent. So, all the children of the weatherContent div tag will be replaced with the content specified by the second tac:replaceChildren tag. The content comes from the weatherTable.jsp file (Listing 8-5), which simply builds the table containing the weather forecast.

In this example, each tac:replaceChildren tag has an attribute named parseOnServer. This is an optional attribute that defaults to true if the attribute is omitted. A value of true instructs Taconite to parse the specified content into JavaScript on the server and to send the JavaScript back to the browser embedded within the response XML. A false value indicates that the parsing of the content to JavaScript will occur on the browser.

It should now be clear why the weather forecast was split into so many separate JSP files. The main weatherForecast.jsp file renders the weather forecast component the first time the entire Ajax Dashboard page is rendered. The weatherForecastAjax.jsp file handles the Ajax updates of the forecast component. Both JSPs need to render the forecast location and the forecast itself. You want to avoid writing duplicate code, so the forecast location and forecast table are separated into their own JSP files, which are included into the weatherForecast.jsp and weatherForecastAjax.jsp files. In this way, updating the forecast location or the forecast table will automatically be the same whether it's rendered when the Ajax Dashboard first loads or whether it's updated by an Ajax request.

What exactly is the output of the weatherForecastAjax.jsp file? Listing 8-8 shows an example of the XML response rendered by weatherForecastAjax.jsp and returned to the browser.

Listing 8-8. weatherForecast.jsp

```
<taconite-root>

    <taconite-replace-children contextNodeID="forecastLocation"
                                              parseInBrowser="false">
        <![CDATA[
            var element0 = document.createDocumentFragment();
            element0.appendChild(document.createTextNode
                                        ("Weather for NEW ULM, MN"));
            while (document.getElementById("forecastLocation")
                                        .childNodes.length > 0) {
                document.getElementById("forecastLocation").removeChild
                    (document.getElementById("forecastLocation").childNodes[0]);
            }
            document.getElementById("forecastLocation").appendChild(element0);
        ]]>
    </taconite-replace-children>

    <taconite-replace-children contextNodeID="weatherContent"
                                              parseInBrowser="false">
        <![CDATA[
            var element0 = document.createDocumentFragment();
            var element1 = document.createElement("table");
            element0.appendChild(element1);
            var element2 = document.createElement("tbody");
            element1.appendChild(element2);
            var element3 = document.createElement("tr");
            element2.appendChild(element3);
            var element4 = document.createElement("td");
            element3.appendChild(element4);
            element4.appendChild(document.createTextNode("Sun. 08/28"));
            var element5 = document.createElement("br");
            element4.appendChild(element5);
            element4.appendChild(document.createTextNode("High: 78"));
            element5 = document.createElement("br");
            element4.appendChild(element5);
            element4.appendChild(document.createTextNode("Low: 54"));
            element5 = document.createElement("br");
            element4.appendChild(element5);
            element5 = document.createElement("img");
            element5.setAttribute("src",
                    "http://www.nws.noaa.gov/weather/images/fcicons/sct.jpg");
            element5.setAttribute("alt", "forecast image");
            element4.appendChild(element5);

            <!-- Other cells omitted for brevity -->
```

```
        while (document.getElementById("weatherContent").childNodes
                                            .length > 0) {
            document.getElementById("weatherContent").removeChild
                    (document.getElementById("weatherContent").childNodes[0]);
        }
        document.getElementById("weatherContent").appendChild(element0);
    ]]>
  </taconite-replace-children>
```

```
</taconite-root>
```

Note how the XML begins with a `taconite-root` tag that has two `taconite-replace-children` tags, which is similar to the structure of the tags in Listing 8-7. Each `taconite-replace-children` tag has a `CDATA` section that contains the embedded JavaScript to appropriately update the page's content. If you carefully read the embedded JavaScript in Listing 8-8, you'll easily be able to see exactly what the JavaScript is doing. In fact, it's likely identical to the JavaScript you would write to update the page! Upon receiving this XML response from the server, the Taconite browser-side library automatically extracts and executes the embedded JavaScript using the `eval` function.

Analyzing the Headline News Component

The headline news component is the simplest component of the Ajax Dashboard. The component polls the server at set intervals and updates its contents with the current headline news stories. Unlike the other three components, the news component never sends any data to the server. Instead, it simply asks for the most current news items and displays them. Since no data is being sent to the server, the amount of code needed to actually send the request is ridiculously small, as shown here:

```
function updateNewsItems() {
    var ajaxRequest = new AjaxRequest("UpdateNewsItems");
    ajaxRequest.sendRequest();
}
```

This component is implemented slightly differently than the weather forecast component. Both rely on the Taconite framework to dynamically create content that is specified within the body of a JSP. The weather forecast component uses Taconite's JSP tags to build the response that is returned to the server. The news component, in contrast, eschews the use of Taconite's JSP tags and instead relies on the developer to build the XML response that is returned to the client. In this scenario, the parsing of the HTML to JavaScript will occur within the browser rather than on the server.

What are the benefits of avoiding the use of Taconite's JSP tags? The main benefit is that this approach demonstrates how the Taconite framework can be server-side technology agnostic. As long as the tools used on the server can generate an XML document, you can use this approach along with the Taconite framework.

A side benefit of using the browser-side parser instead of the server-side parser is lower bandwidth usage. When using the JavaScript parser, the desired HTML content is returned to the browser as just that—HTML. When using the server-side Java parser, the HTML content is translated into several JavaScript commands that are returned to the browser to be executed.

The JavaScript commands are far more verbose than the HTML content they represent, so if bandwidth is a problem, you may want to perform the parsing using the JavaScript parser. Keep in mind, though, that the Java parser is likely faster than the JavaScript parser, so in situations where performance is key (and you're in a Java environment), you may want to use the Java parser.

Listing 8-9 shows the `newsItems.jsp` file that renders the news component. Like the weather forecast component, it has an outer `div` element representing the component window, followed by another `div` element that acts as the component's colored title bar.

Listing 8-9. `newsItems.jsp`

```jsp
<%@taglib uri="http://java.sun.com/jsp/jstl/core" prefix="c"%>

<div id="newsItemsRoot" style="left:400px; top:300px;">
    <div id="newsItemsHandle">
        <table width="100%" border="0" class="textbox">
            <tr>
                <td align="left" class="controls">
                    Top News Stories Powered by Yahoo!
                </td>
                <td align="right">
                    <a class="controls"
                                href="javascript:minimize('newsItemsContent');">
                        -
                    </a>
                     
                    <a class="controls"
                                href="javascript:maximize('newsItemsContent');">
                        +
                    </a>
                </td>
            </tr>
        </table>
    </div>

    <div id="newsItemsContent" class="newsItemsContent">

        <%@include file="newsItemsDetail.jsp"%>

    </div>

</div>
```

Notice the `div` element with an `id` attribute value of `newsItemContent`. Inside that `div` is a JSP include for another JSP file named `newsItemsDetail.jsp`. Like the weather forecast component, the news component is broken out into separate JSP files that are included where needed to avoid duplicating any code.

Listing 8-10 shows the contents of the newsItemDetail.jsp file. All this JSP is doing is iterating over all the news items, and for each news item, the JSP creates a link for the news item and places the link within its own div tag.

Listing 8-10. newsItemDetail.jsp

```
<%@ taglib uri="http://java.sun.com/jsp/jstl/core" prefix="c"%>

<c:forEach var="newsItem" items="${newsItems}">
    <div>
        <br/>
        <a href="${newsItem.link}" class="newsLink" target="blank">

            ${newsItem.title}

        </a>
    </div>
</c:forEach>
```

By now you can see how beneficial it is to keep the code organized into separate JSP files. Each JSP file represents a focused unit of work that you can easily reuse by including it in other JSP files, which eases the maintenance burden when it comes time to make changes.

You can reuse the newsItemDetail.jsp file whenever the browser makes an Ajax request to update the news items. You don't need to redraw the entire component. The only thing that you need to update is the contents of the div element that houses the list of news stories. That's where the newsItemsAjax.jsp file comes in.

The newsItemsAjax.jsp file is the JSP that is used when the browser submits an Ajax request asking for the news items to be updated. This file is interested only in updating the news items instead of redrawing the entire news items component. Like the weather forecast example, it will use the Taconite framework, but this time it will avoid using Taconite's JSP tag library in order to demonstrate how the Taconite framework can be used with any server-side technology.

Listing 8-11 shows the newsItemsAjax.jsp file. Since this example does not use any of Taconite's custom JSP tags, you must manually set the Content-Type header of the response to text/xml. Note the similarities to Listing 8-8, which is the actual XML generated by Taconite's JSP tag library.

Listing 8-11. newsItemsAjax.jsp

```
<%@page contentType="text/xml"%>

<taconite-root>
    <taconite-replace-children contextNodeID="newsItemsContent"
                                                parseInBrowser="true">

        <%@include file="newsItemsDetail.jsp"%>

    </taconite-replace-children>

</taconite-root>
```

Instead of using the tac:taconiteRoot and tac:replaceChildren JSP tags, this example simply writes the XML tags itself, without relying on Taconite's custom JSP tag library to do it. Note how just like the tac:replaceChildren JSP tag, the taconite-replace-children tag has a contextNodeID attribute that specifies the existing element on the page that will have its contents replaced with the specified content. The parseInBrowser attribute with a value of true indicates to the Taconite JavaScript client that the HTML content must first be parsed into JavaScript commands before the commands can be executed.

Nested within the taconite-replace-children tag is a JSP include for the newsItemsDetail.jsp file. As you saw previously, this file performs the actual generation of the HTML content that renders the news items links.

The XML rendered by newsItemsAjax.jsp is returned to the browser as the response to the Ajax request. The Taconite client reads the response and notices that the taconite-replace-children tag's parseInBrowser attribute is set to true. Thus, the Taconite client knows that the taconite-replace-children tag does not contain JavaScript that's ready to be executed. Instead, its content is HTML that first needs to be parsed into JavaScript. The taconite-parser.js file contains the JavaScript code that parses the HTML into the equivalent JavaScript commands.

How Does the Automatic Refreshing Work?

The weather forecast, stock quote, and headline news components on the Ajax Dashboard automatically refresh themselves at predefined intervals. The weather forecast and stock quote components also update themselves each time the user edits their properties. You may be asking yourself how this automatic updating is implemented.

To make the automatic updating work, you need some sort of timer that will execute a specified JavaScript function at set intervals. Fortunately, such a timer is built right into the window object. While not specified by any official standard, the window.setInterval method is supported by all the modern browsers.

The window.setInterval method takes two arguments. The first argument is a string indicating the JavaScript function that should be called at set intervals. The second argument is an integer indicating the number of milliseconds that should pass between calls to the specified function. The window.setInterval method returns an integer representing the unique ID assigned to the interval. You can use this unique ID as the argument to the window.clearInterval method, which is used to stop an interval from being evaluated.

Listing 8-12 shows the stockQuote.js file that handles all the user inputs and manages the automatic updating for the stock quote component.

Listing 8-12. stockQuote.js

```
var stockTickerUpdateIntervalID = 0;

function handleStockTickersChange() {
    clearStockTickerUpdateInterval();
}

function clearStockTickerUpdateInterval() {
    if(stockTickerUpdateIntervalID != 0) {
        window.clearInterval(stockTickerUpdateIntervalID);
    }
```

```
        document.getElementById("trackFlag").checked = false;
}

function updateStockQuote() {
    var ajaxRequest = new AjaxRequest("UpdateStockQuote");
    ajaxRequest.addFormElementsById("stockTickers");
    ajaxRequest.sendRequest();
}

function startUpdateStockQuoteInterval() {
    stockTickerUpdateIntervalID = window.setInterval("updateStockQuote()", 30000);
}

function handleTrackFlagClick() {
    var trackFlag = document.getElementById("trackFlag");

    if(trackFlag.checked) {
        updateStockQuote();
        startUpdateStockQuoteInterval();
    }
    else {
        clearStockTickerUpdateInterval();
    }
}
```

At the top of the file is a global variable named stockTickerUpdateIntervalID. This variable holds the unique ID of the interval that updates the stock quotes. It is initialized to zero.

The automatic refresh is disabled whenever the user edits the contents of the text box that holds the desired stock tickers. The handleStockTickersChange function is called whenever the onkeyup event for the text box fires. The handleStockTickersChange function calls the clearStockTickerUpdateInterval function, which uses the stockTickerUpdateIntervalID to clear the interval and thus stop the automatic refreshing of the stock quotes. The check box is then unchecked to indicate to the user that the automatic refreshing has been temporarily disabled.

The updateStockQuote function is the function that actually performs the Ajax request. Like the previous examples from this chapter, it uses the Taconite JavaScript client to do the dirty work of creating the XMLHttpRequest object, adding the desired parameters to the query string, and sending the request.

The startUpdateStockQuoteInterval function uses the window.setInterval method to start automatic refreshing of the stock quotes. The first parameter in the call to window.setInterval is a string representing the startUpdateStockQuoteInterval function, and the second parameter is an integer representing the time delay, in milliseconds, between calls to the specified function. Notice how the window.setInterval method returns a unique ID of this particular interval, which is stored in the stockTickerUpdateIntervalID variable that is used later when clearing the interval.

Finally, the handleTrackFlagClick function handles the check box's onclick event. If the check box becomes checked, it immediately refreshes the stock quotes by calling the updateStockQuote function, and then it initiates the automatic refreshing by calling the startUpdateStockQuoteInterval function. If the check box becomes unchecked in response to a user's click, then the automatic refreshing is disabled by calling the clearStockTickerUpdateInterval function.

The implementation for automatically refreshing the weather forecast and headline news components is similar to what was described for the stock quote component. As you can see, the automatic refreshing is not terribly difficult to implement. The key is breaking tasks out into small, reusable functions and then building on top of those reusable functions. The entire file is less than 40 lines long. Better yet, thanks to the Taconite framework, only five lines of JavaScript are necessary to perform the Ajax request!

Building a Better Autocomplete

Chapter 4 demonstrated how to build a simple autocomplete feature in which a drop-down list would appear with a list of suggestions each time the user typed into a text box, à la Google Suggest.

The search component of the Ajax Dashboard builds on this example. Unlike the example from Chapter 4, which used hard-coded search "results," this example uses the Yahoo! Search API to perform the search. The Ajax Dashboard also uses the Taconite framework to build the search results.

Listing 8-13 is an excerpt from the autoComplete.html example from Chapter 4. The function shown in Listing 8-13 is the function responsible for building the results drop-down list.

Listing 8-13. *Excerpt of* autoComplete.html *Example from Chapter 4*

```
function setNames(the_names) {
    clearNames();
    var size = the_names.length;
    setOffsets();

    var row, cell, txtNode;
    for (var i = 0; i < size; i++) {
        var nextNode = the_names[i].firstChild.data;
        row = document.createElement("tr");
        cell = document.createElement("td");

        cell.onmouseout = function() {this.className='mouseOver';};
        cell.onmouseover = function() {this.className='mouseOut';};
        cell.setAttribute("bgcolor", "#FFFAFA");
        cell.setAttribute("border", "0");
        cell.onclick = function() { populateName(this); } ;

        txtNode = document.createTextNode(nextNode);
        cell.appendChild(txtNode);
        row.appendChild(cell);
        nameTableBody.appendChild(row);
    }
}
```

The set_names function is responsible for reading the XML returned by the server and building the results. The JavaScript in the set_names function isn't particularly hard; it's just tedious and an unnatural way to write HTML content. Remember, though, that building the onmouseover, onmouseout, and onclick event handlers required nonstandard code; otherwise, it wouldn't work in all major browsers. Had you not known the workaround, you may not have figured out why the example worked in some browsers but not others.

Now, compare the code in Listing 8-13 with the code in Listing 8-14, which shows searchAutocomplete.jsp. Listing 8-14 demonstrates how you build the content of the results drop-down list using the Taconite framework.

Listing 8-14. searchAutocomplete.jsp

```
<%@ taglib uri="http://java.sun.com/jsp/jstl/core" prefix="c"%>
<%@ taglib uri="http://taconite.sf.net/tags" prefix="tac" %>

<tac:taconiteRoot>

    <tac:replaceChildren contextNodeID="popup" parseOnServer="true">

        <c:forEach var="result" items="${results}">
            <div onmouseover="hilite(this);" onmouseout="unhilite(this);">
                <a href="${result.url}" class="autocomplete" target="_blank">
                    ${result.title}
                </a>
            </div>
        </c:forEach>

    </tac:replaceChildren>

</tac:taconiteRoot>
```

The code in Listings 8-13 and 8-14 performs the same task. Each variant builds the results that appear in the results drop-down list. (The JavaScript in Listing 8-13 places each result in a table row, and the JSP in Listing 8-14 places each result in a div element.) Not only is the JSP/Taconite method slightly shorter (18 lines versus 23 lines), but you'll surely agree that the code in Listing 8-14 looks much more natural and easier to write. You'll appreciate writing HTML markup using HTML markup rather than creating it programmatically through JavaScript.

Better yet, remember those pesky workarounds for the onmouseover, onmouseout, and onclick event handlers? In searchAutocomplete.jsp, the event handlers are written as simple attributes on the HTML elements. Taconite automatically generates cross-browser JavaScript to create these event handlers, freeing you from the responsibility of remembering what the various workarounds are.

The search component contains a number of enhancements over the autocomplete example from Chapter 4. The Chapter 4 autocomplete example performed an Ajax request every time the user typed a character into the text box. People who type fast create a higher frequency of Ajax requests, increasing the load on the server with little benefit for the user, since rapid typing leaves little time between keystrokes to display the updated results.

The search component handles this problem differently. Instead of responding to every keystroke made in the text box, once the user starts typing, an Ajax request is made at predefined intervals to update the results drop-down list, and then the Ajax request is made only if the contents of the text box have changed since the last time a request was issued.

Summary

Now that we've shown you how easy Ajax can be, we hope you'll start using these techniques in your applications. In this chapter, we showed you a more involved example that illustrates some of the benefits of Ajax, and we discussed a number of resources you can use to further your understanding. By showing you some common patterns, we hope you'll see some places you can put Ajax to use for yourself, keeping in mind the common gotchas expressed in this chapter. Finally, frameworks such as Taconite can greatly simplify Ajax development work, and we think you'll agree they are worth using.

■ ■ ■

Developing Cross-Browser JavaScript

Browsers have come a long way since 1999. Thanks to standards bodies such as the W3C and ECMA and a revival of competition in the browser market, modern browsers have largely eliminated the proprietary extensions and behaviors that plagued browsers in the late 1990s. Gone are the days when developers had to spend countless hours tweaking HTML layout and JavaScript code to get an application to function properly across different browsers. Today, developers who write code that adheres to standards can be assured that the code will function properly in any standards-compliant browser.

Implementing Ajax techniques in your application will likely dictate that you use JavaScript to dynamically update the page content, whether it be by creating new content, deleting existing content, or changing existing content. Unfortunately, some quirks do still exist in certain browsers, causing erratic behavior and giving developers headaches.

The most frequent offender of these quirks is Internet Explorer. Internet Explorer's HTML-rendering engine and JavaScript environment have received few updates in the past several years, and thus Internet Explorer is the least standards-compliant browser today. However, since Internet Explorer continues to maintain most of the browser market, you must write JavaScript code that works effectively in Internet Explorer as well as other browsers.

The scenarios in this appendix are situations in which you're likely to see browser incompatibilities. This is not an exhaustive list but rather the scenarios you're most likely to encounter when implementing Ajax techniques. These workarounds should behave as expected in all modern browsers.

Appending Rows to a Table

At some point in your experiences with Ajax, you're likely to want to append a row to an existing table using JavaScript or to create a new table with rows from scratch. The `document.createElement` and `document.appendChild` methods make this easy to do. You just create table cells using `document.createElement`, and you add the table cells to table rows using `document.appendChild`. The next logical step is to append the rows to the table using `document.appendChild`.

This works as expected in modern browsers such as Firefox, Safari, and Opera. Using Internet Explorer, however, the rows never show up in the table. Worse yet, Internet Explorer doesn't even throw any errors or give you a clue as to why the rows are not displayed even though they are appended to the table.

In this case, the workaround is simple. Internet Explorer will allow `tr` elements to be added to a `tbody` element, just not directly to the `table` element. For example, if you defined an empty table like this:

```
<table id="myTable">
    <tbody id="myTableBody"></tbody>
</table>
```

the correct way to add a row to the table would be to add the row to the table body instead of to the table, like so:

```
var cell = document.createElement("td").appendChild(document.createTextNode("foo"));
var row = document.createElement("tr").appendChild(cell);
document.getElementById("myTableBody").appendChild(row);
```

Fortunately, this method works in all modern browsers, including Internet Explorer. Stay in the habit of always using table bodies within your tables, and you'll never have to worry about this issue.

Setting an Element's Style via JavaScript

Ajax techniques allow developers to create Web applications that can seamlessly communicate with the server without a complete page refresh. Users of such applications will expect to see the page flicker whenever data is sent to or from the server. This flicker does not occur during Ajax requests, so the user may not know when data has been updated on the page. You'll likely change the style of some elements to indicate that some data on the page has changed; for example, you may highlight the name of a stock whose price was seamlessly updated via an Ajax request.

You should set the style of an element through JavaScript using the `setAttribute` method of the element. For example, to change the text within a `span` element to be displayed in bold and in red, use the `setAttribute` method as follows:

```
var spanElement = document.getElementById("mySpan");
spanElement.setAttribute("style", "font-weight:bold; color:red;");
```

This works well in all modern browsers except Internet Explorer. The workaround for Internet Explorer is to use the nonstandard but widely supported `cssText` property of the element's `style` object to set the desired style, as follows:

```
var spanElement = document.getElementById("mySpan");
spanElement.style.cssText = "font-weight:bold; color:red;";
```

This method works well in Internet Explorer and most other browsers except Opera. To make the code portable across *all* modern browsers, use the `setAttribute` method in addition to the `cssText` property of the element's `style` object, like so:

```
var spanElement = document.getElementById("mySpan");
spanElement.setAttribute("style", "font-weight:bold; color:red;");
spanElement.style.cssText = "font-weight:bold; color:red;";
```

Now setting the style on the element in question will function as expected in all modern browsers.

Setting an Element's class Attribute

After reading the previous section about setting an element's inline style via JavaScript, you've probably decided that simply setting the element's class attribute must be the easiest way to go. Unfortunately, that is not correct. As with setting an element's inline style, quirks also exist when setting an element's class dynamically via JavaScript.

As you've probably guessed by now, Internet Explorer is the oddball amongst other modern browsers, although the workaround is rather simple. Browsers such as Firefox and Safari allow you to set an element's class attribute using the element's setAttribute method, like so:

```
var element = document.getElementById("myElement");
element.setAttribute("class", "styleClass");
```

Oddly enough, Internet Explorer does not set the element's class attribute when using the setAttribute method and class as the attribute name. Instead, Internet Explorer recognizes the className attribute when used in conjunction with the setAttribute method.

The complete workaround for this situation is to use both class and className as the attribute names when using the element's setAttribute method, like so:

```
var element = document.getElementById("myElement");
element.setAttribute("class", "styleClass");
element.setAttribute("className", "styleClass");
```

Most modern browsers will use the class attribute name and ignore className, and Internet Explorer will do the opposite.

Creating Input Elements

Input elements provide a way for a user to interact with the page. HTML natively has a limited set of input elements, including single-line text boxes, multiline text areas, select boxes, buttons, check boxes, and radio buttons. You'll likely want to create some of these input elements dynamically using JavaScript as part of your Ajax implementations.

You create single-line text boxes, buttons, check boxes, and radio buttons all with an input element; only the value of the type attribute differs. Select boxes and text areas have their own unique tags. Creating input elements dynamically via JavaScript is straightforward (except for radio buttons, which are explained in the "Creating Radio Buttons" section), as long as you follow a few simple rules. You can easily create select boxes and text areas using the document.createElement method, passing to document.createElement the element's tag name such as select or textarea.

Single-line text boxes, buttons, check boxes, and radio buttons are a little trickier because they all share the same element name of input and differ only in the value of the type attribute. So, to create these elements, you'll need to use the document.createElement method followed by the element's setAttribute method to set the value of the type attribute. This is not difficult, but it does require an extra line of code.

You must also be careful regarding the order of the `document.createElement` and `setAttribute` statements with regard to where you add the newly created input element to its parent. In some browsers, you can add the newly created element only to its parent element after the element has been created and the `type` attribute has been correctly set. For instance, the following code snippet may behave unexpectedly in some browsers:

```
document.getElementById("formElement").appendChild(button);
button.setAttribute("type", "button");
```

To avoid potentially erratic behavior, be sure to create the input element and set all its attributes, especially the `type` attribute, before adding it to the parent, like so:

```
var button = document.createElement("input");
button.setAttribute("type", "button");
document.getElementById("formElement").appendChild(button);
```

Following this simple rule can help eliminate difficult-to-diagnose problems that may arise later.

Adding Event Handlers to Input Elements

Adding an event handler to an input element should be as easy as using the `setAttribute` method and specifying the event handler name and the name of the desired function handler, right? Wrong. The standard way of setting an element's event handler uses the element's `setAttribute` method; it uses the event name as the attribute name and the function handler as the attribute value, as follows:

```
var formElement = document.getElementById("formElement");
formElement.setAttribute("onclick", "doFoo();");
```

The previous code works in all modern browsers except Internet Explorer. To set an element's event handler using JavaScript in Internet Explorer, you must reference the desired event handler via dot notation from the element and assign it to an anonymous function that calls the desired event handler, like so:

```
var formElement = document.getElementById("formElement");
formElement.onclick = function() { doFoo(); };
```

Note how the `onclick` event handler is referenced via dot notation from `formElement`. The `onclick` event handler is assigned to an anonymous function that simply calls the desired event handler, in this case `doFoo`.

Fortunately, this technique is supported by Internet Explorer and apparently other modern browsers, so you have no reason to avoid setting a form element's event handler dynamically via JavaScript.

Creating Radio Buttons

We've saved the best one for last. Creating a radio button dynamically via JavaScript is a particularly arduous task because Internet Explorer's method of creating a radio button is far different from any other browser's method.

All modern browsers except Internet Explorer allow a radio button to be created using the following expected methods:

```
var radioButton = document.createElement("input");
radioButton.setAttribute("type", "radio");
radioButton.setAttribute("name", "radioButton");
radioButton.setAttribute("value", "checked");
```

The radio button will be created and behave normally in all modern browsers except Internet Explorer. In Internet Explorer, the radio button will be displayed, but it's unable to be checked, because clicking the radio button does not check the radio button as it should.

The method for creating an Internet Explorer radio button is different from the other browsers and totally incompatible. You can build the radio button built previously as follows for Internet Explorer:

```
var radioButton = document.createElement("<input type='radio' name='radioButton'
    value='checked'>");
```

The good news is that it is possible to create a radio button dynamically via JavaScript in Internet Explorer— it's just that it's difficult and incompatible with other browsers.

How can you overcome this limitation? The short answer is that some type of browser-sniffing mechanism is required so the script knows which method to use when creating the radio button. Fortunately, you don't need to check for a multitude of different browsers. Assuming only modern browsers are in use, the script needs to differentiate only between Internet Explorer and *everything else*.

Internet Explorer recognizes a proprietary attribute of the document object named uniqueID. Internet Explorer is the only browser that recognizes this property, which makes uniqueID a perfect fit for determining whether the browser in which the script is running is Internet Explorer.

Using the document.uniqueID property to determine the browser in which the script is running, you can combine the Internet Explorer–specific method with the standards-compliant method to produce this code:

```
if(document.uniqueID) {
    //Internet Explorer
    var radioButton = document.createElement("<input type='radio'
        name='radioButton' value='checked'>");
}
else {
    //Standards Compliant
    var radioButton = document.createElement("input");
    radioButton.setAttribute("type", "radio");
    radioButton.setAttribute("name", "radioButton");
    radioButton.setAttribute("value", "checked");
}
```

Summary

Web development with JavaScript is no longer as painful as it was even a few short years ago. Today, modern browsers are remarkably similar in their implementation of the W3C DOM standards and JavaScript. Some workarounds are still necessary, though—mostly because of Internet Explorer. The tips offered in this appendix will help you write JavaScript that will work correctly on most modern browsers. By following the techniques outlined here, you'll save yourself countless hours of debugging and testing. Happy scripting!

Introducing Ajax Frameworks

By now, you may have noticed that a fair amount of plumbing is involved in programming with Ajax. If you have to support multiple browsers (and who doesn't these days?), you will inevitably run into incompatibilities. Just look at the simple act of creating an instance of the XMLHttpRequest object—it requires a browser test. As soon as you start experimenting with Ajax techniques, you will quickly notice that you are performing the same tasks repeatedly. Of course, you'll probably put together some libraries of common code, or maybe you'll even create your own framework. Before you do, though, you may want to take a look at what's already available.

Like any good technology, Ajax has already spawned a number of frameworks to make life easier for mere mortals. We want to stress that Ajax is new and dynamic—so too is the framework landscape. New entrants appear seemingly daily, and right now none is a clear winner. Few of the frameworks existed before mid-2003, so expect to see significant changes in the coming months.

Some frameworks are based on the client side, and some are based on the server side. Some are designed for specific languages, and others are language agnostic. The majority have open-source implementations, but a few are proprietary. We won't cover every framework, and we certainly won't go into a great deal of depth on the ones we do touch on; still, we wanted to give you a flavor of what is available. By the time you read this appendix, some of the toolkits mentioned will be dormant, and others will have been created. Which framework is right for you? Only you can say; however, you may want to take a conservative stance until the framework area solidifies. An effort is even underway to merge the various frameworks together—it'll be interesting to see how this plays out! By the time you read this, the picture should be clearer, but you will want to keep a close eye on this space.

Browser-Side Frameworks

The following sections cover the browser-based frameworks.

Dojo

Dojo is one of the oldest frameworks, having begun development in September 2004. The project's goal is to build a DHTML toolkit that leverages XHR while focusing on usability issues. Dojo involves only a couple of files, and rather than deal with the setup for XHR, you simply call a `bind` method and pass in the URL you want to call and the callback method. That's it. You can also use the `bind` method to submit entire forms.

One feature that sets Dojo apart is its support for back and forward buttons. Though the feature does not work on every browser (unfortunately, Safari is the odd duck), you can actually register a callback method that will fire if the user clicks either the back button or the forward button. Dojo also attempts to answer the bookmarking issue that is inherent with Ajax by providing a changeURL flag.

Dojo seems to be one of the more mature toolkits, and its focus on usability is refreshing. It appears to be pretty stable, and it has some momentum behind it. Dojo has a fairly active mailing list, but some additional documentation would be helpful. You can find more information at dojotoolkit.org.

Rico

Rico is one of the newest frameworks on the market; it was developed at Sabre Airline Solutions and then made into an open-source implementation. Of course, *rico* is Spanish for *rich*, which indicates the project's overall goal of providing a suite of components for developing rich Internet applications. Browser support is fairly strong, though surprisingly Safari[1] is omitted.

Where Dojo is clearly focused on usability, Rico seems designed for drag-and-drop actions, data grids, and what they term *cinematic effects* (moving widgets, fading a div, and so on). The Rico Web site has a number of interesting demos where the code is outlined—a nice touch for developers looking to get something up and running quickly. The documentation is a bit sparse, but that is likely to change as the framework matures.

You can download Rico as a single file, though you will also need the Prototype JS library. You can find more information at openrico.org/home.page.

qooxdoo

qooxdoo is another new entry to the Ajax framework field that picks up where HTML leaves off by providing a JavaScript-based toolkit. Though in the early alpha stage, qooxdoo offers some polished widgets. Using qooxdoo, you can mimic many of the features found on standard thick clients such as menu bars, tooltips, grid layouts, and drag-and-drop support.

qooxdoo does have some useful documentation, including a helpful explanation of the details under the hood. qooxdoo's strength is clearly its sophisticated widgets. If your goal is to create a thin application that can barely be discerned from its thick cousin, you should try qooxdoo. You can find more information at qooxdoo.oss.schlund.de.

TIBET

Depending on your interpretation of when Ajax first appeared, TIBET may be the oldest framework in existence. According to the documentation, the TIBET team has been working on this toolkit since 1997 with the goal of providing enterprise-class Ajax support. TIBET looks to go beyond just simply wrapping the XMLHttpRequest object; it provides support for Web Services, low-level protocols, and prebuilt wrappers for Google, Amazon, and many other commonly used services.

---

1. Internet Explorer rightly receives the majority of the complaints when it comes to nonstandard behavior with Ajax techniques—just ask the authors! That said, while developing this book, we did find a surprising amount of "odd" behavior in Safari (which greatly disappointed the recent Mac convert in the pair).

What really sets TIBET apart from its peers, though, is the fully interactive browser-based IDE that simplifies development, debugging, and unit testing. You can find more information at `www.technicalpursuit.com`.

Flash/JavaScript Integration Kit

Before Ajax, there was Flash, and many Web sites have been built on the Flash platform. Those with heavy investments in Flash can still take advantage of Ajax techniques with this open-source project. The toolkit works in all the major browsers and allows JavaScript to invoke ActionScript, and vice versa. You can pass a number of objects back and forth, including dates, strings, and arrays.

Installation involves a handful of JavaScript files plus a couple of library functions that need to be present on the Flash side of things. Calling an ActionScript function from your page involves only a couple of lines. Documentation is a little sparse, but if you want to access Flash using Ajax, this kit is worth investigating. You can find more information at `weblogs.macromedia.com/flashjavascript/`.

Google AJAXSLT

Based on work done with Google Maps, Google AJAXSLT is a JavaScript implementation of XSL Transformations (XSLT) using XPath. XSLT transforms XML documents into other languages such as HTML. AJAXSLT lets you perform these transformations directly on the browser using JavaScript.

Google AJAXSLT works in all the major browsers and is released under the Berkeley Software Distribution (BSD) license. The kit is small, consisting of a handful of JavaScript files and handy test pages. Google AJAXSLT isn't perfect, but if Google Suggest is any indication, we expect its shortcomings will soon be solved. Because Google is a pioneer of Ajax usage, it will be interesting to see what else it adds to the public space in the coming months. You can find more information at `goog-ajaxslt.sourceforge.net`.

libXmlRequest

The libXmlRequest framework is among the oldest of the bunch; it was originally released in 2003. The framework consists of a single JavaScript file that acts as a wrapper around the XMLHttpRequest object by exposing two overloaded request functions: `getXml` and `postXml`. Several attributes deal with pooling and caching, and several utility functions handle common tasks such as parsing the XML from the server and modifying the DOM.

It's not clear what browsers this toolkit works in, and the documentation is a bit sparse. The work is copyrighted by its author Stephen W. Cote, and there is no mention of licensing; therefore, you may want to use this work only as a source of inspiration. You can find more information at `www.whitefrost.com/index.jsp`.

RSLite

RSLite is an implementation of remote scripting by Brent Ashley. Technically, this does not leverage the XMLHttpRequest object at the heart of Ajax, but the browser support is much more widespread. If you need to support legacy browsers that do not support the

XMLHttpRequest object, you'll want to look into RSLite. RSLite is extremely lightweight and dates from 2000.[2] You can find more information at www.ashleyit.com/rs/rslite/.

SACK

The Simple Ajax Code Kit (SACK) was developed as a thin wrapper around the XMLHttpRequest object. Its author, Gregory Wild-Smith, thought many of the other frameworks were too complex and attempted to perform tasks they shouldn't, so he created SACK to simplify Ajax development. SACK consists of a handful of methods that simplify calling the server. In fewer lines than it takes to actually create a proper instance of an XMLHttpRequest object, you can send data to the server and handle the response.

SACK consists of a single JavaScript file that contains a surprisingly small amount of code. The software behind SACK is released under a modified X11 license (also known as the MIT license), and like most open-source projects, documentation is not overwhelming; still, you'll certainly find enough to get started. The real strength of SACK is its simplicity—if all you're looking for is a basic wrapper, try SACK. You can find more information at twilightuniverse.com/projects/sack/.

sarrisa

sarissa attacks Ajax by wrapping support for the XML APIs in a browser-independent manner. The framework makes creating and working with XMLHttpRequest objects a breeze (no need to do a browser check; it's handled for you). However, sarissa also offers support for working with the DOM. Like Google AJAXSLT, sarissa provides support for XSLT by emulating Mozilla's processor on Internet Explorer.

sarissa consists of just a handful of classes, and it's released under the GPL. Browser support for sarissa is strongest in Mozilla/Firefox and Internet Explorer with some functions unavailable in Opera, Konqueror, and Safari. You can find more information at sarissa.sourceforge.net/doc/.

XHConn

XHConn is similar to SACK in that it acts as a simple wrapper around the XMLHttpRequest object. Instead of working directly with the XMLHttpRequest object, you instantiate an instance of XHConn, working with it in much the same way you would XHR. That said, it does eliminate the browser check and provides a simple way to determine whether the browser even supports XHR (which is particularly handy for sites that need to degrade gracefully).

XHConn works in Safari, Internet Explorer, Mozilla, Firefox, and Opera. Like the majority of the Ajax frameworks, it is an open-source implementation, which is released under a Creative Commons License. XHConn is a single file that contains little code, but it does what it sets out to do: simplify Ajax. You can find more information at xkr.us/code/javascript/XHConn/.

---

2. We know we said the Ajax frameworks date from 2003, and yet here we are talking about something from 2000. However, RSLite is about remote scripting, a predecessor to Ajax.

Server-Side Frameworks

The following sections cover the frameworks that are based on the server.

CPAINT

Cross-Platform Asynchronous Interface Toolkit (CPAINT) implements Ajax on the server side by returning either text or DOM document objects to the client to be manipulated with JavaScript. CPAINT works with most major browsers, supports remote scripting, and is released under the GPL. The project documentation is fairly complete; however, CPAINT supports only PHP and ASP. You can find more information at `sourceforge.net/projects/cpaint/`.

Sajax

Sajax allows you to directly call server-side code from your JavaScript. Sajax supports a number of languages including Perl, Python, Ruby, and ASP (though it is surprising that Java is not currently supported). Setting up Sajax is pretty straightforward; it involves a simple library for your particular server language. Sajax seems to have a fairly vibrant developer community. Confirmed browser support is limited to Internet Explorer 6 and Mozilla/Firefox, though the authors believe it will work with Safari. You can find more information at `www.modernmethod.com/sajax`.

JSON/JSON-RPC

JavaScript Object Notation (JSON) is a text format that can be used to exchange data much like XML does. JSON is designed to be easy for humans to read and easy for machines to parse while using conventions familiar to the C family of languages. Of more relevance to this discussion, JSON-RPC is a remote procedure call (RPC) protocol that is like XML-RPC but for the JSON language. JSON-RPC is a specification with implementations in several languages (including Java, Ruby, Python, and Perl).

Since JSON-RPC is a specification, you will need to read about the specific implementation that is appropriate for your environment. Depending on the implementation, documentation runs from quite complete to essentially nonexistent. Developer involvement also varies widely. It appears that conversations about the JSON-RPC specification have stagnated somewhat. You can find more information at `www.crockford.com/JSON/index.html`.

Direct Web Remoting

Direct Web Remoting (DWR) allows you to call Java methods from JavaScript as if they were local to the browser. Though limited strictly to a Java backend, DWR is one of the more popular frameworks. DWR's documentation is top-notch, with a number of useful examples to get you started.

Installation isn't hard, but it does involve editing your Web application's deployment descriptor as well as a DWR-specific file. The DWR configuration file specifies which classes can be created and called remotely, and the documentation does warn users about the security implications of calling the server from the browser. Along with the JAR file containing the server-side code, two JavaScript files contain a number of helper functions. DWR fits into common Web frameworks such as Struts and Tapestry and is released under the Apache license. If you are looking for a way to call Java methods from your Web pages, DWR will help you do it. You can find more information at getahead.ltd.uk/dwr/index.

SWATO

Shift Web Applications TO (SWATO) is another Java-based Ajax framework solution. SWATO works in any Servlet 2.3 or higher container and, like DWR, requires some configuration file updates. Interestingly, SWATO utilizes JSON to marshal data between the client and server and, like some of the other options discussed in this appendix, allows you to call server-side Java from a browser. To aid developers, SWATO includes a number of reusable components such as autocomplete text boxes.

Using SWATO is a bit more involved than using other frameworks—the classes you want to make accessible implement a SWATO interface; however, the documentation is more than complete enough to get you started. SWATO is designed to use Spring to wire up the services, but you are not required to do so. You can find more information at https://swato.dev.java.net/doc/html/.

Java BluePrints

The BluePrints team at Sun has been busy adding Ajax to its catalog. The Solutions Catalog includes good documentation on using basic Ajax, implementing autocomplete, creating a progress bar, and validating forms. It also includes JavaServer Faces components. The code developed for the BluePrints Solutions Catalog is available at the www.java.net site.

Ajax.Net

Ajax.Net is to Microsoft .NET as SAJAX, DWR, and SWATO are to Java—they allow you to call .NET methods from a JavaScript client. Ajax.Net involves a single DLL that can be used with either VB .NET or C#. The documentation for Ajax.Net does an excellent job showing solutions for various scenarios. The source is available; however, the licensing of Ajax.Net is ambiguous. You can find more information at ajax.net.

Microsoft's Project Atlas

Microsoft has been active with Ajax for some time; after all, Microsoft did invent the XMLHttpRequest object and has used it in the Web version of Outlook since 1998. Microsoft is focusing on making things easier for developers by providing a more robust development environment. Microsoft wants to deliver quite a bit, including a client-side scripting framework, ASP.NET controls, and Web Service integration. It should release Project Atlas as part of the preview release of ASP.NET 2.0. With Microsoft entering the fray, expect developer toolsets to drastically improve from where they are today. You can find more information at beta.asp.net/default.aspx?tabindex=7&tabid=47.

Ruby on Rails

Rails is an exciting new Web framework based on the Ruby language. Rails has been getting a tremendous amount of attention these days (just "google" *rolling with Rails* to find out more) because of its ability to allow rapid development of Web-based applications. While developing Basecamp, the team at 37signals pulled out a framework called Rails. Basecamp is a prime example of an Ajax application, so it should come as no surprise that Rails has excellent support for Ajax baked right in. Rails has several built-in JavaScript libraries that wrap many common features; it also contains a module that wraps JavaScript calls in Ruby. If you're working in Rails, you'll find Ajax a snap. You can find more information at www.rubyonrails.org.

Index